IMAGE-BUILDING IN CANADIAN MUNICIPALITIES

FIELDS OF GOVERNANCE:
POLICY MAKING IN CANADIAN MUNICIPALITIES
Series editor: Robert Young

Policy making in the modern world has become a complex matter. Much policy is formed through negotiations between governments at several different levels, because each has particular resources that can be brought to bear on problems. At the same time, non-governmental organizations make demands about policy and can help in policy formation and implementation. In this context, works in this series explore how policy is made within municipalities through processes of intergovernmental relations and with the involvement of social forces of all kinds.

The Fields of Governance series arises from a large research project, funded mainly by the Social Sciences and Humanities Research Council of Canada, entitled Multilevel Governance and Public Policy in Canadian Municipalities. This project has involved more than eighty scholars and a large number of student assistants. At its core are studies of several policy fields, each of which was examined in a variety of municipalities. Our objectives are not only to account for the nature of the policies but also to assess their quality and to suggest improvements in policy and in the policy-making process.

The Fields of Governance series is designed for scholars, practitioners, and interested readers from many backgrounds and places.

1 *Immigrant Settlement Policy in Canadian Municipalities*
Edited by Erin Tolley and Robert Young

2 *Urban Aboriginal Policy Making in Canadian Municipalities*
Edited by Evelyn J. Peters

3 *Sites of Governance Multilevel Governance and Policy Making in Canada's Big Cities*
Edited by Martin Horak and Robert Young

4 *Image-building in Canadian Municipalities*
Edited by Jean Harvey and Robert Young

Image-building in Canadian Municipalities

Edited by
JEAN HARVEY AND ROBERT YOUNG

McGill-Queen's University Press
Montreal & Kingston • London • Ithaca

© McGill-Queen's University Press 2012

ISBN 978-0-7735-4096-5 (cloth)
ISBN 978-0-7735-4097-2 (paper)

Legal deposit fourth quarter 2012
Bibliothèque nationale du Québec

Printed in Canada on acid-free paper that is 100% ancient forest free
(100% post-consumer recycled), processed chlorine free

McGill-Queen's University Press acknowledges the support of the
Canada Council for the Arts for our publishing program. We also
acknowledge the financial support of the Government of Canada
through the Canada Book Fund for our publishing activities.

Library and Archives Canada Cataloguing in Publication Data

Image building in Canadian municipalities / edited by Jean Harvey
and Robert Young.

(Fields of governance: policy making in Canadian municipalities ; 4)
Includes bibliographical references and index.
ISBN 978-0-7735-4096-5 (bound). – ISBN 978-0-7735-4097-2 (pbk.)

  1. City promotion – Canada. 2. Municipal government – Public
relations – Canada. 3. Place marketing – Canada. I. Harvey, Jean
II. Young, Robert III. Series: Fields of governance ; 4

HT325.I43 2013   659.2'9307760971   C2012-905451-8

Typeset by Jay Tee Graphics Ltd. in 10.5/13 Sabon

Contents

Preface

This is a collection of papers about how municipalities in Canada construct and project their images. This is a fascinating field for those interested in municipal government, and also for those concerned with public policy. The authors here treat image-building as a policy and focus on how images are constructed. They investigate two main determinants of policy. The first is the set of relationships between governmental actors at the municipal, provincial, and federal levels; that is, the sets of intergovernmental relations that help produce the policies. The second is the array of "social forces" (more or less organized interests of all kinds) that are concerned about the image of their municipality, and that aim to influence image-building policy.

Global forces have brought image-building to the fore in many municipalities. Localities face challenges of economic restructuring and are often competing for incoming investments and immigrants. The Internet has made it possible for all municipalities, even very small ones, to project themselves on a regional, national, and global scale. This book covers some large cities, but it also explores image-building in small and medium-sized towns, and the chapters in this book clearly show that municipalities of all sizes are conscious of their images and devote attention to optimizing them.

This collection presents original research by expert scholars that stands alone and makes a significant contribution to our knowledge about image-building in Canadian municipalities. But the work collected here is also part of a much larger project, one that explores multilevel governance and public policy in Canadian municipalities. This project has many components, but most of the work has been done on six policy areas, one of which is image-building. This project also covers all the provinces and municipalities of different sizes, as in the studies presented here. The objectives of the whole project are to document what policies exist in a variety of fields, and to explain their character by focusing on the processes of inter-governmental relations through which they were shaped, and on the social forces that were involved – or not involved – in the policy process. More information about the overall project is available at www.ppm-ppm.ca.

Some acknowledgements are in order. First, we thank the Social Sciences and Humanities Research Council of Canada for its support through the Major Collaborative Research Initiatives program. The University of Western Ontario and other universities have contributed generously to the project. At research meetings about image-building, Viv Nelles was a pleasant and very constructive presence. We thank McGill-Queen's University Press for its continued interest in our research. Ms Kelly McCarthy has served as manager for the project. She coordinated various meetings of the image-building research team and also helped with the initial preparation of the manuscript. The manuscript was much improved by Ms Nicole Wellsbury, who handled the layout and formatting, and who checked references assiduously. Jen Lajoie also helped with these tasks, and she expertly compiled the index.

Jean Harvey and Robert Young

IMAGE-BUILDING IN CANADIAN MUNICIPALITIES

Introduction

JEAN HARVEY

FOREWORD

Mega-events; Olympic Games; world cups or championships; expos; world fairs; "world-class" cultural events; blockbusters; film or music festivals; and mega-historical celebrations, such as the Vancouver Olympic Games in 2010, the four hundredth anniversary of Quebec City in 2008, the Toronto Film Festival, and the Montreal Jazz Festival are large-scale, highly visible initiatives undertaken in order to promote Canada's largest cities as world-class destinations. They are aimed at attracting tourists, investors, and new residents through the images they project to the world. However, image-building is not only outward looking. It also serves a function of boosting civic pride and generating social cohesion. There is an expanding literature about the increasing importance for big cities to compete to attract mega-events for specific economic goals, or for more fluid objectives, such as their status as "world-class" cities (Essex and Chalkley 2004; Friedman et al. 2004; Hannigan 2003; Harvey 2001; Kong 2007; Roche 2000; Whitson 2004; Yeoh 2005). It is important to point out that smaller cities and towns, as well as rural municipalities, are also involved in a variety of place promotion strategies, branding their attributes not only to the regional, national, or global levels, but also to their own citizens or prospective citizens (Black 2008; Fagnoni 2004; Gratton et al. 2005; Law 2009; Whitson 2004). Such municipalities will be the main focus of this book (though not the exclusive one). We know very little about their image-building activities.

Through different active and reactive strategies, both municipalities and large cities are projecting a myriad of images about their singular qualities as places to live, to visit, or to invest in. These strategies include branding exercises, hosting cultural or sport events and festivals of all forms, plain marketing initiatives, tourism promotion, and even immigration campaigns. Through image-building, municipalities make themselves known to their neighbours and to the world. From image-building, they expect both civic pride and economic development, the latter being the major motive for local boosters and champions, chambers of commerce, and tourism and hospitality operators.

Municipal image-building is not made in a vacuum. In addition to intense competition from other municipalities, tourism promotion campaigns, cultural and sports events, and festivals almost always involve the interplay of all levels of government – municipal, provincial, and federal – sometimes directly, sometimes indirectly. When, for example, the city of Vancouver agreed to bid to host the 2010 Winter Olympics, the project needed the approval of (and large financial investments by) the province of British Columbia and the federal government, as well as the adoption of a multipartite agreement that laid out specific governance mechanisms for hosting that mega-event. When each year, Carleton-sur-Mer, a municipality of 4,400 residents in the Gaspé area of Quebec, hosts its Maximum Blues Festival, a complex set of financial contributions comes from the upper levels of government, through Canadian Heritage, the Conseil des arts et des lettres du Québec, Québec Tourism, and so forth, not forgetting partners from the private sector. Indeed, as argued by Black (2008), flagship events are often seen by cities as opportunities to tap the public finances of higher levels of government.

From one province to another, from rural municipalities to the largest Canadian cities, from tourism to cultural festivals, multilevel governance mechanisms take different forms, as does the interplay of social forces with governments vary considerably. Moreover, provinces and the federal government are themselves engaged in various image-building initiatives. For example, each year as the winter draws to a close, the Canadian Tourism Commission, along with almost every province's tourism authority or department, deploys massive advertising campaigns projecting multiple images of places to visit and spaces to discover, aiming to attract tourists from all across Canada and abroad, selling here the great Canadian wilderness, there, the buoyant multicultural life of cities, and elsewhere, some local cultural festival. This kaleidoscope of images speaks to the complexity of image-building and to the issues and mechanisms of multilevel governance at play.

Most of the academic literature on image-building has focused on the branding strategies of major and second-tier large cities, tracing their transformation into urban entertainment destinations, and analyzing the impact of mega-events and landmark infrastructures in the promotion of these places. Almost all the literature on image-building involves cities, their image-building strategies, policies and programs, and their various impacts locally. In this book, we focus principally on mid-size to rural municipalities, and examine an aspect that has been left almost untouched: the interaction between these municipalities and other levels of government. We are centrally concerned with how multilevel government processes are at play in the image-building of smaller cities and municipalities. This book also pays careful attention to the social forces – organized interests and societal actors of all kinds – that may play a central role at every stage of the policy cycle. This book features chapters analyzing municipalities in Prince Edward Island, Manitoba, and Saskatchewan, three of the less populated Canadian provinces, as well as a chapter on the federal government policies and programs that impact upon municipal image-building (MIB). This provides novel insights into the branding of cities, as for the first time, a book focuses on the interaction of several levels of government and social forces in this field of policy-making.

This book has four main objectives. First, it provides several case studies of municipalities of various sizes in order to assess the variability of municipal image-building from one municipality to another and to get a sense of the various types of image built, as well as to explore the factors that come into play in the selection and projection of municipal images. Second, this book documents how MIB varies across provinces in its importance and in the interplay between the various levels of government and social forces. Our methodology permits systematic comparison. Third, we want to draw general theoretical lessons from our empirical work. We frame our research with respect to general questions, the answers to which have significance well beyond the municipalities studied here and Canada itself. Finally, a fourth aim of this book is to identify factors that make good MIB in order to help policy-makers develop the best possible policies and programs in this sector.

This introductory chapter provides an overview of what MIB is and how it is potentially important in contemporary municipal policy. First, I will briefly develop a working definition of MIB, a definition that roughly guides the chapters included in this book. Second, through a quick review of literature, I wish to point out how changes in the political economy of cities in the last three decades have created a context in which image-building gained an importance that arguably it never had before. Third, I will have another look at the importance of image-building through a discussion of the policy fields it contributes to or may have an influence on. I will also address the issues of the kaleidoscopic nature of cities' images and of the potential impacts of MIB. Fourth, I will turn my attention to definitions of public policies and of multilevel governance. Then I will develop the theoretical setting within which the case studies are based and to which they will contribute. As well, the methodology of the investigation is explained here. Finally, I will provide some guideposts to help the reader anticipate the chapters that follow.

PLACE PROMOTION, PLACE BRANDING, OR MIB?

Place promotion, place branding, place making, image-building, and the marketing of cities are all terms being used in the literature. Indeed, there is hardly any consensus on what the meanings of these concepts are and what distinguishes one from another. In fact, most of the contributions to the literature do not present any definition at all of the concepts they use. The semantic confusion and definitional rarity is a function of the variety of disciplines – sociology, urban studies, geography, marketing, political science, economics, semiotics – from which image-building is studied. They are also a function of the various theoretical frameworks used: political economy, postmodernism, structuralism, governmentality, cultural studies, and so on. A full understanding of these subtleties is obviously beyond the scope of this introduction. Rather, I shall present some extant definitions of some of these terms to provide a sense of the semantic field they cover, and will quickly close in on a working definition that delineates the focus of this book.

Drawing from Gold and Ward (1994), Watkins and Herbert (2003, 252) define place promotion as "the use of publicity and marketing to create selective images of specific localities targeted at specific populations." During the 1980s, they argue, industrial cities started to change their promotion strategies from an industrial focus towards a focus on tourism. New images started to proliferate "with a persistent set of general aims concerned with attracting visitors, appealing to inward investors, increasing local pride, identity and self-confidence, and countering negative perceptions. Cities were in competition with each other and each sought an image that was different and distinctive" (Watkins and Herbert 2003, 252).

At its most basic level, according to Kavaratzis and Ashworth (2005, 508), "place branding is merely the application of product branding to places." In their paper focusing on how places like cities can be branded they argue that

> all branding tries to endow a product with a specific and more distinctive identity and that is, in essence, what most city marketing seeks to do for cities. A place needs to be differentiated through unique brand identity if it wants to be, first, recognized as existing, second, perceived in the minds of place customers as possessing qualities superior to those of competitors, and third, consumed in a manner commensurate with the objectives of the place. (510)

From a different theoretical angle, Hannigan (2003, 352) adds that branding has three interrelated dimensions. First, it requires instant recognition; hence the emphasis on "synergies" with the sports and entertainment industries, with their rosters of high-octane celebrities. Second, successfully branded leisure spaces play on our desire for both comfort and certainty, key attributes of Disney-like theme parks. Finally, branded environments provide a point of identification for consumers in an increasingly crowded marketplace.

For the purpose of this book, the notion of MIB will be used throughout as an umbrella concept that includes public policies and programs (terms that I shall define later on) designed by (or for) municipalities in order to promote inward and/or outward images for the pursuit of various political ends, such as tourism promotion, economic renewal, or civic identity. Defined that way, the scope that represents MIB allows studying efforts to sell municipalities to investors, to tourists, to potential immigrants, and to the current and prospective residents in a competitive market. This focus also puts the emphasis on political contests about how the municipality represents itself to the regional, national, and global worlds.

CONTEXT

While the most recent literature places a strong emphasis on the increasing importance of MIB, it is also recognized that

> places have long felt a need to differentiate themselves from each other, to assert their individuality in pursuit of various economic, political, or socio-psychological objectives. The conscious attempt of governments to shape a specifically designed place identity and promote it to identified markets, whether external or internal, is almost as old as civic government itself. (Kavaratzis and Ashworth 2005, 506)

As a matter of fact, not only municipal governments have been concerned with their image. Canada's history is replete with examples of place promotion. Canada's expansion in the West relied heavily on extensive promotion abroad about the opportunities Canada could offer to new immigrants. In their overview of image-building and place promotion literature, Lehr and Lehr (2007) remind us that place promotion played a large role in the colonization of Canada, attracting European migrants, Mennonites, Ukrainians, and so on. Boosterism was also widespread in the nineteenth and twentieth centuries in order to attract investors and residents to burgeoning mine towns and industrial centres. If MIB is as old as municipalities, why is it so important now, as suggested by the literature I have referred to so far? Has MIB gained unprecedented importance or has it simply changed form? Reading through that same literature, three major factors stand out: economic transformation, the fiscal crisis of cities, and globalization. In combination, these factors have led to the emergence of a new neoliberal regime of accumulation and urban governance (Harvey 2007) in which MIB has become almost a necessity for public authorities in order to "sell" their city in an increasingly crowded worldwide market. Here is how Hannigan (2003, 353) sums up this situation:

> In the late 1980s and early 1990s a fiscal crisis across Europe and North America caused by the triple problems of deindustrialization, a falling tax base, and declining public expenditure had some serious implications for cities. Not only were factories closing and jobs disappearing, but the mass industrial culture

that had prevailed since the end of the Second World War was steadily weakening. During the same era, we witnessed the re-emergence of political structures and ideologies based around the notions of privatization and deregulation, and the rise of a new urban lifestyle in which visual images and myths were relentlessly packaged and presented. In combination, these forces provoked the emergence of a new entrepreneurial style of local economic development in which image promotion was privileged as being central by planners and politicians.

Broudehoux (2007, 230) adds that, according to David Harvey (2001), "this new entrepreneurialism is characterized by the central role of public-private partnerships, the speculative nature of the projects undertaken, and a shift away from concerns of collective consumption to the political economy of place." All in all, "in these early years of the twenty-first century, the contemporary city has become a prime site for consumption-related activities related to tourism, sports, culture, and entertainment" (Hannigan 2003, 352).

These authors focus their attention mainly on large cities, but it is important to emphasize the fact that globalization and industrial restructuring have strongly affected smaller municipalities and the rural areas of countries like Canada, leading to population and employment decline. In a recent study, Alasia et al. (2008, 3) underline that "over the last two decades, about one-third of Canadian communities experienced continuous population decline," and argue that these trends are not going to disappear in the near future. Moreover, they show that "exposure to global restructuring trends increases community vulnerability to population and employment decline." The importance of MIB is also stressed in the literature dealing with smaller cities and rural municipalities. Law's (2009) comparative study of Collingwood, Ontario and Kimberly, British Columbia, a former shipbuilding community and a former mining town respectively, illustrates the importance and the hardships of cities trying to develop a new image in their efforts to offset economic decline. Wamsley (2003) underlines how place promotion is vital to small municipalities in rural Australia, where the importance of tourism seems to be inversely proportional to their size. He adds that globalization also affects smaller cities as markets are now worldwide and closely interconnected, notably through the Internet.

The authors of the chapters that follow are well aware of larger global events, and of the theoretical work that aims to comprehend them. Occasionally they refer to globalization, economic restructuring, neo-liberalism, and other deep explanatory factors, but the content of most chapters is largely empirical. The authors are exploring new territory, and the emphasis is on what happens in the communities that we have selected to study. Chapters deal with image-building initiatives, processes, and agents – individuals, politicians, officials, and associations. What guides the studies theoretically are not the grand currents that deal, perhaps, with the ultimate causes of events and policies – the forces of globalization, changes in cultural values, demographic change, and technological innovations. Instead we focus on two sets of explanatory factors that are important in shaping the policies that exist within Canadian municipalities. These are, first, the processes of intergovernmental relations involved in making policy about image-building, and second, the social forces that attempt to influence or even direct image-building policies. We work with a set of questions about intergovernmental relations and social forces. Our point of departure is that the images associated with municipalities are a function of these variables. Put another way, we think that these proximate causes are very important in determining the actual shape of real policies about the image of municipalities. Structural forces, such as heightened international economic integration, may dictate the need for municipal image-building; others may affect its possibilities and the way it is carried out. (The Internet is important here.) We started with the view that intergovernmental relations and the play of social forces would affect municipal policy about image-building, and we started with a set of questions about these factors. Of course, the authors of the provincial chapters did not slavishly work to answer a predetermined set of questions. Our approach is strongly inductive, which is appropriate in an area about which so little is known. The central questions are laid out below, and they are taken up in the conclusion in light of the empirical findings of our research.

IMPORTANCE

The last three decades of change in the political economy of cities have led to a renewed and transformed interest in MIB by urban planners and politicians. The importance of the policy field is also

Table 1
Relation of MIB to various policy fields

Field	Target	
	Inward	*Outward*
Infrastructure	Local investment Local consumption	External investment
Tourism	Local tourism	Leisure travel Business travel Entertainment
Recreation		
Culture	Participation	Leisure travel
Sport	Consumption	External investment
Citizenship		
Population	Belonging Cohesion Participation	Immigrants
Inclusion	Special populations Immigrants Aboriginals	
Heritage and Conservation	Belonging Cohesion	Leisure travel Business travel

underlined by its potential impact on various other areas of municipal policy. Indeed, MIB is rarely an end by itself, or a specific standalone objective. Rather, MIB is a tool toward different political ends. Moreover, MIB can be directed as much inwards as outwards. Table 1 summarizes the potential interactions of MIB with other, often interconnected, aspects of municipal policy.

MIB can be a major catalyst in cities' infrastructure development or urban renewal. Conversely, infrastructure development is often related to the preservation of municipal images or to their renewal. Infrastructures related to urban renewal may instill local investments. For example, not only can shops get revamped or transformed, but local developers also see in MIB opportunities to make major investments in tourism amenities or entertainment facilities. Leisure and entertainment infrastructure may also lead locals to consume these spaces and the products they offer. As a plethora of academic work suggests (Bradley et al. 2002; Chapin 2004; Eisinger 2000; Friedman et al. 2004; Haningan 2003; Reid 2006; Richards at al. 2004), MIB plays a major role in attracting external investments in hospitality, entertainment, housing, and administrative and industrial development. The relation between MIB and tourists is among the most evident cases. Inwardly, MIB may incite citizens to be tourists in their own locality, to visit other neighbourhoods, museums, and various landmark spaces or venues. Arguably, MIB's most important function is to attract leisure travellers, sport tourists, culture tourists, and business travellers. Bradly et al. (2002) argue that the city image can be both an encouragement and a deterrent in attracting conventions and "meetings tourism," though it is not the only factor in the location decision-making process.

While landmark cultural and heritage events and venues are closely related to outward MIB, inwardly, recreation policy has a strong influence on the image residents have of the city they live in. Community recreation centres and municipal sporting facilities are often the prime locations where city residents participate in the civic life of their city. Allegedly, recreation is a dimension where social capital may build, and conversely, where social exclusion may become exacerbated (Dyreson 2001; Harvey et al. 2007; Smith and Ingham 2003). Hence, MIB is related to the citizenship policy field, which can be divided into two categories: population and inclusion. MIB affects the relationships a city builds with its residents. The city's image may have an influence on citizens' sense of belonging and civic pride, which may impact upon social cohesion and civic participation in the city or the closer neighbourhood community. As well, MIB is sometimes deliberately designed to attract migrants who are looking for a good place to live and raise a family, or (a recent trend) to retire. MIB is also related to the inclusion of diverse populations. The inclusion of populations that do not fit the mold of the majority group and of the able-bodied is often a great challenge for municipalities' image-building policies. Finally, MIB is linked to heritage conservation policy. Landmark heritage buildings, old city centres, and plentiful natural settings are obvious tourist attractions. Heritage is also linked to civic pride and the sense of belonging because it projects the image of a community that has roots in history. It signals the genetic code of a place that speaks to the citizens' sense of community.

Table 1 focuses on how MIB can be seen as a positive tool or asset for various policy fields. However, it cannot be overemphasized that these impacts can be negative, and also that positive impacts may be restricted to only a few segments of the population. Such is often the case with the development of new sports or cultural mega-infrastructures. For example, Broudehoux (2007) underlines that

Table 2
Image layers

Level	Target	Event or Venue Scale
Global	Foreign tourists and investors, immigrants	Mega-international
International	Foreign tourists, investors	International International region
National/Provincial/ Territorial	National, regional	National Regional
Local	Regional, local	Regional Local

most of the new leisure infrastructure developed for the Beijing Olympic Games was going to be accessible only for the entertainment of the upper classes. Moreover, there are endless examples of renewal initiatives destined at projecting a new image, which had the effect of gentrifying these cities' neighbourhoods and consequently evicting their poorest residents, such as was the case with the Vancouver Olympic Games.

A final vision of the importance of MIB is given by Vanollo's (2008, 231) description of the different forms and vehicles used toward the development and promotion of favourable images:

> The importance of image-building as a policy and strategic tool is highlighted by promotional materials, such as brochures, websites, booklets, videos, and pictures explicitly built to attract tourists, economic operators, and investments, so as to create positive, appealing, and charming images of the city. In addition, many policy documents set out specific visions for the future and present a strong emphasis on the definition, communication, and shaping of particular images for the future. They do this through a multitude of texts, slogans, pictures, discourses, and data. In this respect they act as a sort of metaphor, describing some features of the principal element, i.e. the general image (idea) of the city through different elements and discourses.

Another dimension that adds to the complexity of MIB is the fact that different layers of images coexist and sometimes compete in an increasingly crowded market. This is because different audiences are targeted, and the layers are a function of the size of the city or municipality. Table 2 offers a general overview of the different layers of MIB. A first tier is formed by mega-events or venues that play the role of "signaling" the city's global image scope. For Maurice Roche (2000, 1) mega-events are

> large-scale cultural (including commercial and sporting) events which have a dramatic character, mass popular appeal, and international significance. They are typically organized by variable combinations of national governmental and international nongovernmental organizations, and thus can be said to be important elements in "official" versions of public culture.

A second tier is formed by international events or cultural infrastructure of lesser magnitude, aiming to draw the attention of a region of the globe or of a specific international community, such as the countries of the Commonwealth or the Francophonie. Also falling into this category are international events, such as a single sport's world championship. A third tier is formed by national, provincial and territorial events, and infrastructures that are mostly aimed at citizens from all over the country, as well as attracting a few international consumers. Conversely, events and venues of a national or local nature are aimed at corresponding citizens, tourists, consumers, investors, and immigrants. The literature clearly suggests that not only mega-cities are engaged in the competition for a status image (Whitson 2004; Black 2008). Specific layers of images are accessible or manageable as a function of the size of the cities, signaling at the same time both their specific "brand" and their status in the international division of cities' images.

The idea of the kaleidoscopic nature of MIB comes from the immense variety of images and slogans that are put forward. Festivals of all kinds (about identities, foods, cultures, cars, planes, technologies, and so on), celebrations of specific community ethnic backgrounds, heritage specificities, music, sports and entertainment amenities, natural landscapes, landmark events, and more: all constitute a vast prism of images that compete on the market.

In this section, I have focused on the various aspects of MIB in general and on its potential importance in municipal policy. It is now time to turn our attention to MIB as public policy, and to the issues of multilevel governance involved.

IMAGE-BUILDING AS PUBLIC POLICY

Is MIB a simple marketing trick used by municipalities to sell themselves to consumers and investors, or should MIB be considered as a specific domain of municipal policy? How are other levels of government involved in this sector? What social forces are active in MIB?

First, it is important to define what we consider as policies or public policy. Again, there is no consensus on one precise definition of public policy. For our current purposes, Page (2006) and Pal (2006) provide what we need. For Page (2006, 210), "*Policies* can be considered as intentions or actions, or more likely a mix of the two."

Insofar as they arise from conscious reflection and deliberation, policies may reflect a variety of intentions and ideas: some vague, some specific, some conflicting, some unarticulated. They can ... even be unintended or undeliberated consequences of professional practices or bureaucratic routines. Such intentions, practices, and ideas can in turn be shaped by a vast array of different environmental circumstances, ranging from an immediate specific cue or impetus to a more general spirit of the time or even a belief in a self-evident universal truth. (Page 2006, 207–8)

Page adds that these intentions and actions can be viewed at four levels of abstraction. At the most general level, policy *intentions* take the form of principles or general views about how to run public affairs. Somewhat less general intentions are policy *lines*, or strategies about how to manage specific issues or topics. Moving to actions, "*measures* are the specific instruments [or tools] that give effect to distinct policy lines" (Page 2006, 211). Finally, "*practices* are the behavior of officials normally expected to carry out policy measures" (Page 2006, 211).

For Pal (2006), public policy includes intentions and actions, but also inactions. Policies are "a course of action or inaction chosen by public authorities to address a given problem or interrelated set of problems" (Pal 2006, 2). It is important to emphasize Pal's point that a decision by a government not to act on a specific issue is often, by itself, a policy. Finally, Pal (2006) argues that there is a fine line between programs and policies. Policies are mostly "guides to a range of related actions in a given field" (Pal 2006, 2), while *programs* are the specific courses of action taken in order to fulfill the goals of a policy. Here, one important point needs to be added. While the definitions quoted underline the importance of intentions, there are circumstances where public policies are not intended by public authorities, but rather are the result of actions by specific social forces or by other levels of government. In such cases, there is no policy intention or action, but a *de facto* public policy exists. For example, MIB initiatives may be taken by local boosters or by organizations, such as planning boards or tourism commissions, without input by local politicians. Similarly, an effort at image-building by provincial or federal governments helps frame whatever the municipality puts in place. Given all of this, for the purpose of our work, *public policies* are defined as intentions, actions, or inactions either chosen by or accepted by municipal public authorities. Therefore, the chapters included in this book pay attention not only to explicit policies, programs, and actions taken by municipalities, but also to implicit ones.

Governance is another notion in common currency that is now used by various academic disciplines with different meanings. Simply put, governance, according to Kooiman (1993), is a term that refers to the plurality of governing actors, and to the interactions between political actors and civil society in the government of public affairs. He explains the role of interaction as follows:

> Instead of relying on the state or on the market, social political governance is directed at the creation of patterns of interaction in which the political, and the traditional and hierarchical governing and social self-organization are complementary, in which responsibility and accountability for interventions is spread over public and private actors. (Kooiman 1993, 252)

In other words, governance is a notion used in the context of a less central role for formal government institutions and actors, and a larger role for civil society in decision making through a variety of arrangements, such as partnerships, networks, private-public commissions, and so on. If governance refers to patterns of interaction between political and civil society, *multilevel governance* refers to

> a system of continuous negotiations among nested governments at several territorial tiers ... as a result of a broad process of institutional creation and decisional reallocation that has pulled some

previously centralized functions of the state up to the supra-
national level and some down to the local/regional level. (Marks
1993, 392)

More concretely, following Painter (1991), two forms of intergovernmental relationships have always existed in Canada: competitive federalism, in which each level of government fights to keep
its jurisdictional prerogatives, and collaborative federalism, where
the different levels of government negotiate their respective roles on
a given dossier or a broad policy field. In this system, Canadian
municipalities are not in a strong position. First, they are "creatures
of the provinces," so provincial governments define what municipal
structures and functions will be. Second, they increasingly lack the
fiscal and other resources to fulfill their obligations because of rising
costs, the downloading of functions from other governments, and
their reliance on the property tax.

In most federations, central governments have become driven
into intervening in the municipal field, either through the provinces
or through direct mechanisms that allow them to bypass second-
tier levels of government. In Canada, this occurs largely through
the federal spending power, but we know little about how this relationship works in practice. Provinces play different roles in managing municipal-federal relations: monitoring, advocacy, mediation,
regulation, or partnership (Garcea and Pontikes 2006). Putting the
emphasis on multilevel governance, this book examines these intergovernmental relations in the field of image-building in the context
of growing policy complexity with governments and social forces
participating in decision making and policy implementation. A principal aim of this book is to investigate intergovernmental mechanisms in MIB, to analyze how these mechanisms work, and to see how
they can account for image-building policy in municipalities.

We are interested in several intergovernmental issues. Most basically, we want to investigate the links between municipal governments and the federal government. This relationship has long been
neglected, and there are signs that Ottawa has developed a renewed
interest in municipalities (Young and Leuprecht 2006), so we want
to track federal involvement and influence in municipal image-
building. Second, we cannot neglect the provincial governments,
"with their virtually total control over the terms and conditions
under which cities are governed, and their demonstrated willingness

to intervene when they deem it necessary" (Cameron 2002, 307). Provincial governments supervise municipalities and their relationships with the federal government, but the intensity of oversight varies considerably. We want to explore this variation and its causes in the image-building field. Third, we are interested in the role of politicians in this field. The normal interactions between levels of government involve officials who often can work smoothly together because of shared expertise. Politicians establish the program parameters within which officials work, but they also become involved in decision-making, and they can champion issues and causes. So what is the role of politicians in image-building and what effect do they have on the character of policy?

Intergovernmental relations are conducted by actors with resources and goals. All of them must mobilize and pursue resources in today's constrained public sector. As Rhodes put it, "no organization is an island" (1999, 71). Actors bring resources to bear in intergovernmental relations, and the distribution and deployment of them is critical in shaping the resulting policy. We are interested in the resources at the disposal of municipal, federal, and provincial actors. In particular, we want to understand how the relative balance of resources affects the character of public policy.

A final issue is collaboration between municipalities and their agencies. The main focus of the research presented here is on vertical relationships between levels of government. But there is also a trend toward horizontal collaboration between municipal governments and other municipalities, special service boards, development agencies, and other bodies. Through careful fieldwork, Agranoff and McGuire (2003) identified many collaborative activities in the field of economic development. They also found a strong relationship between vertical and horizontal collaboration, with each stimulating and strengthening the other. We are interested in the extent of collaboration among municipalities in image-building, and in particular, in whether relationships with the provincial and federal governments stimulate it.

Multilevel governance refers to the interplay of governments, and of civil society or "social forces." By this term we mean a wide range of more or less formally organized associations – interest groups, voluntary associations, trade unions, members of social movements, religious groups, business associations, and groups representing First Nations and cultural and other minorities. As discussed, the term "governance" refers to the collaboration of such social forces with formal government organizations – departments, agencies, and politicians (Rhodes 1996). There are many reasons for such collaboration to have increased, for example, the precepts of New Public Management, the resource constraints faced by governments, and the need for information for policy-making. Here, we are not interested in the causes, but we are concerned with the power relations among social forces and with their influence on the images built by municipalities.

The interplay of social forces and governments appears to be particularly multi-faceted within MIB. On the one side, at each level of government, MIB may involve several departments, such as tourism, parks and recreation, culture, and infrastructure. All have established clientele groups. MIB is also often the concern of several quasi-autonomous agencies that have the promotion of the city at the centre of their activity. Such is the case with tourism commissions, or organizations like Montréal International (a large and complex agency that promotes the city and its development). At the same time, many social forces are active on the MIB front, and often they are the driving forces. Chambers of commerce and other civic boosters or champions of business are the most obvious social forces in this field. Some sectors of business, such as tour operators, hotels and restaurants, and recreation have a clear and direct stake in image-building policy. These interests can transcend individual municipalities, for example, in the growing industry of sport tourism operators, which we find organized into the Sport Tourism Alliance of Canada. Their goal is to have cities and other levels of government subsidize their initiatives because of the positive image that would be built and the tangible economic benefits that would accrue to local economies and governments themselves. This is to be expected. But it is also the case that all businesses within a municipality have an interest in the image of the place, and in the visitors, investments, and immigrants that a good image supposedly attracts.

Another set of social forces consists of a wide range of community groups, social movements, heritage societies, and environmental groups. Their political visions often clash with those of civic boosters and champions of business. They may fight for the preservation of city neighbourhoods where affordable housing can still be found, for the protection of sensitive habitats for specific animal species or vegetation, for heritage buildings or sectors that are in the way of major redevelopments, and for urban renewal that will bring benefits to the wider population. There are also groups that fight for the interests of art, culture, and sport, and for special populations such as urban Aboriginals, cultural minorities, and so on. Such social forces are interested in constructing municipal images that reinforce the local characteristics that they wish to preserve, promote, and strengthen.

We have several research questions about the role of social forces in the process of image-building. We first need to know what groups are involved. Then our interest turns to the stages of the policy process: agenda setting, proposing alternatives, decision making, and implementation (Pal 2006). We want to assess when different social forces are involved, because earlier involvement normally means that influence on the policy is greater. How does the pattern of involvement affect the character of municipal images?

Our primary area of interest concerns business. There is a very large body of literature about the connection of business interests with the local state. Some argue for a "growth machine" model where redistribution at the local level is not possible (Fainstein and Fainstein 1986; Peterson 1981). Others argue for "urban regimes," where business can form coalitions with other social forces (Stone 1989; Sites 1997). Still others argue for a pluralist model, where policy is fragmented and no one interest dominates all fields (Dowding 2001). We are searching for evidence about whether business dominates policy-making at the local level and in intergovernmental policy-making. We also want to know whether other social forces engage in policy conflicts with business interests and whether they can win policy concessions. These are critical questions to ask about image-building policy.

The final objective of this research is to assess the quality of municipal image-building. Can we identify good MIB policies and initiatives? Are there changes in the process of image-building, especially in the conduct of intergovernmental relations and the participation of social forces, that would produce better policies? How can policy be improved? As in all policy research these practical questions are important ones.

SETTING THE STAGE

This book begins with an overview of federal policies that affect municipal image-building. The bulk of the work, however, consists of sixteen case studies of image-building in Canadian municipalities. These cases are in Manitoba, Prince Edward Island, and Saskatchewan. We chose these provinces for several reasons. Tourism is exceedingly important in PEI, so we expected a lot of effort to be spent on image-building. In Manitoba and Saskatchewan, on the other hand, we did not anticipate that image-building would be central in the concerns of most municipalities, and so our findings might be more representative of the Canadian norm. Further, in both provinces, many municipalities struggle with the problem of retaining population, and this demographic issue is important in the peripheral regions of every Canadian province. The authors chose four municipalities in each province. They were to be of various sizes and were to include the largest city in the province. The precise choices took into consideration the factors of regional representativeness, special characteristics, and accessibility.

Why did we focus on relatively small cities and towns, and even rural municipalities, rather than on the big cities? There are several reasons. First, small towns in Canada have not been the subject of research about image-building, branding, or indeed most policy areas. Yet according to the 2006 Census, 19.8 per cent of Canadians lived in rural areas. It is often said that Canada is 80 per cent urban, but for Statistics Canada, any area with a population of at least one thousand people and a density of at least four hundred people per square kilometer is urban. All else is rural. This means that "urban" includes many municipalities that do not have most of the characteristics that we normally associate with big cities. Some 7.2 per cent of "urban" Canadians live in towns with fewer than ten thousand people, and 15.9 per cent live in towns smaller than fifty thousand people. Therefore, these areas are worth studying. We will see that in some cases smaller places have unique characteristics; in other instances the process of image-building seems to be just a microcosm of what happens in larger places. Finally, as part of the larger research project described in the preface, other scholars studied image-building in the seven other provinces, focusing on the largest city in each. Some of the material gathered in that work will be brought to bear in the conclusion, especially when issues about municipal size and image-building are addressed.

A wide variety of sources and techniques were used in the research presented here. The authors of the chapters consulted government documents, press releases, studies of various kinds, newspaper and magazine coverage, and any extant scholarly literature. They also studied websites and other material used in image-building, such as print advertisements, brochures, and posters. The most significant, perhaps, was interviewing. In each locale, interviews were conducted with officials from all three levels of government. A particular effort was made to contact municipal officials and politicians. Many people representing various social forces were also interviewed. Hence there was a lot of new and original material that could be brought to bear on our research questions.

The book begins with Caroline Andrew's study of federal policies that affect municipal image-building. These are essentially of two types. The first is Ottawa's own advertising, which is aimed to convey an attractive image of the whole country. This is a constraint to MIB because its initiatives are not always in line with the images that cities and their provinces want to project. The second is the federal government's support for events and installations that facilitate municipal image-building. Andrew analyzes spending on culture and sports. This is extensive, and it is deployed in smaller communities as well as in big cities, perhaps disproportionately so.

The first case study by John Lehr and Karla Zubrycki is about Manitoba. The chapter covers MIB with respect to tourism, economic development, and immigration. One of its major contributions is the illustration of how image-building has been embraced by all levels of government since the earliest days of the development of this province. In Manitoba it seems that most image-building is actually done by social forces, with policies being accepted by public authorities. Image-building seems to be little influenced by partisan politics. It appears to be more difficult to achieve consensus about images in larger municipalities, but there can be disagreement in even the smallest ones.

The second provincial case study by Judy Lynn Richards and her collaborators focuses on Prince Edward Island, the smallest of Canadian provinces both in size and population, making it a mostly rural province. In PEI, tourism is one of the largest industries, therefore image-building is a major issue. In this case, small size induces municipalities, the province, and the federal government to play different roles than they do in bigger provinces. Smallness matters, as a good deal of political interaction is informal. Here, though, the provincial government is particularly dominant.

The third case study by Cristine de Clercy and Peter Ferguson is about Saskatchewan. This chapter delineates and explores three types of MIB policies: events and partnerships policy, branding policy, and economic development policy. While demonstrating the complex multilevel governance landscape in that province, the authors also show that the history of its localities cannot be understood without the need for image-building to attract immigrants. Moreover, a key function of image-building is to maintain a positive image among existing residents because out-migration is a threat in much of Saskatchewan. Municipal governments seem to have a relatively free hand in devoting resources to MIB, but the process clearly is led by business; community groups have little direct influence, and Aboriginals and anti-poverty groups are excluded.

In the conclusion, Robert Young sums up the findings and brings them to bear on our original theoretical preoccupations. He trances the general characteristics of image-building in Canada through comparative analysis. He then addresses our questions about intergovernmental relations and social forces in image-building. Next is an evaluation of the quality of the policies in the field. Finally, Young assesses avenues for improving the process of image-building in Canadian municipalities.

In sum, through the overview and the case studies presented here, this book provides an original focus on municipal image-building, and on the mechanisms of intergovernmental relations and governance at play in this area of public policy. It covers a range of municipalities that is rarely considered in depth in the literature on MIB. Through careful research, we are able to report some new and unexpected findings that we hope will interest our readers.

REFERENCES

Agranoff, Robert, and Michael McGuire. 2003. *Collaborative Public Management: New Strategies for Local Governments*. Washington: Georgetown University Press.

Alasia, Allesandro, Ray Bollman, John Parkins, and Bill Reimer. 2008. *An Index of Community Vulnerability: Conceptual Framework and Application to Population and Employment Changes, 1981 to 2001*. Ottawa: Statistics Canada, Agriculture and rural working paper series, Catalogue no. 21-601-MIE- No.088 http://www.statcan.ca/english/research/21-601-MIE/21-601-MIE2008088.pdf

Black, David. 2008. "Dreaming Big: The Pursuit of Second Order Games as a Strategic Response to Globalization." *Sport and Society* 11, no. 4: 467–79.

Bradley, Andrew, Tim Hall, and Margaret Harrison. 2002. "Selling Cities: Promoting New Images for Meetings Tourism." *Cities* 19, no. 1: 61–70.

Broudehoux, Anne-Marie. 2007. "Spectacular Beijing: The Conspicuous Construction of an Olympic Metropolis." *Journal of Urban Affairs* 2, no. 4: 383–99.

Cameron, Ken. 2002. "Some Puppets; Some Shoestrings! The Changing Intergovernmental Context." In *Urban Affairs: Back on the Policy Agenda*, edited by Caroline Andrew, Katherine A. Graham and Susan D. Phillips. Montreal and Kingston: McGill-Queen's University Press.

Chapin, Timothy. 2004. "Sports Facilities as Urban Redevelopment Catalysts: Baltimore's Camden Yards and Cleveland's Gateway." *Journal of the American Planning Association* 70, no. 2: 193–209.

Dowding, Keith. 2001. "Explaining Urban Regimes." *International Journal of Urban and Regional Research* 25, no. 1: 7–19.

Dyreson, Mark. 2001. "Maybe it's Better to Bowl Alone: Sport, Community and Democracy in American Thought." *Culture, Sport, Society* 4, no. 1: 19–30.

Eisinger, Peter. 2000. "The Politics of Bread and Circuses: Building the City for the Visitor Class." *Urban Affairs Review* 3, no. 3: 316–33.

Essex, Stephen, and Brian Chalkley. 2004. "Mega-sporting Events in Urban and Regional Policy: A History of the Winter Olympics." *Planning Perspectives* 19, no. 2: 201–32.

Fagnoni, Edith. 2004. "Amnéville, from Old Industrial City to Leisure-Tourism City: Which Future for Deserted Urban Grounds?" *Mondes en Développement* 32, no. 1: 51–66, 109.

Fainstein, Norman I., and Susan S. Fainstein. 1986. "Regime Strategies, Communal Resistance, and Economic Forces," in rev. ed. Susan S. Fainstein et al., *Restructuring the City: The Political Economy of Urban Redevelopment*. New York and London: Longman.

Friedman, Michael, David Andrews, and Michael L. Silk. 2004. "Sport and the Façade of Redevelopment in the Postindustrial City." *Sociology of Sport Journal* 21, no. 2: 119–39.

Garcea, Joseph, and Ken Pontikes. 2004. "Federal-Municipal-Provincial Relations in Saskatchewan: Provincial Roles, Approaches, and Mechanisms," in Robert Young and Christian Leuprecht, eds., *Municipal-*

Federal-Provincial Relations in Canada. Montreal and Kingston: McGill-Queen's University Press.

Gratton, Chris, Simon Shibli, and Richard Coleman. 2005. "Sport and Economic Regeneration in Cities." *Urban Studies* 42, no. 5&6: 985–99.

Hannigan, John. 2003. "Symposium on Branding, the Entertainment Economy and Urban Place Building." *International Journal of Urban and Regional Research* 27, no. 2: 352–60.

Harvey, David. 2001. "From Managerialism to Entrepreneurialism: The Transformation in Urban Governance in Late Capitalism." In *Spaces of Capital: Towards a Critical Geography*. New York: Routledge, 345–68.

– 2007. *A Brief History of Neoliberalism*. Oxford: Oxford University Press.

Harvey, Jean, Maurice Lévesque, and Peter Donnelly 2007. "Sport Volunteerism and Social Capital." *Sociology of Sport Journal* 24, no. 2: 206–23.

Kavaratzis, Michalis, and G. J. Ashworth. 2005. "City Branding: An Effective Assertion of Identity or a Transitory Marketing Trick?" *Tijdschrift voor Economische en Sociale Geografie* 96, no. 5: 506–14.

Kooiman, Jan. 1993. *Modern Governance: New Government-Society Interactions*. London: Sage.

Kong, Lily. 2007. "Cultural Icons and Urban Development in Asia: Economic Imperative, National Identity, and Global City Status." *Political Geography* 26, no. 4: 383–404.

Law, Alan. 2009. "Monumental Changes: Archives of Community in Leisurescape." *Annals of Leisure Research* 12, no. 3: 350–376.

Lehr, John S., and John C. Lehr. 2007. Image-building and Place Promotion: a Literature Review. Unpublished working paper.

Page, Edward C. 2006. "The Origins of Policy." In *The Oxford Handbook of Public Policy*, edited by Michael Moran, Martin Rein, and Robert Goodin. Oxford: Oxford University Press, 207–27.

Painter, Martin. 1991. "Intergovernmental Relations in Canada: An Institutional Analysis." *Canadian Journal of Political Science*, 24, no. 2: 269–88.

Pal, Leslie. 2006. *Beyond Policy Analysis: Public Issues Management in Turbulent Times, Third Edition*. Toronto: Nelson.

Peterson, Paul E. 1981. *City Limits*. Chicago: University of Chicago Press.

Reid, Gavin. 2006. "The Politics of City Imaging: A Case Study of the MTV Europe Music Awards Edinburgh 03." *Event Management* 10, no. 1: 35–46.

Rhodes, R.A.W. 1996. "The New Governance: Governing without Government." *Political Studies* 44: 652–667.

– 1999. *Control and Power in Central-Local Relations*, Second Edition. Aldershot: Ashgate.

Richards, Greg, and Julie Wilson. 2004. "The Impact of Cultural Events on City Image: Rotterdam, Cultural Capital of Europe 2001." *Urban Studies* 41, no. 10: 1931–51.

Roche, Maurice. 2000. *Mega-events and Modernity: Olympics and Expos in the Growth of Global Culture*. London: Routledge.

Sites, William. 1997. "The Limits of Urban Regime Theory: New York City Under Koch, Dinkins, and Giuliani." *Urban Affairs Review* 32, no. 4: 536–57.

Smith, Jason M., and Alan G. Ingham. 2003. "On the Waterfront: Retrospectives on the Relationship between Sport and Communities." *Sociology of Sport Journal* 20: 252–74.

Stone, Clarence N. 1989. *Regime Politics: Governing Atlanta, 1946–1988*. Lawrence: University Press of Kansas.

Watkins, Helen, and David Herbert. 2003. "Cultural Policy and Place Promotion: Swansea and Dylan Thomas." *Geoforum* 34, no. 2: 249–66.

Whitson, David. 2004. "Bringing the World to Canada: 'The Periphery of the Centre.'" *Third World Quarterly* 25, no. 7: 1215–32.

Yeoh, Brenda S.A. 2005. "The Global Cultural City? Spatial Imagineering and Politics in the (multi)Cultural Marketplaces of South-East Asia." *Urban Studies* 42, no. 5&6: 945–58.

Young, Robert, and Christian Leuprecht. 2006. *Municipal-Federal-Provincial Relations in Canada*. Montreal and Kingston: McGill-Queen's University Press.

2

Federal Policies on Image-building: Very Much Cities and Communities

CAROLINE ANDREW

As a child growing up in British Columbia, much of the "branding" of Canada seemed somewhat bizarre. We did have maple trees but they didn't really go scarlet in the fall, more often brown before falling. "*Quelques arpents de neige*" didn't resonate with Vancouver's climate – "*arpents de pluie*" would have been a better description. The central dramatic image of our history books was the wheat fields meeting the trains (only later did I realize that this was a socio-economic perspective, and perhaps preferable to the previous "great man tradition"), and I couldn't connect to this at all. In BC, we didn't have wheat fields, and certainly no longer took the train.

The intent of these examples is to suggest the importance of images, and therefore the importance of understanding public policies that promote the development and reinforcement of national and sub-national images. These examples also suggest that the central policy question is the relationship, or the fit, between the images and those receiving the images. We will pursue the question somewhat later on about who are the intended targets for receiving the images, but first we must justify our definition of the public policies to be examined.

Our focus, given the relationship of this chapter to the overall aim of the project of understanding good municipal public policy, is to analyze the ways in which federal government policies and policy areas that are related concretely to image-building promote images that convey representations of municipal Canada. In other words, we analyze representations of the full range of human settlements in which Canadians live.

We want to understand who is represented and how are they represented. In particular, we are interested in questions of size –

does federal image-building represent metropolitan areas, large cities, small cities, small communities, rural communities, or all of the above? Is there more, or better, representation of big-city Canada or of small-town Canada? This is an important issue because the image projected by the federal government may form the frame within which municipalities (and provinces) have to work when defining their own images. Second, we want to examine federal programs that can help municipalities in their image-building efforts. How are these benefits distributed? Are the large cities favoured, or is there also assistance for smaller communities? The literature on image-building is abundant and rich, as Jean Harvey has demonstrated in the introduction to this book. One of the interesting questions it raises is that of the audience for image-building: is it those who are external to the place building its image that are targeted (be they tourists, investors, or immigrants choosing a destination), or is it the local residents whose civic pride is to be developed and strengthened by seeing their municipality through a new lens? This is an important question when thinking about image-building, and it is certainly important for analyzing federal policies. In looking at the various policies, we need to think of whether the target audience is clear and whether the message is coherent in terms of its target. It may be that certain images can serve multiple audiences, but this may not always be true.

   This chapter will first look at the ways in which Canada has been represented at the international level before turning to the analysis of domestically focused programs. At the international level, our interest is more on the question of branding, and particularly on the branding of Canada as a tourist destination, while at the domestic level, we will be looking more at patterns of federal spending. Our specific examples in the second section will be programs relating to sport and to culture. We conclude by returning to our central question about what is good public policy in image-building.

BRANDING CANADA ON THE INTERNATIONAL STAGE

Theoretically, one could propose an almost unlimited list of federal policies, programs, and activities related to image-building. In a *Globe and Mail* article from 1 July 2010 entitled, "Oh, Canada, Get a Brand" (Houpt 2010, 1, 6), the regulation of Canada's financial sector, and Agriculture Canada programs relating to domestically produced food stuffs were given as pertinent examples of building

Canada's image on the international scene. These two examples certainly enlarge the scope of possible policies to analyze. Even our focus on the representation of municipal Canada, or Canadian human settlements, does not substantially narrow the potential list of policies. In order to begin to define the scope of this chapter, I will use Evan Potter's (2009) useful categorization of five dimensions through which the representation of Canada takes place at the international level. The dimensions are as follows: culture, tourist destination, economic power, openness to immigration, and how Canada governs itself. We will examine each of these briefly in order to see to what extent these dimensions lead to a representation of communities in Canada, and what sizes of communities would fit most logically into these different definitions.

If we look first at culture, it is striking how many of the iconic images of Canadian culture are of nature and not of communities. The traditional importance of the Group of Seven was certainly a portrayal of the wilderness of northern Canada, and even the less wilderness-focused Quebec painters of the same period were painting pastoral scenes of rural Quebec. More recently, Aboriginal art has become one of the symbols of Canadian culture, and although, in reality, half of the Aboriginal population lives in urban areas, the images still possess an intimate relationship to nature.

CANADA AS A TOURIST DESTINATION: WHAT IMAGES DOMINATE?

Potter's second dimension, tourist destination, is affected by public sector policies, and certainly the federal government plays an important role in tourist promotion. The federal agency is the Canadian Tourism Commission (CTC). Created in 1995 and transformed into a Crown corporation in 2001, its mandate is four-fold: sustain a vibrant tourist industry; market Canada as a destination; support a cooperative relationship between the private sector, the government of Canada, and the provinces and territories; and provide information about Canadian tourism to the private sector and the government.

In terms of our interest in image-building, it is the marketing of Canada that is of the greatest interest. In 2004, the Canadian Tourism Commission came up with a new branding: "Canada. Keep Exploring." Described as a "brand built for explorers," the description goes on to state, "we attract travellers who want the freedom to express themselves through travel" (see http://en-corporate.canada.travel/markets).

The main images included in "Canada. Keep Exploring" are of single individuals in landscapes. Of the principal visual images that were connected to the new branding, one is a woman with a kayak and the other is a man bicycling through a forest. "Self-expression and the freedom to explore" was another of the principal messages, and the major dimensions were described as culture (illustrated by two images – of two people sitting at a small table, and another image of two people beside a totem pole), and geography (illustrated by two images – of a woman with a kayak, and another image of a man bicycling in a forest). Tourism is, for the most part, seen as self-expression, and it is primarily visualized as individuals being active in nature and secondarily as socializing in restaurants or cafés.

In July 2010, the CTC's website highlighted the "Canada. Keep Exploring" campaign as the Canadian brand. A tourism brand is described as "the imagination and emotion a country inspires in visitors; a set of beliefs and associations they hold about a place. A tourism brand is a promise of what to expect when you visit." Five unique selling propositions were then outlined, and the first had a clear urban focus, "vibrant cities on the edge of nature." This was followed by personal journeys by land, water, and air; active adventure among awe-inspiring natural wonders; local cuisine; and, finally, connecting with Canadians. The urban focus was limited to the first proposition of "vibrant cities on the edge of nature," whereas the last theme of "connecting to Canadians," for example, gave the following four place-based references, all with small-town or rural connotations: "You can meet a friendly Maritime fisherman on the docks of Lunenberg, Nova Scotia. Share stories with a local at the Yukon Storytelling Festival. Learn the traditional life of the Great Plains people at Alberta's famous buffalo jump. Meet a third-generation cheese-maker along *la route des fromages* in Quebec."

There is also a huge bank of images on the CTC website providing every possible representation of Canada available. However, the images linked to the "Canada. Keep Exploring" brand are more about individuals than collectivities, and the only explicitly urban image is seen as closely related to nature. "Nature is more than a backdrop in Canadian cities. It's a symbol of freedom – the freedom to explore and be yourself. Think Canada's got edge? You bet it does." It is not about empty spaces, it is about human beings in contact with nature.

The federal government's branding is a good illustration of one of the central messages of the tourism literature, that tourists want specificity and familiarity at the same time (Judd and Fainstein 1999; Maitland and Ritchie 2009). They want to feel that they are somewhat specific, but at the same time, they want to feel completely at home and with a sense of understanding their environment. The "Canada. Keep Exploring" campaign seems to do this nicely; it suggests the discovery of new places and/or new understandings of self, but within a framework of well-known ideas that fit with some of the stereotypes about Canada, held both by Canadians and non-Canadians. "And that friendly reputation? Well, we decided to show off the real face of Canada – authentic, witty, informal, and, yes, friendly" (Canadian Tourism Commission, 2010).

However, the CTC is also constrained by the reasons why tourists want to come to Canada. On an international scale, the image of Canada is very much linked to wilderness, nature, and outdoor activities. The two central images of "Canada. Keep Exploring" certainly build on this understanding of Canada: kayaking and bicycling, both in attractive natural settings that do not suggest any proximity to other human beings or to any form of settlement. Canadian cities are tourist destinations and are seen to be safe and clean, but they certainly do not rank with the great cultural capitals of the world, and it would be counterproductive to advertise Canada as a predominantly urban destination. They do include some visual images of urban life, largely associated with eating and drinking in company with other adults, but these are minor themes compared to the images of individuals in contact with nature.

The third set of images that Evan Potter discusses are those associated with Canada as an economic power, and here again, the references are more to the natural resources of Canada, and associated more with rural and remote Canada. Canada's recent economic profile is more about the potential of its natural resources than about its urban-based manufacturing or high technology industries, and this, too, suggests a non-urban profile.

The fourth dimension of Potter's images of Canada is the openness to immigration, and here the connections to urban images should be clear: the big cities have been, and continue to be, the major destinations of new immigrants, and certainly the major Canadian cities have been transformed in terms of the overall composition of their populations. Visual images of Toronto, Vancouver, and Montreal convey an openness to immigration in that the very multiple origins of the population are obvious.

Finally, Potter describes the Canadian government's interest in explaining how Canada is governed, and in representing Canada as a vibrant democracy concerned with human rights. This is an image about governmental processes, but the image is also influenced by the content of government policies. For example, the Canadian government's policy on climate change or on the involvement of Canada in the war in Afghanistan have certainly created a negative international reaction to the vibrancy of Canadian democracy and the priority attached by the Canadian government to human rights. The federal government is interested in greater international and national recognition of our experience in the processes of democratic government.

Another interesting example of the federal government's role in articulating the Canadian governmental experience at an international level had been Canada's creation and initial support of the Forum of Federations, an international NGO whose role is to communicate information about the contribution federalism makes, and can make, to the maintenance and construction of democratic societies and governments, and to create networks of practitioners of federalism, including existing federations and countries seeking to introduce federal elements into their governance structures. Following the first International Conference on Federalism in 1999, the forum was created as an initiative of then-federal minister, Stéphane Dion, and certainly was part of the federal government's strategy in its relations with Quebec. The federation has developed over time, and the Fourth International Conference on Federalism was organized by the Indian government in 2007. One of its four main themes was the question of local government and metropolitan regions in federal countries. However, the work of the forum on municipal governments is a very small component of the overall message about the importance of federalism as a tool for responding to democratisation by managing diversity, geographical space, and different legal and political regimes through the division of legislative responsibilities between national and state and/or provincial entities. Integrating the third level of government into the practice of federalism is very minor compared to the understanding of federalism as involving two levels of government: national and sub-national. The Fifth International Conference on Federalism, held in Ethiopia in December 2010, focused on sustainable development and federalism, and not at all about the role of municipal institutions (Forum of Federations 2010).

Certainly the understanding at home and abroad of Canadian federalism is of a relationship between the federal government and the provinces. Indeed, this image has, in the twentieth century, led to urban Canada being largely invisible within the understanding of the Canadian political system. The governing of cities is not a visible part of the image of Canadians governing themselves. This is true internationally and it is dramatically true within Canada. City governments are beginning to be described but the dominant image of our system of government remains that of classical federalism: the relationship of the federal government to the provincial governments. It should be noted that the Canadian government has now ended its support to the Forum of Federations.

In summarizing our use of Evan Potter's categories of the main fields of image-building by the Canadian government on the international scene, we can conclude that only one of the five – the openness of Canada to immigration – is a primarily urban image. All of the others – culture, tourist destination, economic power, and how Canada governs itself – essentially lend themselves to images of natural settings or of relationships to nature, or, finally, of images of federal-provincial accommodations. They do not exclude urban images, but the obvious associations are not with the visualization of urban Canada.

In order to attempt to understand the "take up" of these images projected by the federal government internationally, one can look at one form of reaction: the choices of topics made by scholars outside Canada applying for financial support through the International Council of Canadian Studies (ICCS) to come to Canada to pursue those research topics. The ICCS, founded in 1981, is supported by several federal agencies led by the Department of Foreign Affairs and International Trade Canada (DFAIT). The ICCS brings together the twenty-one national and multi-national associations of Canadian studies, and the six associate members in thirty-nine countries. Through its Understanding Canada program, it offers support to researchers and students who wish to study in Canada, to teach a course with significant Canadian content, to publish an article developing Canadian material, or, finally, to conduct research pertinent to a doctoral thesis. Applicants are encouraged to choose a topic with policy relevance in one of the following areas: economic development, environmental sustainability, democracy and rule of law, managing diversity, North American partnership, and peace and security. In the 2010 competition, the largest number of projects focused on the theme of managing diversity, with many relating to the topic of Aboriginal Canada, either in terms of exploring Aboriginal culture, or in terms of relationships between Canadian public policy and Aboriginal reality. There were also a number of proposals that looked at Canadian writers, either in terms of gender or ethnocultural diversity. In most cases, these projects were not specifically located in cities, but rather focused on the particular writer's choice of location. The proposals dealing with environmental sustainability were often explicitly related to northern locations and almost always non-urban. The very high number of proposals relating to the theme of managing diversity suggests that this is the international dimension of the Canadian image that resonates most clearly among scholars at the present time. The Canadian experience, with its Aboriginal populations, the recent immigrant population, and the experience of trying to establish women's equality through public policy, have all been visible internationally. The specifically urban dimension of these issues could be argued (particularly in terms of immigration and gender), but this has not been a significantly visible dimension of the research areas being submitted. The ICCS program is admittedly a very "niche" program and therefore has a very limited angle into the international branding of Canada, but it does provide insight into what people living outside Canada, who are particularly interested in Canada, think is worth investigating about Canada. To this extent, it gives an additional perspective on the ways in which the representations of Canada are received by international audiences. As of May 2012 the Canadian government has indicated its intent to cancel this program.

We have been looking at federal policies around image-building that are open-ended in the sense of creating images that will be built upon by those receiving the images. Our description of the Canadian Tourism Commission is clear in this regard: Canadian tourism publicity encompasses a wide variety of different messages, although some are more central to their campaign. Those receiving the images then choose to come to Canada, and choose their destinations within Canada, by constructing links between the images presented and their own priorities. This is also the angle of analysis that we have done in regard of the subjects chosen by Canadianists around the world – they relate to areas of academic interest of the individuals concerned, and to the ways in which the images of Canada relate to these areas of interest. These have tended to suggest that the images of Canada that resonate internationally are those of natural beauty and interesting experiences in managing diversity. These experiences relating to diversity do tend to take place in the large cities of Canada, but the urban character of the setting is not an explicit emphasis.

DOMESTIC IMAGE-BUILDING POLICIES

Moving from the international level to the domestic level, we move from thinking about images to thinking about patterns of federal spending, and the program regulations that structure and orient these expenditure patterns. We have chosen to look at programs relating to sports events and to cultural infrastructure, as these two sets of programs involve spending that is place-based. In both cases, the federal government has elaborated policies and programs that involve explicit categorization by size of locality. These are, therefore, directly pertinent to our interest in understanding the federal vision of municipal Canada and how this is constructed. More specifically, does federal spending advantage urban Canada or small-town Canada? This will be our principal focus in looking at sports policy and cultural policy.

We are interested in the results of the programs – the extent to which these programs produce, spending patterns that privilege urban Canada, or, conversely, spending patterns that privilege small-town Canada. We are also interested in the administrative processes involved, and therefore, in the extent to which the question of the size of community is explicitly part of the program. As one part of this question, we want to know whether municipal governments and/or social forces play any direct or indirect role in the program, in its conception, formulation, and/or delivery.

This is not to argue that the portrayal of Canada as urban could only be done if big city municipal governments were directly involved in the program, but simply to make the point that our interest is both in the results of federal policy-making and in the administrative procedures. We are interested in the relation between the framing of federal policies and the involvement of different sets of actors in the operations of the program, but we do not presume that involvement in the program will necessarily lead to an impact on the results. Taking our specific example, it is not necessarily true that a large urban municipality would necessarily depict themselves as about many different people in busy streets. They could also be caught up in the view that Canada is wilderness and pristine nature, and want only to portray their parks and empty walkways.

Municipal policy-making and sport, culture, and tourism have all been central elements in municipal "branding." The literature on municipal image-building, or "branding," is extensive and offers an understanding about the particular importance of image-building in the present period, while recognizing that cities have been concerned with image-building for a very long time. Indeed, the Canadian literature on municipal boosterism is much more about the nineteenth century than the twenty-first, although research is expanding on present-day examples (Whitson and Horne 2006; Gibson and Lowes 2007).

Globalization and the neo-liberal downsizing of the welfare state have meant that cities are placed in a much more competitive situation. The stage is increasingly global, as opposed to national, and the national level cannot be counted on to the same extent to provide stable levels of support as it had in the previous period. It increasingly supports "winners," rather than providing support equally across growing and declining areas. Cities and smaller communities are increasingly devising strategies for economic development that play out on a global scale. Increasingly, and perhaps an indication of a shift from neo-liberalism to inclusive liberation, these strategies make arguments about the quality of life and the liveability of their community. Both Richard Florida (2002) and Allen Scott (2007), to mention only two authors, have abundantly debated the ways in which quality of life, networks of social solidarity, and economic development are interrelated in present-day urban settings.

Sport Policies

We will look at the federal policies that relate to the location of sports facilities and the holding of different categories of sports events. Sport can be important in municipal image-building because it can bring the place to the consciousness of large numbers of people. The mere fact of being known helps image-building. Beyond this, the facilities constructed for sporting events can attract visitors in the future while providing recreational opportunities for the municipal residents.

Sport Canada has three funding programs: the Athlete Assistance Program, the Sport Support Program (funding national sport and multi-sport organizations), and the Hosting Program. Our major interest is in the Hosting Program, as it supports the holding of sport events and, therefore, has a place-based focus.

The Hosting Program was initially adopted in 1983, revised in 1996, and then again in 2008. The impetus for program development was clear: increasing numbers of sports events and their increasing costs. There are four delivery components to this program: international major multi-sport games, international single-sport events, international strategic focus events (this refers to events that are focused on underrepresented groups that face systemic barriers), and, finally, the Canada Games.

As of January 2008, an updated version of the international component of this program had been put into place. The policy document explaining the updated version articulated the benefits of hosting:

- contribution to enhanced athlete excellence, and to the development of sport programming and infrastructure legacies, particularly for targeted Olympic and Paralympic sports with the greatest potential for podium performance;
- increased capacity for high-performance sport through providing opportunities for Canadians to improve their skills and leadership;
- enhancement of Canada's role as a leading sport nation through the delivery of technically and ethically sound sport events reflecting Canadian culture and values;
- promotion of social, cultural, and community benefits, including enhanced voluntarism, active citizenship and civic participation, cultural programs reflecting Canadian diversity, physical activity, and healthy communities; and
- promotion of economic benefits for the community in which the event is hosted, as well as for the province/territory and country (Government of Canada, Canadian Heritage 2008, 3).

The first three objectives relate to the sport component, whereas the last two objectives deal with the community impact, expressed first in terms of active citizenship and healthy communities, and secondly in terms of the economic impact. In 2004, Canadian Heritage conducted a summative evaluation of the hosting policy (Government of Canada, Canadian Heritage 2004), focusing on the need to demonstrate the link between hosting sports events and sport development. The first two recommendations of the evaluation underlined this point: "sport development is the key expected outcome for each event and the department's hosting program as a whole," and "sports events must be shown to support sport development" (Government of Canada, Canadian Heritage 2004, 5–6). The report went on to state that "sport development should be defined to encompass the development of athletes, coaches, officials, and volunteers, as well as increasing viewer participation" (Government of Canada, Canadian Heritage 2004, 5). The evaluation argued that the hosting program must develop performance measurements that related hosting events to sport development. As the evaluation stated, "without this, the rationale for the program disappears" (Government of Canada, Canadian Heritage 2004). To this extent, the location of the event is secondary to its impact on sports development.

However, this evaluation did lead to making clear distinctions in terms of the size and scope of the event and its organization. Smaller events were to report on sport development outcomes alone, whereas large events, measured in terms of federal financial support, were to report on sport development outcomes, community impacts, economic impact following the specific Sport Tourism Economic Assessment Model (STEAM), and social impacts, including the legacies that had been created.

This policy on the reporting on outcomes by size of event can be interpreted in a variety of ways: as facilitating the participation of smaller communities; as realistically evaluating the potential of accurate outcome-reporting from smaller communities; as wanting to hang on to economic indicators despite the explicit program emphasis on sport development; as reinforcing the obligation for major events to think about legacies; and as linking to other federal priorities, such as the Results-based Management and Accountability Framework (RMAF).

Amounts provided vary considerably, as the evaluation indicated for the three-year period from 2000–01 to 2002–03 (Government of Canada, Canadian Heritage 2004, 18). The Canada Games component is covered by a federal-provincial agreement called the Clear Lake Resolution, signed in 1997, which determines a breakdown for the intergovernmental division of costs. The London Games of 2002 received $7.9 million from the federal government, and the Bathurst-Campbellton Games of 2003, $7.5 million. The strategic focus component covered the North American Indigenous Games (NAIG) with an overall federal contribution of $2.5 million, the Arctic Winter Games, $0.6 million, and les Jeux de la Francophonie, $16.9 million. In the international single-sport events, many small events were funded (between twenty-three and thirty-six per year), but the major expenditures were for the 2001 Edmonton World Championships in Athletics ($38 million), the 2003 Hamilton World Cycling Championships ($8.5 million), and the 2005 Montréal Fédération Internationale de Natation (FINA) ($16 million).

The summative evaluation report was followed shortly in 2004 by the adoption of the Strategic Framework for Hosting International Sport Events, endorsed by the federal-provincial/territorial (F-P/T) ministers responsible for sport, recreation, and fitness. The framework is also one product of the 2002–05 F-P/T priorities for collaborative action. Since the 1980s, F-P/T ministers responsible for sport, fitness, and recreation meet annually to manage intergovernmental issues. For the purpose of preparing for these conferences, and for the implementation of their decisions, a F-P/T mechanism for sport development has been put in place, including a deputy ministers' committee, a deputy ministers' work group, as well as different working groups whose mandates evolve with the decisions taken at the ministers meetings.

As this mechanism is centred on F-P/T relationships, officially municipalities do not have a voice at this level. However, one of the main objectives of the 2004 framework was to strengthen relationships between the three levels of government, as well as with the sport community in hosting sport events. One unstated objective of the framework was to attempt to manage the constant influx of requests by local organizing committees wishing to host such events, and, of course, all requesting provincial and federal support. In order to do this, the framework set a maximum number of events that would be supported in different categories over a large number of years. For example, two major international multi-sport events (e.g. Olympic Games or Commonwealth Games) could receive government support over the period of ten years.

While the F-P/T collaborative mechanism is the major instrument of intergovernmental relationships in sport, fitness, and recreation, other mechanisms exist. As stated earlier, the 1997 Clear Lake Resolution provided the mechanism for the three levels of government to interact with regards to the Canada Games. The prospect of hosting the Vancouver Olympic and Paralympic Games led to the adoption, in November 2002, of a multi-party agreement, including the federal and BC governments, the municipalities of Vancouver and Whistler, the Canadian Olympic and Paralympic committees, as well as the bidding committee that attracted the Games. That agreement set up the governance rules of the organizing committee for the Games, according to IOC rules.

In conclusion, one can say that the largest federal contributions do go to large urban centres for the large international events. However, for the federal government, these events are described in terms of the organizations behind the events and not explicitly as place-based. And, indeed, the structuring of the hosting policy around the categorization of types of events can be seen as an effort to make sure that the benefits of sporting events, be they social, or for athletic or economic development, are distributed across Canada.

Cultural Policies

Culture has an obvious relation to image-building. Almost by definition, events highlighting art, music, dance, and distinctive cultural elements of the place contribute to a positive image for the municipality. They attract tourists and arouse local enthusiasm. Cultural events and infrastructure can also provide a legacy around which future images can be built.

So, in culture do we find a pattern similar to that in the sports area? The programs also fall under Canadian Heritage, and this suggests that the findings may be similar to those for sports events. We will look at three programs that fund programming (Arts Presentation Canada [APC]),[1] physical infrastructure (Cultural Spaces Canada [CSC]), and capacity building (Canadian Arts and Heritage Sustainability Program [CAHSP]). Overall, there are five components to CAHSP, however, two components that are relevant here are the Cultural Capitals program, which aims at integrating culture into municipal policy, and the Network Initiatives component, which supports national projects that strengthen the environment for the arts and heritage. The other three components relate to capacity-building within arts and heritage organizations, and the encouragement of private sector support to these organizations as such, are not place-based. The programs being examined are relatively new – APC and CSC in 2001 and the Cultural Capitals and Networking Initiatives in 2002 – but in general, they were built on previous programs.

Both Arts Presentation Canada, which provides financial assistance to arts presenter organizations, arts festivals, and presenter support organizations, and Cultural Spaces Canada, which provides financial assistance for the improvement, renovation, and construction of arts and heritage facilities, support activities across the full range of sizes of communities.

Arts Presentation Canada has given funding to 224 communities and cities from 2001-02 to 2006-07 (Government of Canada, Canadian Heritage, Annual Reports). One example of broad distribution is for 2006-07 for New Brunswick, which equalled twenty-seven projects in fourteen localities. Caraquet received the largest number of projects (six), including the two largest grants: $80,000 and $60,000. Fredericton received five projects, and Moncton, four. A rather different pattern was true in Saskatchewan, where Regina and Saskatoon received the vast majority of the approved projects. The amounts given by the Arts Presentation Canada program are often small and there are considerable numbers of projects. Measurement is further complicated by the fact that many of the projects going to the largest centres are, in fact, for province-wide activities or associations.

Cultural Spaces Canada is easier to analyze in terms of distribution, as physical infrastructure is necessarily fixed in space. From 2001-02 to 2006-07, the program funded 533 projects (Government of Canada, Canadian Heritage, Annual Reports). In most provinces, the largest project was not in the largest urban centre. In BC, Nanaimo received the largest project ($2.2 million); in Alberta it was the Banff Centre ($5.8 million); in New Brunswick, Caraquet received $1.5 million; in Ontario, the Great Canadian Theatre Company in Ottawa received $3 million, but Parry Sound received $2.9 million. The largest project in Newfoundland was given to the provincial Department of Tourism ($1.9 million). In Quebec, Wendake received $2.3 million (in two separate projects), and in Saskatchewan, Moose Jaw received $1.2 million.

The 2003 evaluation of these programs did not look specifically at the distribution by size of community, but it did examine
the capacity of the different program components to support underrepresented groups. A survey was done of regional managers and the
results indicated that respondents felt that Arts Presentation Canada
had been the most successful in terms of diversifying audiences. "It
[APC] has contributed to the diversification of programming among
targeted communities and has supported an increasing number of
outreach initiatives targeting youth, Aboriginal, culturally diverse,
and francophone audiences" (Government of Canada, Canadian
Heritage 2003, 65).

The report went on to explain why Aboriginal groups faced the
most obstacles and were therefore the least well-served by the programs. The obstacles were the limited resources to prepare applications and to implement projects, the reporting requirements that
were seen as burdensome, and program criteria that did not take
into account the realities of the groups and their ways of doing
things. Therefore, federal program requirements effectively limited
the capacity of social forces to be involved in the programs.

The Cultural Capitals program component is potentially the most
interesting for this chapter, as it explicitly attempts to engage with
municipal governments. The intent of the program was municipal capacity-building in the area of cultural policy. The aims were
to reward municipalities that had developed significant activity
in the cultural sphere, encourage municipal governments to think
of investing more in arts and cultural policies, and increase and
improve municipal cultural services. The program was announced
by the minister of Canadian heritage at the 2002 annual meeting
of the Federation of Canadian Municipalities (FCM) and cancelled
in 2012. Designations of up to five cultural capitals a year were
announced. Three population levels were established:

- below 50,000 – two awards per year and a maximum of $250,000
  per award;
- between 50,000 and 125,000 – one award per year and a maximum of $500,000;
- above 125,000 – one award per year and a maximum of $500,000.

A fourth category, the Award for Innovative Cultural Bridges,
was for two or more municipalities from at least two provinces or

territories that would develop exchanges and partnerships (again with a maximum of $500,000). If this award was not given, another Cultural Capital designation could be made.

The program was modelled on similar existing programs, such as the European Union's Cities of Culture program, and the American Capital of Culture Initiative. Consultations were held with the FCM and the Canadian Conference of the Arts in developing the program. The initial criteria certainly did not advantage the large urban centres, as the largest category included all municipalities above 125,000 in population. Interestingly, the 2005 evaluation recommended the creation of a new category of municipalities above 500,000 in population, but this was not adopted.

In the first six years of the program, twenty-eight communities were designated and one Cultural Bridges Award was given. The largest municipalities that had been designated were Vancouver, Regina, Toronto, Edmonton, and Victoria. The smaller municipalities included Rivière-du-Loup, Powell River, Annapolis Royal, and Saint-Jean-Port-Joli.

At its inception, the federal contribution had to be matched by the municipality. However, numbers of applications decreased over the first few years, and the 2005 evaluation indicated that the matching requirement was a major problem for many municipalities (Government of Canada, Canadian Heritage 2005, 10). The evaluation indicated that Canadian Heritage was aware of this and was considering increasing its share. This was done, and the 2006 guidelines indicated that the federal contribution represented 75 per cent of eligible costs, up to a maximum of $2 million for municipalities above 125,000 in population; a maximum of $750,000 for the category of 50,000 to 125,000 in population; and a maximum of $500,000 for the category of municipalities under 50,000 population.

The Networking Initiatives funds went originally to the Creative City Network, and to the Arts Network for Children and Youth. The Creative City Network is an organization of municipal employees working in areas of arts, culture, and heritage, and the federal funds allowed it to develop activities, and thereby strengthen the connections between municipal arts, culture, and heritage policy-makers across Canada. The 2005 evaluation recommended the development of a strategy to ensure that the networking projects continued after the end of departmental funding. This recommendation was not accepted by the department, and instead, Canadian Heritage indicated simply that "the program will be working with these organizations to ensure that they develop strategies to further partnerships and diversify sources of funding" (Government of Canada, Canadian Heritage 2005, 26). In other words, the department felt no obligation to develop a government-led strategy to ensure the projects continued.

The two funding sources for cultural programming and physical infrastructure do not give priority to the large urban centres. The Cultural Capitals program, designed to build arts and culture capacity within municipal governments, is explicitly organized to encourage the participation of smaller municipalities. Those under 50,000 in population receive two of the four designations annually, although the federal contribution is less than that going to the category of municipalities above 125,000. The suggestion of creating a category for municipalities above 500,000 was not acted upon. Over the first six years, all provinces except Prince Edward Island have received at least one Cultural Capital designation, which suggests a certain concern for spreading the designations across the country. Overall, the distribution of federal cultural funds appears to reflect a preoccupation to facilitate the access of smaller municipalities to federal financial support. A certain opening to social forces is evidenced by the consultation that took place with the FCM and the Canadian Conferences of the Arts before the program was launched, but clearly the program implementation was more directed to governments, and in this case, to municipal governments.

In summarizing our analysis of sport and cultural policies, the principal conclusion is that federal policies are much more about enabling municipal and local activity than about a clear federal policy. In terms of the distinction made by Neil Bradford (2007) between an explicit urban policy and an implicit urban presence, the policies are certainly not explicitly urban and, indeed, most of the programs examined are primarily concerned with facilitating the access of smaller communities. Indeed, Bradford goes on to describe the fact that "in the policy roll-out" of the federal urban agenda (Government of Canada, Canadian Heritage 2004, 10), the addition of "communities" to "cities" meant that any focus on larger urban centres was eliminated and resources would be distributed across the entire country. Our analysis of federal programs suggests that this has indeed been the pattern of allocation. Federal policy would seem to be oriented towards enabling communities of all sizes to apply for federal support. Federal image-building is therefore more about process than content; the content comes, or does not come, from the municipal or community use of the programs.

DISCUSSION: WHO BENEFITS FROM BRANDING?

Before concluding on the impact of federal policies, it is useful to refer briefly to the literature that attempts to explain municipal initiatives in branding.

There are two very different streams of literature. First is the critical, largely university-based research that relates municipal efforts to the larger socio-economic context of capitalist development in a neo-liberal era. Within the flourishing international literature on these questions, Canadian researchers have been active and visible participants. The title of an article by David Whitson and John Horne indicates the overall conclusions of these studies: "Underestimated costs and overestimated benefits? Comparing the outcomes of sports mega-events in Canada and Japan" (Whitson and Horne 2006). Another title of an article in the same special journal issue situates the theoretical framework: "Urban entrepreneurship, corporate interests and sports mega-events: the thin policies of competitiveness within the hard outcomes of neo-liberalism" (Hall 2006). In general, these studies emphasize the relatively small margin of discretion of municipal policies, positioned between the weight of local private sector interests (and often in collusion with these interests), and the weight of global neo-liberal pressures both on the national level of government and on the local level.

The second stream of literature is the "how-to" material, giving practical advice to municipal governments about successful strategies for branding. One such example comes from CEOs for Cities entitled, "Branding Your City" (2006, 21–3). It lists a number of guiding principles, such as, "look beyond words," "make it emotional," and "it takes time," and ends with emphasizing the importance of involving stakeholders and keeping them informed. Both kinds of studies basically share the same analysis and acknowledge the relatively limited margin of discretion held by municipal governments. The "how-to" literature is more positive about municipal activity, but also acknowledges the limits of municipal action.

This brings us back to our original questions: What is good public policy in this area? Who bears the costs and who gets the benefits? Does the hosting policy for sports events encourage municipalities to bid for events that overestimate benefits and underestimate costs? Or does it, and the programs for cultural spaces and activities, give access to activities that would be out of reach for many Canadians without further assistance? Whitson and Horne (2006, 83) see a double dimension to mega-events: "A mega-event, therefore, is not only about showing the city off to the world; it is also about putting the global on show for the locals, and inviting them to take on new identities as citizens of the world – identities that will henceforth be lived in the production and consumption of global products."

Becoming world citizens is given a negative connotation in the above example, as it is defined as becoming full participants in global capitalism. But one can also see becoming a citizen of the world in a more positive light as being able to see oneself as equal to others who were previously seen as superior. Indeed, Whitson and Horne (2006, 83) include the example of Brisbane, where the holding of mega-events was interpreted as "the arrival of once marginal communities into membership in the dominant world order."

The analysis of marginalization also raises the question of the distribution of costs and benefits across different groups within individual communities, for example, the difficulties experienced by Aboriginal associations in accessing many of the cultural programs. Which groups within communities are benefiting from greater access to federal government support?

The examination of federal programs of image-building raises questions, it does not provide the answers, which must come from the municipal and community studies. The federal programs are perhaps enablers, but what they enable must be the focus for understanding image-building in Canada. In general, our conclusion is that the federal government enables both large cities and smaller communities to participate in, and benefit from, programs that facilitate image-building by local governments. However, to understand the image-building that is happening, one must look directly at the municipal level. The following chapters do exactly this.

NOTE

1 On 26 June 2009, the Arts Presentation Canada Program was renamed the Canada Arts Presentation Fund. The program's mandate and objectives remain the same.

REFERENCES

Andrew, Caroline. 2007. "Branding Canada Urban?" Presentation, Canadian Political Science Association Annual Meeting. Saskatoon.

Bradford, Neil. 2007. "Whither the Federal Urban Agenda? A New Deal in Transition," *Canadian Policy Research Networks*, Research Report F/65 Family Network.

CEOs for Cities. 2008. *Branding Your City.* http://www.ceosforcities.org/work/branding_your_city

Florida, Richard. 2002. *The Rise of the Creative Class: and How it's Transforming Work, Leisure, Community and Everyday Life.* New York: Basic Books.

Gibson, T., and M. Lowes. 2007. *Urban Communication.* Lanham, Maryland: Rowman and Littlefield.

Government of Canada, Canadian Heritage. 2003. *Joint Formative Evaluation of Arts Presentation Canada, Cultural Spaces Canada, and the Canadian Arts and Heritage Sustainability Program.* http://pch.gc.ca/pgm/pac-apc/index-eng.cfm

– 2004. *Summative Evaluation of the Department of Canadian Heritage's Sport Hosting Program.*

– 2005. *Report on a Formative Evaluation of Two Canadian Arts and Heritage Sustainability Program Components: Cultural Capitals of Canada and Networking Initiatives.*

– 2008. "Federal Policy for Hosting International Events." January. http://www.pch.gc.ca/pgm/sc/pol/acc/2008/accueil-host_2008-eng.pdf

Government of Canada, Canadian Tourism Commission. 2010. "Inspiring the World to Explore Canada." http://en-corporate.canada.travel/

Forum of Federations. 2010. Forum of Federations: The Global Network on Federalism. http://www.forumfed.org/en/index.php

Hall, C. Michael. 2006. "Urban Entrepreneurship, Corporate Interests and Sports Mega-events: the Thin Policies of Competitiveness within the Hard Outcomes of Neoliberalism." *The Sociological Review* 54, no. 2: 59–70.

Houpt, Simon. 2010. "Oh, Canada, Get a Brand." *The Globe and Mail*, Report on Business. 1 July, pp. 1, 6.

Judd, Dennis, and Susan Fainstein. 1999. *The Tourist City.* New Haven, Connecticut: Yale University Press.

Maitland, Robert, and Brent Ritchie. 2009. *City Tourism: National Capital Perspectives.* Cambridge, Massachusetts: CABI Publishing.

Potter, Evan H. 2008. *Branding Canada: Projecting Canada's Soft Power Through Public Diplomacy.* Montreal and Kingston: McGill-Queen's University Press.

Scott, Allen J. 2007. "Capitalism and Urbanization in a New Key? The Cognitive-Cultural Dimension." *Social Forces* 85, no. 4: 1465–82.

Whitson, David, and John Horne. 2006. "Underestimated Costs and Over-estimated Benefits? Comparing the Outcomes of Sports Mega-events in Canada and Japan." *The Sociological Review* 54, no. 2: 73–89.

3

Image-building in Manitoba

JOHN C. LEHR AND KARLA ZUBRYCKI

You don't want to just look at what these small towns are, you want to
look at what they're aiming to become, and they all got an ambition that
in the long run is going to make 'em the finest spots on earth.

Sinclair Lewis, 1922

Manitoba has a long history of image-building. During its early days
as a province its communities attempted to foster their development,
and that of their regions, by the unabashed embrace of boosterism,
a synonym for self-promotion. Boosterism operated at various levels. The federal government promoted the settlement of the West
through vigorous campaigns aimed at convincing potential settlers from the United States, eastern Canada, and Europe to immigrate into western Canada and contribute to its development (Peel
1966; Lehr 1983; Stich 1976). Land and railway companies also
participated in the quest for immigrants and tourists (Hart 1983;
Ward 1998, 10–28). Communities ranging in size from Winnipeg,
the provincial capital, down to small station halts on branch lines,
shamelessly paraded themselves as "the next Chicago," the "future
capital of the Northwest," or the "Chicago of the North," competing with other destinations within Canada and the United States
(Artibise 1970; Rees 1988). Immigrants were lured into the West
and induced to invest in speculative real estate deals backed by little
more than enthusiastic self-promotion, an unswerving conviction
that this was the land of opportunity, and that this specific community was the place to realize maximum profits.

Times have changed: the prairie boom collapsed in 1913, and
many of the promises and claims so ardently voiced in the boom-
time years proved to be chimeras based more on blind faith than

substance (Blanchard 2005). Although yesterday's hyperbole has given way to more measured language, the promotion of place continues to be a vital component of economic development in Manitoba and elsewhere.

Places seek to impress themselves on the public's consciousness for good reason. Places that are known are generally regarded more positively than those that are not. With places, familiarity does not breed contempt. On the contrary, a place that enjoys a favourable position in the collective consciousness is advantaged in the competition for capital and people (Gould and White 1974, 175–8). Communities today seek to promote or market themselves by establishing personalities or images. This image is not necessarily reflective of reality, but can be manufactured by a skilled promoter. George Warren (1927), a place promoter who was mostly responsible for building Victoria's image as "a little bit of Olde England," put it quite bluntly:

> The power to make a community is not luck. It is not alone a
> question of nature, or kindness, nor is it a matter of chance,
> on the contrary, communities are built ... where men (sic) want
> them, where men of business initiative, imagination, and business
> co-operation, determine where they shall be built using advertis-
> ing or publicity as one of the principal mediums.

For Warren, the key was the creation of a sense of place, which he described as "personality." He was also convinced that the "personality of a community, when corrected, broadened, or capitalized" would determine a community's future. In short, if it wished to accelerate its growth, a community had to pay attention to the ways in which its image was built, and aggressively project this packaged image to a carefully targeted audience. This commodification of place was deplored by many, but is still "regarded by marketers, somewhat disarmingly, as the starting point for their work" (Ward 1998, 6).

Place identity, or sense of place, incorporates the notion of a symbiotic relationship between person and place, and involves perceptions of qualities that imbue places with a particular character (Peterson and Saarinen 1986). Different people perceive places differently because in their assessment of places, they draw on key physical features, cultural attributes, historical associations, the built environment, and their own experiences while in that place. The more distinctive an image of place, the more successful the place will be in attracting attention (Gartrell 1988, 27). Place identity, as Warren (1927) pointed out, can be created, although more commonly, identity is a function of pre-existing attributes. These may be accentuated in the public's mind by orchestrated campaigns directing attention to them, and establishing a perceptual association between a place and a quality or value.

The image of a place is the sum of beliefs, ideas, and impressions that people have of a place, and they represent the simplification of a plethora of associations and pieces of information that are connected with that place (Kotler et al. 1993). Such images are highly personal and vary greatly between individuals. To be effectively employed as a marketing tool they should be carefully targeted at a specific audience.

The past few decades have seen a spread of interest in the potential for place promotion and image marketing. Once mostly confined to tourist destinations, place promotion is now seen as an integral part of economic development by places that are not generally regarded as desirable destinations by the tourist industry. Places, even small rural communities, now seek to position themselves within the markets for immigrants, visitors, investors, industry, corporate headquarters, entrepreneurs, and extra-regional purchasers (Niedomysl 2004, 1991–3), and shape their images according to the targeted market. Each sector responds to different elements of an image, although all are generally responsive to an overarching sense of vitality and a "can-do" attitude.

Cultural homogeneity – the by-product of modernism – is creating places that lack a sense of place or even regional identity (Kunstler 1993; Zukin 1991, 12–14; Relph 1976). In response, atavistic and anachronistic elements are commonly incorporated into new developments in an attempt to suggest links to an often imagined past, and to impart a sense of individuality that is vital if a sense of place is to develop (Lowenthal 1975). Much tinkering with ordinary landscapes is undertaken by individuals unaware of the subliminal messages projected through the improvement of their property's aesthetic appeal. Orchestrated campaigns directed at developing a sense of place within a community frequently employ similar strategies, such as creating heritage-themed streetscapes designed to project a sense of permanence, history, and continuity (Hall 2007, 322). In the quest to combat the aesthetic erosion of old commercial centres, Heritage Canada encourages the "retro-fitting" of small-town "Main Streets" to recreate their appearance in the pre-automobile era. The objectives of such projects are interdependent and inseparable: aesthetic enhancement, development of heritage resources, and commercial revitalization. The creation or recreation of local identity and sense of place is a fundamental concern. Image-building has thus assumed a crucial role in many aspects of social and economic development.

In a search for distinction, places may seek to assume the characteristics of consumer products to establish a brand image, and to associate themselves with specific attributes represented by their brand. As Urry (1991, 2) pointed out, places are consumed, at least visually, by tourists, seasonal visitors, and residents. Occasionally, places will adopt a persona and manipulate the built environment to reflect a specific theme or concept. In British Columbia, Osoyoos has embraced a Spanish motif, and Kimberley has themed itself as a Bavarian village in order to attract tourists. Neither community is dominated by the culture that the theme promotes. Concept marketing of this type has become a common practice in North America (Phillips 2002, 10–11, 45). Landscapes are fabricated and place becomes a commodity to be marketed, trademarked, and sold like any commercial product. Successful promotion demands establishing an image in the minds of consumers, just as marketing of material goods requires that consumers associate certain qualities with specific brands. Place branding relies on building a strong image of place, and using advertising techniques to implant this image in the public's consciousness. When the market reciprocates by associating specific characteristics with a place, it has been successfully branded.

The practice of place promotion embraces the many approaches used by public, private, and non-governmental organizations to build and sell the image of communities. Image-building is affected by the actions of the public sector. The provision of a wide range of services, investment in infrastructure, and support of professional sports and the arts are integral to the process of image-building, affecting the place-promotion ethos, and the political environment of the community. Phillips (2002) argues that since politics is essentially about control, the public sector becomes a major participant or player in the creation and marketing of places through its influence on policy. Place marketing is an aspect of public and quasi-public policy and, as such, should ideally achieve its objectives without any negative effect upon other communities within the same political jurisdiction, yet it is an activity that by its very nature is, or at least appears to be, highly competitive. Because of its nebulous nature, for the purposes of this research, image-building has been examined primarily from the point of view of its relationship to policies affecting tourism, economic development, and immigration.

This chapter examines the role of public policy in the image-building and place promotion process in four Manitoban communities: the rural municipality (RM) of Stuartburn in southeastern Manitoba; the RM of Swan River in north-central Manitoba; the city of Winkler in south-central Manitoba; and the city of Winnipeg, the capital and primary city of the province. These four municipalities were chosen principally to reflect the variability in the size of municipalities within the province: Stuartburn is a thinly populated rural municipality whereas Swan River includes a larger town, as well as several neighbouring municipalities. Winkler is a small city, and Winnipeg is the capital of Manitoba and its largest city by far. The four municipalities also represent very different regions of the province. They differ economically and socially, and provide a fair representation of a diverse province.

COMMUNITY PROFILES

The Rural Municipality of Stuartburn

The RM of Stuartburn is located in the southeastern quadrant of the province. Ukrainian immigrants from the former Austro-Hungarian Empire settled the area in the last decade of the nineteenth century (Kaye 1964). Until 1902 the district was a part of the RM of Franklin. When it broke away it was saddled with high debt and for years the municipality remained locked in poverty. When it went bankrupt during the depression, it was "disorganized" and administered by the Public Trustee from 1944 until 1997.[1] Much of the area is poorly drained, low-lying, stony land classified by the Canada Land Inventory as Class 6 agricultural land with little economic potential for agriculture. It was one of the last areas in Manitoba to be electrified, and even today is poorly served by some major telecommunications companies. Mixed farming, with an emphasis on beef and dairy cattle, is the predominant activity. Considerable areas within the municipality that were once cultivated have now reverted to grass. The Prairie Farm Rehabilitation Agency (PFRA) acquired several sections of such land, which it operated as a community pasture. Some parts of the municipality that were never cultivated constitute the remnants of the tall grass prairie. The Nature Conservancy of Canada (NCC) purchased some of these lands to operate as protected areas, and is currently expanding its holdings. The only settlement of any size within the municipality is Vita, a village of some three hundred people with a few stores, a regional high school, hospital, and the administrative offices of the municipality.

Rural depopulation has seen out-migration of the descendents of the original Ukrainian settlers, and immigration of many non-Ukrainians, principally Mennonites, so the social character of the municipality, once solidly Ukrainian, has changed considerably since the 1970s. Economically, little has changed, though a fairly recent innovation has been the introduction of intensive livestock operations into the district (Heald 2005). Further development of intensive hog operations has been halted by a provincially declared moratorium. The municipality continues to rely heavily on agriculture supplemented by off-farm work.

In the 1920s, Stuartburn district was described as the "homebrew capital of Canada" and was portrayed in the Ukrainian-language press in Canada as a dysfunctional community rent by religious rivalries. These old-country legacies began to fade in the 1950s and Stuartburn is now anxious to represent itself in a more positive fashion.

The RM of Stuartburn has only given serious thought to image-building since 2006. Driven in part by a change in council membership, some results are becoming apparent, although no formal image-building policy has yet been articulated. For example, each community within the municipality now has a standardized sign welcoming people at the entrance of the community. Within Vita, signs placed at the major intersections within the settlement directionally indicate the principal public buildings, such as the municipal office, the hospital, and school. The RM commissioned these signs when it became aware that visitors to the community were unable to immediately locate crucial services. Vita is a very small community of less than ten blocks and, at first, it seemed to some local residents that there was little point to this initiative, as "everyone knew where everything was" (Respondent F 2007). However, it was pointed out that not everyone who required access to these places was local.

In the 1980s, change started to take place in Stuartburn on two fronts. Firstly, the Nature Conservancy of Canada began to acquire remnants of tall grass prairie that were left undisturbed and uncultivated due to the low agricultural potential of the land. The NCC's intention of developing this resource was the first time the region had any real potential for attracting outside visitors for tourism. Secondly, in the 1990s, Parks Canada expressed interest in developing a national historic site to commemorate Ukrainian settlement on the prairies. They partnered with the Gardenton Museum to acquire the Korol homestead situated two miles south of Gardenton. This was a protracted process and by the time the land had been acquired the building proved to be unsalvageable. The project collapsed and the abandoned house deteriorated past the point of restoration.

In a 2005 study of Gardenton, a small community of about fifty people within the municipality, Heald assessed its options for development and concluded that place-making was vital for the community's future. This, she advocated, should centre on its rural qualities, the Tall Grass Prairie Preserve, and the relative absence of intensive livestock operations.

Recent development has centred on the presence of the Western Prairie Fringed Orchid, a rare and endangered plant that, in Canada, occurs only in the RM of Stuartburn. The reeve and council are enthusiastic about using the orchid as a symbol for the RM, and are hopeful that it could be an attraction for nature tourism. This is not an unreasonable expectation, as the RM has already received numerous visits from nature-oriented groups. Unfortunately, the municipality's population is split on the desirability of promoting the orchid as an attraction. Farmers are generally opposed to the idea, as they see the orchid as a threat to their livelihood; they fear that, as it is an endangered species, their ability to cultivate will be restricted and they will face heavy fines if they inadvertently destroy one. As yet, the only action that has been taken by the council is to produce a souvenir pin that stylizes the orchid and bears the name of the municipality. Orchid sites are not yet marked and visitors are left to their own devices to locate them.

One attempt at image-building in the mid-1990s was a response to a perceived threat rather than an attempt to develop a particular natural attribute. There were proposals to build hog farms in the municipality. Developers were attracted to the area by its relatively low population, the low cost of land, and the area's proximity to Winnipeg. Those opposed to hog barns cited environmental concerns, principally fears of contaminating the relatively high water table, and also concerns over waste disposal and odour. They formed the Concerned Citizens of Gardenton to present a united front against further hog barn development in the municipality. Some felt that Gardenton and Stuartburn could be marketed as a "hog-free" RM for those wishing to live outside of, but near to, Winnipeg. All residents of the RM do not share this opinion. In fact, Vita tends to be quite supportive of hog barn operations, whereas Gardenton tends to be more opposed (Shewchuk 2006; Reeves 2007). This split in attitudes between the two communities reflects the relative ability of each to profit from such operations. Vita has a commercial service function, whereas Gardenton does not. Thus, Vita is in a position to benefit from the injection of capital associated with intensive livestock operations; Gardenton, on the other hand, could at best benefit from the creation of one or two jobs, but would possibly lose amenity value through the environmental consequences of hog farms, such as odour problems and possible negative effects on the relatively high water table.

The RM of Stuartburn faces some very real difficulties in using heritage development to build its image. Although there are many potential heritage sites within the RM, including cemeteries, old churches, and a few pioneer houses, the district lacks a broad volunteer base necessary for the development of these resources. Furthermore, the ethnic character of the area is changing, and most newcomers from outside the district often have no association with Ukrainian culture and little feeling for the history of the area. Rural depopulation exacerbates the situation. It is difficult to assemble sufficient people with the experience, interest and skills to be effective advocates for heritage preservation.

The Stuartburn case shows that higher-level governments can potentially help image-building efforts, even in the smallest communities. However, such places may have few resources to bring to the intergovernmental table, or, indeed, to employ in any way. Even in small and remote places, the need for positive image-building is apparent to officials and citizens, but even here a lack of consensus can stymie the creation of such policies.

Swan River

The town of Swan River was incorporated in 1908 and serves as a hub for the surrounding communities of Minitonas, Benito, Bowsman, Kenville, and Durban. It is located approximately 410 kilometres away from the nearest twenty-four-hour border crossing and, as such, represents the most northerly community in this study. It has a population of 3,859 with about 2,800 more people in the surrounding rural municipality of Swan River (Statistics Canada 2006). The entire Swan Valley, which extends outside the RM to include six other towns and RMs (identified and discussed below), expands the population to 11,350 people. Swan River, nestled between the Porcupine Mountains to the north and the Duck Mountains to the south, is approximately 370 kilometres from the provincial capital of Winnipeg. The land of the Swan Valley itself is rolling, which is one of its appeals to tourists. One of the economic sources for the town and the RM is tourism, with many services and businesses catering to the industry. Outdoor activities, from fishing to skiing, are one of the driving factors in tourism.

The fertile soil of the valley also allows for a range of agricultural activities on the surrounding land. Cereal farming, oilseed farming, and mixed farming of cattle, dairy, and pigs are some of the mainstays of the agricultural economy. In addition, forestry is a major industry in the area; Swan River was awarded the title of Forest Capital of Canada in 1998 due to its forestry activities, which include major forestry employers, such as Louisiana Pacific and Spruce Products Limited.

POLICY OVERVIEW

Image-building policy for Swan River embraces the town of Swan River, the rural municipality, and beyond to include the entire Swan River Valley region. The Swan Valley Enterprise Centre (SVEC) is primarily responsible for the image-building process. Perhaps the most interesting aspect of this case study is that seven entities – the towns of Swan River, Minitonas, and Benito; the village of Bowsman; and the RMs of Mountain, Minitonas, and Swan River – work together to build the area's image, both for tourism and economic development. They do not each undertake image-building on their own, but rather, contribute to SVEC, pooling their resources. Darlis Collinge

(2006), economic development manager for SVEC, explains they are creating a brand. "I think it [image-building] is a very valuable exercise for a community. I think all communities should do it so that they know where they fit and what their niche is."

The image-building strategy is encompassed in SVEC's 2006 Investment Attraction Marketing Plan. It was born in part out of a need to counteract some of the problems facing Swan Valley, such as depopulation, an aging population, a struggling agricultural sector, and the need to attract more youth and jobs, including employment in more diversified sectors. The plan identifies three main goals: "attracting new residents, specifically immigrants to Canada; attracting entrepreneurs; and attracting industry aligned with the existing forestry, agriculture, and tourism sectors within the region" (Swan Valley Enterprise Centre Inc. 2006). Therefore, it takes a broad view of image-building, encompassing both tourism and economics.

The marketing materials that were produced brand the Swan Valley visually from an environmental slant: "What we decided to focus on is blue skies, clear air, and pristine lakes … We're presenting ourselves as a healthy, environmentally conscious, clean way to be" (Collinge 2006). The marketing plan identifies these characteristics as key to attracting European immigrants, a sub-strategy further discussed below.

In addition, the tagline, "a community within communities," was created to lend cohesion to the valley, and to emphasize friendliness and community values. Rick Reich (2006), reeve of Swan River, strongly approves of the phrase. "I'm a firm believer that our valley is one. We do have several municipalities, and we try to have seven different identities, but we are one … we have to work together or we won't survive."

While Reich supports the strategy, and Collinge (2006) says he stops by her office "about once a month," she wishes local governments would be more involved in the image-building process. Local governments provide 25–35 per cent of funding for SVEC, but she says they have not been active contributors to the development of the strategy. They provide financial aid, but are less willing to provide feedback, ideas, people, and time.

When the need for an investment and image program was realized in 2005, SVEC formed an investment attraction committee. Local councils were invited to have representatives on the committee, but Collinge says there was little interest. The only government-affiliated representative was someone from the office of Rosann Wowchuk, the provincial member of the legislative assembly (MLA). This lack of interest from local government disappointed Collinge: "You would think that the municipalities would be more involved in how they're represented, but they're not."

Councils learned about the marketing activities in several ways. First, each municipality had a member sit on SVEC's general board. This board dealt with many matters, only one of which was the marketing plan. The council representatives were supposed to be liaisons between SVEC and the councils, but this link did not always work well; many times the councils were not told much about SVEC's activities, and rarely did councillors bring to their respective councils news of the marketing plan (Collinge 2006). Therefore, the larger contribution to the marketing plan by these councillors was during SVEC's board meetings. Collinge (2006) admitted that marketing discussions at the meetings led to useful ideas, such as which groups might be targeted for marketing. In these cases, local government was involved in non-financial ways.

When SVEC would approach the seven councils directly for feedback, Collinge (2006) was usually disappointed. Once some feedback materials were developed, SVEC sent information and questionnaires to each council. For communication with them, she went through the chief administrative officers (CAOs), and even this proved to be a roadblock; one of the CAOs told her, "our agenda is pretty full. I don't think I can put it on." Of the seven information packages that were sent out, only two came back with some responses, and these were not detailed. For instance, when a choice was given, a responding council may have specified their choice, however, the open-ended answers were often left blank. Reich (2006) characterized his council's input succinctly: "We got to pick the colours." Although he supports SVEC's activities, he sees the councils' roles as being apart from image-building. "As for economic development, council lets the enterprise centre do the image stuff and council itself goes after keeping lower taxes, attracting industry, and attracting more jobs." Collinge would have preferred them to be more involved in the concepts, details, and strategies. She notes that she dealt more with the CAOs for the marketing activities, rather than the councils. Sometimes, the CAOs were willing to provide personal opinions on the plan.

For the most part, the provincial and federal levels were involved only through monetary contributions (Collinge 2006). The province funded the regional development corporation, from which SVEC received funds. Federally, SVEC got funding through a federal program for innovation in sustainable communities.

SVEC's initiative to bring immigrants to Swan River required some federal involvement; attracting immigrants was one of the thrusts of the investment attraction plan. SVEC representatives went to an immigration trade fair in the United Kingdom in February 2006, armed with the promotional materials they had developed. Collinge (2006) feels it was a good move and led to some success; two couples at the fair planned on coming the following fall to "see if would be a good fit for them." She said that even for those who did not immigrate, it was also important to get the Swan Valley's name "out there." She explains, "we now have more people in this world who have heard of the Swan Valley who hadn't heard of it before." A total of fifteen thousand people came through the doors at the fair, many of them prospective immigrants, people looking for opportunities abroad. SVEC feels their area provides for those "seeking high quality rural lifestyles" (Swan Valley Enterprise Centre Inc. 2006), a desire that Collinge feels is strong in some Europeans. These people, who choose to move to the country rather than follow the migration trend to the city are termed "anti-urbanites" (Mitchell 1981). Even before the fair, an article written in a German publication attracted one family with five children from Germany, which demonstrates the importance of getting one's community known. The family now operates an apiary.

While SVEC has carried out the most concerted and comprehensive effort at image-building in Swan River, there are other parties that have carried out separate image-building efforts too. Real estate developer, Darin McKay (2006), wanted to brand the town of Swan River as a retirement community. Like SVEC's branding, his reasoning related to the surrounding land. He felt the varied activities in the region, including enjoying the mountains, hunting, fishing, and hiking, would appeal to many retirees. However, when asked, he said that he does not work with SVEC at all and had not seen many results from its activities. When asked about his opinion on SVEC's marketing plan, McKay had little to say. Additionally, he did not think there was much competition for image-building. "It's unfortunate that there is *not* much competition. There are other areas that could be pursued, but nobody is doing so that I can see," he says. This implies that SVEC might not be letting its community know about their activities. Collinge (2006) said they've tried, but have not had much success.

For his own projects, McKay says he does not work with local government very much, and not at all with the provincial or federal governments. He has made some requests of them, usually by attending council meetings, but he says their arms are "not as open" to development ideas as other Manitoban communities in which he has worked, such as Dauphin and The Pas (2006). For instance, the town of Swan River council refused to alter some by-laws to facilitate the construction of a residential complex he wanted to build; the architectural drawings included balconies that were four inches over the current by-law allowance. McKay feels an exception should have been made. "I'm confused why our elected representatives aren't working ... vigorously to get people to work and invest here," he says. "A more progressive, business-minded council would be a real attraction to anyone considering development in Swan River or neighbouring municipalities" (2006).

Similarly, when McKay was trying to build an "ideal, downtown location" that was easily accessible for pedestrians and seniors, he encountered problems with council. "I wasn't planning on building a nuclear power plant downtown, or to divert the river," he says. In his opinion, seniors would be more attracted to a community where they could walk to all services.

In the case of Swan River, image-building is part of a coherent economic development strategy that targets immigrants, entrepreneurs, tourists, and particular kinds of industry. There is considerable horizontal co-operation among municipalities; this is not achieved directly, but through the medium of a specialized regional body that enjoys some support from the provincial and federal governments.

The City of Winkler

Winkler is located in the northeast area of the former Mennonite West Reserve about ten kilometers east of Morden. The city is situated at the junction of Highway 32 that connects Winkler to the United States' border, and Highway 14 that connects to Morden and Winnipeg via Highway 3.

Winkler was established in 1892, but it was not until 1906 that the settlement formally became a village. Its early success came largely at the expense of other communities in the area. With continuing

Mennonite immigration Winkler enjoyed a steady growth, both economically and demographically.

Although predominantly Mennonite, Winkler had a strong German, Anglo-Saxon, and Jewish presence in its early years. Mennonites gradually took over the political, social, and cultural scene, and have left their distinctive mark in their values and attitudes towards worship, work, and recreation in the city (Werner 2006).

Throughout the twentieth century, Winkler continued to grow, feeding off various waves of Mennonite immigration from Russia, Germany, and South and Central America. Only 27 per cent of Winkler's population identify themselves with either British or Canadian ethnic origins, while 67 per cent affiliate with German, Dutch, or Russian ethnicity. Winkler will likely maintain this ethnic composition as it continues to be a destination for overseas immigrants who identify with German or Mennonite culture. In fact, the majority of immigrants moving to Winkler are Mennonites from Central and South America who still maintain their German language, culture, and heritage.

In promotional material, Winkler claims to have a current population of about nine thousand. Its population pyramid is significantly different from most other rural towns in southern Manitoba as it has a young population and family size above the national average. The success of its program to attract German immigrant families has created a problem for the school district; even with fifteen portable classrooms added, the high school is overcrowded and it will be some years before a new school can be built (*Winnipeg Free Press*, 22 September 2008).

Winkler has a reputation as a highly religious community; it is often referred to as the buckle of Manitoba's Bible belt. Only 3 per cent of Winkler's population claim no religious affiliation. While over the years, orthodox Mennonite beliefs and values have been relaxed, they still play an important role in the fabric of everyday life. Concerts and recreation, once frowned upon, have since worked their way into Winkler and have become a part of the community's promotion. Other beliefs concerning the role of religion in education and the consumption of alcohol have been maintained, despite growing pressure to adopt a more secular policy.

Initially a rural service centre serving an agricultural hinterland, manufacturing is now a significant part of Winkler's economy, accounting for 28 per cent of employment. Its commercial and retail sectors are no longer solely reliant on agriculture; it has several large big-box stores, including a Wal-Mart. As do most other small prairie towns, Winkler receives in-migration from the elderly and infirm from the surrounding rural area that seek its medical and personal care services.

Winkler has enjoyed steady economic and demographic growth for the last several decades. It has industrial parks with serviced lots ready to accept new businesses, and has supply and support services available for new business ventures. The town's population has grown rapidly over the last several decades. Civic officials boast that there are likely three hundred vacant jobs in the community. To meet the demand for labour, Winkler has developed a program to attract Mennonites and other German-speaking immigrants to the community. The community website claims that this program has brought in roughly two thousand people over the past several years.

Winkler has some barriers to development. Within the Mennonite community there is a reluctance to develop aspects of the economy that may introduce secular influences into the community. For example, when the concert hall was constructed, there was some concern about secular influences in the acts that would be performing in the hall (Lehr 2007).

Winkler faces the problem of its population's inability to service its expanding job market. The community's ability to address this may be hampered by its seeming concern to retain Winkler's distinctive social and religious character. Mennonites and German-speaking immigrants are favored as immigrants, as they are perceived to fit well with the community's values and beliefs.

Recent residential development was slowed by delays in extending infrastructure to the west side of the community. Water supply and water quality is a further concern, as lack of water has retarded the development of agricultural processing, causing Winkler to lose in the race to attract this potentially lucrative sector of the economy. Water piped into the community from the Red River was absorbed by residential and non-wet industrial growth.

Housing costs have increased dramatically in Winkler over the last decade. The average cost of a house in Winkler in 2001 was $114,124, about $14,000 more than the average house in Morden, a similar sized community some six miles to the west (Lehr 2007).

Planning and promotion has been an important part of Winkler's economic success for the past thirty years. Elected in 1963, Mayor

Henry Wiebe put Winkler on a path of industrial and residential growth that continues today. The city's council primarily carried out promotion at this time. Today, the council maintains this role but is now aided by the city's development corporation and the chamber of commerce. Winkler continues to pursue industrial growth, and plans for continuing increases in its population.

The City of Winnipeg

Manitoba is unusual among Canadian provinces in that its capital city dominates the province in terms of population and economic power. More than 55 per cent of Manitobans live in the Winnipeg capital region. Brandon is the second largest centre, but with a population of approximately forty-three thousand, it is about 7 per cent the size of Winnipeg. Other centres are tiny in comparison to the capital. Portage la Prairie and Dauphin, with populations of 12,728 and 7,906 respectively, are truly small towns.

In its early years, Winnipeg had a strong image as the gateway to the West. All freight and passengers entering the prairies passed through the city, which developed extensive retailing, wholesaling, and manufacturing functions. It was the centre of the grain trade and the primary city of the prairies (Blanchard 2005). It was a reception area for immigrants, the home of the oldest educational institutions on the prairies, and a centre for government. Its "North End" was, and still is, arguably Canada's most famous cognitive region. Its gritty qualities have become part of the nation's mythology, celebrated in John Marlyn's novel *Under the Ribs of Death*, Bess Kaplan's *Corner Store*, Adele Wiseman's *The Sacrifice*, and immortalized in James Woodsworth's social commentaries *Strangers Within Our Gates* and *My Neighbour*.

Passing through the city in 1913, Rupert Brooke commented on Winnipeg's brisk efficiency and sense of purpose:

Winnipeg is the West ... Winnipeg is a new city ... A new city; a little more American than the other Canadian cities, but not unpleasantly so. The streets are wider and full of a bustle, which keeps clear of hustle. The people have something of the free swing of Americans, without the bumptiousness; a tempered democracy, a mitigated independence of bearing. The manners of Winnipeg, of the West, impress the stranger as better than those of the East, more friendly, more hearty, more certain to achieve graciousness, if not grace. There is, even, in the architecture of Winnipeg, a sort of gauche pride visible. It is hideous, of course, even more hideous than Toronto or Montreal; but cheerily and windily so.

One can't help finding a tiny hope that Winnipeg, the city of buildings and the city of human beings, may yet come to something. It is a slender hope, not to be compared to that of the true Winnipeg man, who, gazing on his city, is fired with the proud and secret ambition that it will soon be twice as big, and after that four times, and then ten times. (Brooke 1978, 85–6)

The end of the boom in 1913 shattered the illusion of infinite growth, and the armistice of 1918 and the return home of discharged veterans brought disillusion. The General Strike of 1919 placed the city in the forefront of the nation's consciousness as a hotbed of radical socialism and a possessor of a large foreign-born population that lived mostly in the North End. Violence and lawlessness became a part of the city's image (Sandemose 2005, 91–2).

In 1972, the city of Winnipeg amalgamated with its surrounding municipalities. Before then, St Boniface, St Vital, St James, Charleswood, Kildonan, and Fort Garry were all separate municipalities with their own civic governments, administrations, school divisions, and services. For a few years, Winnipeg promoted the new unified entity as "Unicity" to stress the unification of governance and the amalgamation of services. As the population became accustomed to the new arrangement this terminology was gradually phased out. Today it is rarely, if ever, encountered.

In the 1980s, even its boosters conceded that Winnipeg had a terrible reputation, as it was generally perceived as "damn cold" and a city that had many down-and-out drunks hanging around Main Street (Squire 1986). The city's location on the prairies, an area with "all kinds of negative associations" in the minds of Canadians from outside the region, was also a barrier to successful promotion. Winnipeg AM (Awareness Motivators), a now-defunct group dedicated to the promotion of the city, admitted that Winnipeggers themselves were a major contributor to the city's bad reputation, being only too ready to brag about how cold it was back home when on winter vacation in Hawaii (Squire 1986, 52–3).

In the late 1970s, following the hydrocarbon boom in Alberta, and, to a lesser extent, in Saskatchewan, Winnipeg attempted to promote itself as a part of the resource-rich Canadian West, using the slogan, "Winnipeg: Where the New West Begins." This New West was defined as "a place where the pioneering spirit lives on as in the old days, but without the attending hardships" (Squire 1986, 54). The New West begins geographically in Winnipeg, and the word "begins" can also suggest a beginning in time, directing attention to the future in which the New West has an increasingly important role.

After a few years when it became quite clear that Manitoba was not a part of the energy boom then transforming the economy of Alberta, the city launched a new, rather ineffective campaign with the slogan, "Love me, Love my Winnipeg." In an attempt to turn a liability into an asset, another campaign, designed to counter the perception that winter was a test of endurance for the city's population, promoted "Wonderful Winter in Winnipeg." In 1984, the Winnipeg Blue Bombers won the Grey Cup for the first time in twenty-two years, spawning the new slogan of "Winnerpeg" that appeared on stickers carried by all city transit busses, and on lapel pins issued by city hall. These campaigns all came and went, and after a hiatus of some years, Mayor Susan Thompson's administration sought to reposition the city by adopting the slogan, "Winnipeg: One Great City." This was accompanied by the introduction of a newly commissioned logo, which is still used today.

Shelagh Squire (1986, 58) identified the variety of agencies then involved in image-building as a barrier to the city's successful promotion. A further concern was a failure to agree on the aspect of the city that should be promoted. Thus, some promotional agencies saw its ethnic and social diversity as an asset, whereas others saw it as a drawback. Furthermore, at the time, the city lacked a clear defining landmark that would serve as a recognizable icon for use in city promotion. The Golden Boy atop the legislative building was essentially a provincial icon, and other landmarks, such as the St Boniface Basilica or the Mint, were either geographically peripheral, or carried commercial or religious associations. In sum, Winnipeg has seen a succession of weak images and transient slogans. Image-building has not been effectively done.

WHO MAKES POLICY?

The nebulous nature of the concept of image-building complicates the task of identifying and isolating policy that is directed to it. Much of what constitutes image-building policy is poorly focused and not identified as such by the administrators who are involved in its formulation. Few local administrators perceive image-building to be a high priority for their municipality. When placed alongside more "practical" concerns, such as infrastructure development, housing, and policing, image-building is seen to be a minor concern. The only exception to this perspective is by those officials and private citizens who are actively involved either in the tourism sector or in economic development. Furthermore, the financial resources available for image-building are generally insignificant when placed alongside those devoted to other more practical concerns. Those who think differently, and who regard image-building as crucial to the long-term social and economic health of a community, often find themselves in a difficult position, as all too often the common opinion is that money is better spent on endeavours that give an immediate, albeit short-term, result. By its very nature, creation of an image requires a long-term commitment, and the results are not going to give an immediate or economic return; in fact, it is often extremely difficult to measure the payback on the investment in image-building.

Nowhere is this problem more apparent than in the smaller, rural municipalities where agriculture is the dominant economic activity, and where image-building is a relatively new concept. In larger centres where there has been a long-standing recognition that a strong image can attract capital and immigrants, and in those municipalities that traditionally have been a destination for vacationers, there is a greater awareness of the importance of image-building.

Although in general, image-building policy is poorly defined and often exists in the breach; all the municipalities considered in this study were, to some degree, aware of the relevance of image-building but generally did not accord it a high priority. Ironically, the effort put into it, and certainly their perception of the need for the formulation of an effective image-building policy, seemed to be inversely proportional to the municipality's size. Stuartburn, for example, although operating with minimal resources, has taken steps to promote its communities through local signage, and is presently debating the best ways to use its environmental and cultural capital to aid in the economic development of the community.

Policy formulation differs markedly between municipalities, reflecting the various agendas that can contribute to the desire to develop the image of a community. For example, in the RM of Stuartburn, a number of individuals are loosely allied in their desire to see the area have a stronger and more positive image, but there is no agreement on how to attain their objectives. The Gardenton Museum wishes to promote the Ukrainian character and historical resources of the area, while others, including the reeve, wish to capitalize on the natural assets of the area, especially the Tall Grass Prairie Preserve. Needless to say, there is also a large portion of the community that is content to continue to rely on agriculture with some off-farm work, and who are not particularly interested in developing any kind of image-building policy.

Swan River's situation is somewhat paradoxical in that while there is a more focused attempt to develop a strong image in order to further tourism, immigration, and economic development, there is no real debate over the best strategy to accomplish this task. Although there is some debate over tactical details, such as the precise design of the logo, there is unanimity on the question of strategy. According to Collinge (2006), its investment attraction committee of eight to ten members, none of whom are members of council, has free rein in developing the area's image. While local councils assist with the funding of SVEC, they have a passive role; rarely do they provide input on the content of the economic development plan.

SVEC is thus essentially representative of social forces rather than of government. The committee was established after a public brainstorming session and an invitation-only meeting; it was formed through volunteers, most of whom attended one of these sessions and were interested in promoting the Swan River Valley. In 2006, representatives included local business people, a member from the chamber of commerce, and interested citizens who volunteered to be part of the board (Collinge 2006). This is a case where initiatives were taken without much input from politicians. There is little or no government action, but, as Jean Harvey noted in the introduction, a *de facto* policy exists and is accepted by the public authorities.

Winkler

Winkler is very fortunate to have a well-developed image as a Mennonite town strongly committed to Christian and family values. Its Mennonite heritage is well-recognized within the region and throughout the province, and carries with it associations of a strong work ethic, conservative values, and self-reliance.

Unlike the other three communities examined in this paper, there has been little need for Winkler to promote its pre-existing image or to modify it. Rather, the greater concern in Winkler seems to be how best to disseminate its image to the widest possible audience. There has been little interest in tinkering with the nature of the image because the image is well-directed to attract the kind of people that Winkler sees as best fitting into its community. For example, Adelgunde Dyck (2007), founder of Star 7 International, an immigration agency dedicated to recruiting and integrating immigrants into Canadian society, says that Winkler is a very appealing destination for Mennonites from Europe and South America, as well as for German-speaking people in general.

Winnipeg

Image-building in Winnipeg can best be described as fragmented and without any real coordination between interested parties. For a complex institution such as the city of Winnipeg, there can be many different images promoted by various social forces and bureaucracies.

According to a 2004 press release, the Winnipeg Chamber of Commerce thinks that there is a need for the city to begin talking about itself in a more positive way, stressing the presence of the aerospace industry, the biotechnology sector, and emphasizing what is taking place in the universities in terms of research and development. "We need to brag about the world-class events we regularly host and the dynamic cultural community that exists here. Instead, we tend to concentrate on the negatives, like mosquitoes, potholes, and crime statistics, all things that could be solved if officials at city hall determined that these were priorities."

Certainly things have changed in Winnipeg since the 1980s, and major initiatives have changed the face of downtown. For example, the Forks Renewal Corporation developed the land around the

Forks National Historic Site in a way that greatly appeals to tourists and locals. New buildings, such as the MTS Centre and the Manitoba Hydro Building, have changed the streetscape of Portage Avenue, while the development of Waterfront Drive along the river, and of Red River College in the Exchange District have certainly enhanced the aesthetic appeal of the downtown.

The chamber (2004) is acutely aware of Winnipeg's negative image. In the last decade it has conducted polls to determine how people across the country view the city. The results are depressing. It is often described as cold, boring, flat, and mosquito-ridden – but friendly. As the chamber remarked, these are "not exactly selling points to attract new business or people to Winnipeg" (2004).

In the opinion of Respondent A (2007), a long-standing middle-level bureaucrat employed by the city of Winnipeg, building the city's image is "up there" in terms of the present and past administration's objectives, but it has not been executed successfully, partly because various administrations have different priorities. A coherent policy has never been articulated and efforts remain poorly focused, uncoordinated, and fragmented. In part, this may be a result of a failure to define clear objectives and to clearly articulate policy, and identify the appropriate channels for its realization.

> The previous administration of Mayor Glen Murray had a vision of the kind of image that it wanted to project to the world: a vision of Winnipeg as an exciting place to live, with street festivals, a flourishing arts community, and a lively downtown. This administration [of Mayor Sam Katz] is all about pipes, police, and potholes. (Respondent A 2007)

Two members of Winnipeg city council (Gerbasi 2007; Smith 2007) echoed this assessment, as did a high-level city bureaucrat, and several other stakeholders in the various quasi-governmental and non-governmental organizations involved in various facets of image-building. Mayor Katz defended the city's efforts to market itself, and dismissed calls for the city to establish a single body to develop and implement a long-term marketing plan (*Winnipeg Free Press*, 20 April 2005). Image-building policy in the city of Winnipeg, if it exists at all, exists only in the abstract, and there is no obvious coordination of efforts to formulate a coherent image that can serve to promote the city, either to its people or to prospective visitors.

On the other hand, Brian Grey (2005), Mayor Katz's director of policy, stated that whereas the former administration took a personal interest in promotion of the city, Mayor Katz prefers to develop Winnipeg's image through economic promotion using a more personal style of face-to-face diplomacy and personal contact. Nevertheless, the city administration responded to widespread indifference to the city's slogan, "One Great City," used since the 1980s, unveiling the new slogan, "Heart of the Continent," in September 2008 (*Winnipeg Free Press*, 6 September 2008).

Because of the diverse nature of image-building, it is difficult to identify key policy-makers. It is clear that some bureaucrats regard the provision of a safe social environment and pothole-free streets as vital to the image of the city. Indeed, the present mayor embraces and is proud of this approach (Gerbasi 2007; Smith 2007). He says there is not a great deal of image-building policy, other than the chamber of commerce's request that cab drivers not bring people to the downtown via the shortest and less attractive route, but instead take the "long way" from the airport, which passes through more scenic areas (2004).

Perhaps the most obvious candidate to be at the centre of Winnipeg's image-building policy is Economic Development Winnipeg (originally called "Destination Winnipeg"), a city-funded arms-length agency dedicated to the promotion of economic development and tourism. Their view is narrowly focused on the provision of information about Winnipeg to prospective visitors and investors. The agency provides assistance for event and convention planners. Its emphasis is upon large-scale visitation, such as group tours, rather than the family or independent traveller. It distributes information provided to it, but does not seem to take an active role in developing Winnipeg's image.

Few communities can develop successful image-building programs based solely on their reputations for economic dynamism. Most successful branding campaigns are multi-faceted and promote the economic, cultural, and environmental attributes of the community. There is little Winnipeg can do to counter the reality of its severe winter climate, but it certainly could do more to tell the world about its vibrant arts scene and its rich architectural legacy.

This is an approach that many feel Economic Development Winnipeg could take, and indeed should take (Gerbasi 2007; Johnson 2007; Respondent A 2007; Respondent B 2007; Smith 2007).

Winnipeg has a remarkable inventory of historic buildings, many of which have survived through historical accident. For example, in 2001, the city commissioned a study to investigate the possibility of securing a World Heritage designation for the Exchange District, which is already a National Historic Site.

The consultant's report suggested that the Exchange District was the best surviving concentration of early twentieth century terra cotta warehouse buildings in the world, and that the various levels of government should co-operate to enable a nomination to be put forward. Nothing was done, despite the report being presented to the city, the province, and to regional representatives of the federal government. This was simply a lack of political will on the part of all three levels of government (Respondent A 2007; Respondent C 2007).

The Provincial Historic Resources Branch is mandated to protect and develop the province's heritage, but tends to focus its operations outside Winnipeg, directing its attention to rural areas and leaving the city to its own devices. To some extent, this is a response to the perception on the part of rural residents that Winnipeg receives more than its fair share of provincial resources and that the rural areas are short-changed. The province has actively encouraged the development of municipal heritage advisory committees (MHACs), of which there are fifty-eight; ten of these are currently active. MHACs attempt to protect and develop municipal heritage resources. They draw upon the expertise of the Provincial Historic Resources Branch when required. The province, however, does not fund these committees.

Within the city of Winnipeg, the most prominent advocacy group for heritage is Heritage Winnipeg. This is a largely privately funded organization dedicated to the preservation and promotion of Winnipeg's built environment. Its activities include intensive lobbying of city and provincial politicians, as well as rallying public support for the preservation of historic buildings. As a heritage organization, it sees its work as central to the maintenance of the historic component of Winnipeg's image.

The Manitoba Historical Society is Western Canada's oldest heritage organization and has a province-wide mandate to promote Manitoba's history. Unfortunately, its membership is aging and shrinking, and it lacks the resources to engage in an advocacy role within the city. The society owns and operates Dalnavert National

Historic Site, which frequently appears as an icon in Manitoba's promotional advertising.

There is no doubt that the heritage community thinks it has a lot to offer but feels that the city has abdicated its leadership role in policy formation. The city's excellent inventory of historic buildings is relatively under-utilized in its promotional literature. Only during "Doors Open Winnipeg," an annual one-day event, does the city showcase its architectural legacy, which is actually organized and administered on their behalf by Heritage Winnipeg.

The way in which the Human Rights Museum was developed illustrates the lack of any clearly defined policy, either for management and interpretation of heritage resources, or the promotion of Winnipeg's image. The museum was initiated by an individual, albeit one with extensive financial backing and equally impressive political connections. Israel Asper, founder of CanWest Global Communications Corporation, proposed the project unilaterally, pursuing funding from all levels of government, rather than seeking to build a logical series of partnerships beginning with the city. In essence, he bypassed it to deal directly with the federal government to achieve his goals. The success of the Asper initiative demonstrates that a dynamic and committed champion is perhaps more important to the success of an initiative than the existence of policy (Stroski 2007). This is perhaps especially true of rural municipalities where the execution of a project is almost totally dependent upon the commitment of a local champion. For example, the initiative to preserve the elevator row at Inglis, although derived by the federal government, could not have been carried through without the dedication of one particular local volunteer. Ironically, it is policy that makes this so. The federal government is committed to the idea of cost-sharing and partnerships, and so demands that local communities put considerable resources into projects that are essentially of national importance.

INTERGOVERNMENTAL RELATIONS

In Manitoba it appears that intergovernmental relations on a local level in terms of image-building tend to be rocky or simply non-existent. Of the three rural municipalities examined here, only Swan River has established a mechanism whereby several municipalities are actively co-operating to promote regional development and formulate a regional image. The relative geographical isolation of Stuartburn was reflected in its lack of interaction with surrounding municipalities, at least in so far as image-building was concerned. Winkler seemed to relish its independence. Not only did it not co-operate with surrounding municipalities, but seemed to have a somewhat antagonistic relationship with the neighbouring town of Morden. As the dominant city in the province, with economic power rivalling that of the provincial government, Winnipeg apparently sees little reason to partner with adjoining municipalities to promote a regional image that might overshadow the city's image.

Of the four populations considered in this study, Swan River demonstrates by far the strongest focus on horizontal co-operation between municipalities. Seven entities in total – the towns of Swan River, Minitonas, and Benito; the village of Bowsman; and the RMs of Mountain, Minitonas, and Swan River – are co-operating, albeit with some friction, to create an overall image for the Swan Valley.

Rick Reich (2006), reeve for the RM of Swan River, has long been an advocate of this approach. He explains that it not only strengthens bonds between communities, but also makes sense economically, as the entities can pool their money. In fact, Reich goes a step further and suggests that the seven political entities can be merged into one. "We have eleven thousand people and forty-two elected officials that look after them," he says, adding that Winnipeg has only fifteen councillors for its population of 633,451. He points out that every council hires an administrator and pays for an office, hydro, insurance, and other necessities. "It doesn't change if you're four hundred people or four thousand. Your basic costs are fairly similar ... It's like having too big a mortgage and the interest eats up all your money instead of making payments." Therefore, Reich is trying to convince the residents of the area that it would be prudent to merge. There are still many who disagree with the idea, but he says more people have begun to agree with him in recent years. Reich contends that if they reduce these costs, money will be freed up for other investments to improve the area, such as for the current goal to construct an indoor swimming pool. He adds that it is already significant that the seven authorities are working together for this initiative. It is more likely that they will get federal-provincial infrastructure funding because all councils passed resolutions supporting co-operation. The local MLA, Rosann Wowchuk, supported them in this approach. Wowchuk finds it helpful to be able to go to her caucus and say that she has seven authorities that want to work together to create one entity that will provide services to all the RMs (Collinge 2006; Reich 2006).

Reich (2006) is also a strong supporter of SVEC's economic attraction initiative and marketing plan, and keeps in touch with Collinge on the topic. He believes a strong, common image is important. "What we have to do is sell ourselves as one. It is image. To me, the perfect image is a strong, financially viable place ... if we can save money and become more cost-effective, we become more viable, which gives us a good image." He notes that while not all councils are getting actively involved in SVEC's work, they are in large part supportive of the view and are "just approaching it from a different angle."

However, it is not always easy for seven political entities to work together. For years, there has been discord between them, much of it focusing on the perception that the town of Swan River gets most of the amenities, while the other towns do not. In fact, several municipalities once pulled out of SVEC because they felt it did not represent them equally (Collinge 2006).

This conflict emerged in an unusual way during the planning of the marketing strategy. For an outsider, it would seem logical to use a swan as the logo. However, it was not that simple for those who live in the valley. Collinge (2006) says the investment attraction board made a conscious decision not to use a swan as a logo so as not to "alienate" the other RMs and towns that did not have names associated with a swan. "We knew that from the outside looking in, a swan would make sense, but we also knew that if we didn't have people from the inside who supported it, it wouldn't matter what it looked like from the outside." Instead, in 2006 the logo was the letter "V" stylized to look like a valley.

The logo debate was more important to some board members than others, however. Don McCrae (2006), a trapper from nearby Cowan, resigned from the board after he became frustrated with the never-ending discussions over the logo. "I drove eighty miles and they spent 90 per cent of the meeting discussing the logo," he says. "The logo doesn't sell trips." While he is glad that SVEC is at least doing something to create a brand for the region – he realizes that other regions are not so fortunate – he feels SVEC's approach is not ideal. Instead of spending a large amount of time on such things as logos, McCrae feels strongly that goals should be set, and then the board should come up with strategies to meet those goals. For instance, he felt that market research into immigrants would have been more beneficial prior to the 2006 trip to the immigration trade fair. "Find people from Scotland who have immigrated to Canada, find out why they came, and why they came to a certain spot instead of another spot," he stresses. He thinks that such research could lead to more immigrants than would selecting the ideal logo. "When you're selling soap, you've got to know the soap. When you're selling fish, you've got to know the fish," he says of the need to know the motivations of immigrants.

In stark contrast to the co-operative model adopted by Swan River stands Winkler, where, according to one provincial bureaucrat, the relationship between it and the adjacent town of Morden mirrors the feud between the "Hatfields and the McCoys" (Einarson 2007). Although there are no significant differences between the two communities in terms of the ethnic composition or their geographical situation, there seems to be a mutual distrust, despite the fact that many people commute from one community to the other on a daily basis. Physically, the two towns are different; Morden has a solid core of fieldstone buildings and more of a "traditional" look to it, whereas Winkler seems to better fit the *Rough Guides*' description of "one of a series of charmless towns in southern Manitoba" (Lehr and Kentner-Hidalgo 1998).

The placement of the hospital midway between the two communities is a physical manifestation of their rivalry, as neither of the two communities was willing to let the other have the advantage of superior medical facilities. Twenty-seven years of bickering passed between the two communities before the provincial health minister finally intervened and decided on the compromise location for the facility (Siemens 2007).

According to Lehr (2007), municipal officials in Morden are quite amenable to co-operating with Winkler in promotion of the Morden-Winkler region, but their interest has not been reciprocated. This is one instance where even the Winkler development officer wishes for the provincial government to take a more active role and force co-operation (Siemens 2007). Many involved in Winkler image-building recognized that community attitudes were hindering development (Siemens 2007; Dyck 2007). Everyone interviewed in Winkler stressed that the community was somewhat unusual in its parochialism and conservatism. There is a strong tradition of

Mennonite in-group self-reliance (Dueck 2007; Dyck 2007; Redekop 2007; Siemens 2007; Respondent D 2007).

Unlike other policy fields that are more central to the political process, such as immigration or infrastructure, image-building does not appear to be firmly anchored to political ideology. Where there are differences of opinion as to the most effective strategy to be adopted, they seem to be essentially local and based upon local economic interests. A case in point is the situation in Stuartburn where two factions disagree on the importance of the municipality's image as either a haven for large-scale livestock operations or a refuge for the Western Prairie Fringed Orchid. For the most part, local politics are not aligned along conventional political party lines. Since image-building decision-making is on a local level, political doctrine seldom comes into play.

In light of the above, changing governments at the federal level have had insignificant impacts upon image-building policy in rural municipalities (August 2007). In large measure, this is reflective of the peripheral involvement of the federal government in image-building efforts of rural Manitoban communities.

A recently announced initiative by the provincial government has provided funding to establish a "regional vision for the capital region" (Manitoba Government 2007). Modest funding of $40,000 has been provided to foster long-term economic and environmental sustainability of communities in the capital region through co-operation, with the intention of having Winnipeg and its surrounding communities "think and act like a region." This initiative is not specifically directed to the image-building process, but if strong intergovernmental linkages were to be developed, it would create an ideal platform for the formulation of strong public policy involving horizontal interjurisdictional collaboration, and presumably the development of stronger ties with higher levels of government.

SOCIAL FORCES

Social forces of various kinds – businesses, service clubs, community organizations, and individual citizens – are usually the instigators of image-building. Various elements of the media also play a crucial role, particularly those elements based outside the region whose stories, opinion pieces, and travel features can do much to shape opinion on a national or international level. In 1982, the German news magazine *Der Spiegel*, ran a series of articles profiling communities in the German Diaspora, including the German community in Winnipeg. The difficulties faced by German immigrants were stressed, and the severity of the Manitoba climate was emphasized and sensationalized. The article identified Winnipeg and Manitoba as the coldest places in a generally cold Canada. One informant described the climate as "pretty nasty ... there are 131 days of frost here, and temperatures below minus 30 degrees Celsius aren't unusual. The record is minus 46.2." Equally galling was the portrayal of Winnipeg as a social and cultural desert, where there was nothing affordable to do.

Although outraged by what it considered to be an inaccurate and unfair portrayal, there was little that the city could do to repudiate this account. Denials are seldom heeded and, even if published, rejoinders seldom receive the attention gathered by the original article.

Politicians and administrators are seldom the catalysts for image-building initiatives. It tends to be the grassroots that conceive of the ideas and advocate their implementation. It is an axiom in this area that politicians are led more than they are leaders. For example, image-building in the town of Swan River was first proposed by SVEC, which is a non-governmental institution. Under their initiative, local politicians were invited to collaborate in the process. Nevertheless, SVEC remained the driving force, and politicians were generally passive observers, neither impeding nor promoting the SVEC initiative (Collinge 2006).

In 1998, Swan River claimed the title, Forest Capital of Canada. Although the mechanism by which this title was awarded is unclear, it seems that it was due to the activities of Louisiana Pacific and Spruce Products Limited, and the community's eager embrace of the companies' presence in the area. Interestingly, forestry activities in the region have also had negative effects on image-building. For instance, the ability of Louisiana Pacific to engage in sustainable forest management in Duck Mountain Provincial Park was questioned by a number of ecological organizations (Soprovich 2006). Louisiana Pacific was also castigated for being one of the continent's worst polluters.

Winkler has traded upon its long-established reputation as a conservative Mennonite community with a strong work ethic, provision of mutual assistance, and level-headed sobriety. The various agencies interested in promoting this image have done little to expand it, although they have all been content to disseminate it without alteration. Star 7 International, for example, draws upon this image to attract German-speaking and Mennonite immigrants from overseas, but significantly, it makes no mention of this image to potential immigrants from the Philippines, knowing full well that this will not be perceived positively by predominantly Roman Catholic immigrants (Dyck 2007; Redekop 2007).

In contrast, social forces are far more active in Winnipeg. The chamber of commerce, The Forks North Portage Renewal Corporation, as well as institutions representing the city's heritage community all feel that they have something to contribute to the development of a more positive image for Winnipeg. Unfortunately, there seems to be a disconnection between these social forces and the executive policy committee of city council. The institution charged with promoting Winnipeg, Economic Development Winnipeg, does not appear to contribute significantly towards the evolution and development of Winnipeg's image. Some city councillors feel that this situation is unfortunate and the relationship needs reformulation. One solution would be to expand its mandate and strengthen its ties to both the community and to the council. Alternatively, a new entity could be established to develop and promote Winnipeg's image on a truly holistic basis (Gerbasi 2007; Smith 2007).

SPORTS AND IMAGE-BUILDING

It was surprising that none of the stakeholders or politicians interviewed during the course of this research raised the role that sport might play in contributing to the image of their community. Clearly, in the case of the smaller municipalities studied (RM of Stuartburn, Swan River), sporting activities serve only the recreational needs of the immediate population. Their facilities, such as they are, do not in any way distinguish them from the surrounding centres. For sports facilities to contribute to the image of a community, they would have to eclipse those available within their hinterland.

For example, Winkler and Swan Valley are both sufficiently large to support hockey arenas, and each hosts a team in the Manitoba Junior Hockey League: the Winkler Flyers and the Swan Valley Stampeders. In terms of image-building, the impact of teams in this league is limited and confined to raising awareness of the community in the league's region.

A place can enhance its image through sport in various ways (Kotler, Haider et al. 1993). One is by hosting a premier team in a major league sport that receives intensive media coverage. Another is for a community to host what is known as a "hallmark event": a one-time "mega-event" of national, hemispheric, or global significance. Examples would include the Pan-American Games held in Winnipeg in 1999, the Winter Olympics held in Calgary in 1988, or the FIFA World Cup held in Germany in 2006. Winkler was fortunate to be selected by the Canadian Broadcasting Corporation (CBC) as the site of the eighth annual Hockey Day in Canada event. Although not truly a hallmark event, "Hockey Day" briefly focused national attention on Winkler, which was selected on the basis of its commitment to hockey.

For three days, from 7–9 February 2008, Winkler was in the national spotlight, as the CBC broadcast live from the city. Local hockey heroes attended, among them Dustin Penner, a member of the 2007 Stanley Cup champions Anaheim Ducks, and currently a member of the Edmonton Oilers of the National Hockey League (NHL). Other personalities attending from the hockey world included broadcasters Ron MacLean and Don Cherry. CBC even broadcast the national news from Winkler, bringing in national news anchor Peter Mansbridge. In addition, Cassie Campbell, captain of the gold-medal-winning 2002 Winter Olympics women's ice hockey team, and retired celebrated sportscaster, Dick Irvin, were featured. Winkler community events coordinator, Deb Penner (2008), claimed the heavy media coverage that accompanied the event "changed the image of Winkler in the minds of many Canadians." Even Ron MacLean stated on air that Winkler was a "dry town," but after being informed his statement was incorrect, his own view of the city changed.

Unlike a classic hallmark event, Hockey Day in Canada left no infrastructural legacy, such as was left by the Montreal Olympics in the form of the Olympic Stadium. The attention devoted to Winkler was intense, but brief, and the long-term impact of the occasion on Winkler's image is difficult to gauge. Nevertheless, the town received communications from across Canada, and even the northern United States, inquiring about and applauding the event (Penner 2008).

Winnipeg hosted the Pan-American Games in 1999, which might be regarded as a hemispheric hallmark event. This major athletic competition attracted athletes from virtually every country in the Americas and placed Winnipeg in the spotlight for the two-week duration of the Games. Whereas the benefits of the influx of government and corporate monies into the city are measurable, the impact of the event on Winnipeg's image is not. Certainly, that 400 million people throughout the Americas watched the closing ceremonies on television suggests that awareness of the city must have received a considerable boost (CBC 1999).

Winnipeg suffered a major blow to its pride in 1996 when the Winnipeg Jets, its NHL franchise, moved to Phoenix, Arizona. Among the arguments raised in favour of keeping the Jets in Winnipeg were the team's injection of capital into the community and its intangible promotion of image. Proponents of publicly subsidizing the Jets argued that having the team carry the city's name was worth millions of dollars of free promotion. They argued further that the very fact that Winnipeg had an NHL franchise testified to its status as a first-rate city. Others were more sceptical; Jim Silver (1996) contended in *Thin Ice* that it was economically impossible and morally wrong for the city to subsidize an NHL team. The matter of the Jets return remained a hot topic. In the provincial election of 2007, the provincial Conservative leader even offered an ill-advised election promise to bring back the Jets if elected. A plethora of websites and Facebook groups bemoaned the absence of NHL hockey, endlessly speculating about the possibility of the Jets returning to Winnipeg.

With the Jets gone, the Winnipeg Blue Bombers became the city's flagship team, but the Canadian Football League (CFL) is confined to central and Western Canada. The Jets' replacement franchise, the Manitoba Moose, played in the American Hockey League, but received little attention from the North American sports media. Even less attention is given to the Winnipeg Goldeyes, a baseball team that plays in a minor eight-team league. With the exception of the Blue Bombers, none of these teams are an effective vehicle for carrying Winnipeg's message that it is an exciting, dynamic city to a national audience, let alone carry its image across the continent.

The announcement in 2011 that the Atlanta Thrashers were purchased by Winnipeg's True North Sports and Entertainment group, and would move to Winnipeg, sent the city into a paroxysm of joy (*Winnipeg Free Press*, 31 May 2011). Despite an indifferent performance in their opening season, the new Jets sold out every game and enjoyed an enthusiastic reception by the city. Their return was credited with changing the psyche of the city, improving its self image, creating a positive outlook and, somewhat paradoxically, igniting enthusiasm for Winnipeg's other sports franchises. No government assistance was involved.

Intergovernmental relationships in regards to sports tend to be focused on the material: the building of arenas and other facilities. The relationship to the image of the city is usually implicit rather than explicit, and the benefits to image-building are difficult to factor in to any cost-benefit analysis.

RESOURCES

Paradoxically, while the higher levels of government have access to greater capital resources for image-building (witness Manitoba's controversial "Spirited Energy" campaign), local governments have access to greater social capital. A community such as Swan River, which lacks access to significant capital reserves, has been able to develop and promote its image simply by the determination and commitment of its local economic development corporation. We suspect that in many communities there is a good deal of latent social capital that could easily be harnessed if good public policy could provide the necessary mechanism and motive. For example, in the RM of Stuartburn, there are a number of individuals and organizations that all have an interest in promoting the area, and yet there is no mechanism for bringing them together as a cohesive, coherent, and effective social force (Shewchuk 2006; Hiebert 2007; Moore 2007; Richenhaller 2007; Respondent E 2007). Not surprisingly, without this, image-building efforts in Stuartburn so far have been less than effective.

As noted earlier, one important resource is the existence of a "local champion," someone who has the vision, energy, and time to develop and promote an idea or project. Without such individuals to drive the process, attempts at image-building can quickly flounder. When entrusted to well-meaning committees, the process tends to stall. Ideas become watered-down in an attempt to accommodate too many visions or to make the image all embracing (Respondent A 2007; Respondent B 2007).

CONCLUSION AND RECOMMENDATIONS

This study has shown that image-building policy by public authorities in the four municipalities examined here is largely absent. Such policy that does exist is rarely driven or formulated by any level of government. More often, policy exists in an unstructured and informal basis, being created, promoted, and implemented by social forces. Largely because of the way in which policy has come to be, the influence of local champions has become crucial to the successful implementation of policy.

However, not every community or RM is fortunate enough to have a dedicated champion. Therefore, it would be useful to have a central coordinating agency, most likely at the provincial level, which would coordinate image-building efforts of both rural municipalities and the city of Winnipeg. This kind of impetus at a provincial level could awaken latent image-building interest in the communities, foster the champions that are so crucial to image-building, and provide a policy structure to define roles and responsibilities in the image-building process.

One barrier to the further development of sound policy is the nebulous concept of image-building, and the failure to appreciate the pivotal role that it can take in economic and social development. It is difficult to convince policy-makers working in different fields that image-building should be considered as part of their mandate, especially when there is no immediate financial return. Image-building spans many different policy fields – education, infrastructure, immigration, investment, tourism, and so forth – hence the difficulty of convincing policy-makers in each of these fields that they should take responsibility for developing and promoting community image as part of their mandate. Even if policy-makers in a certain field recognize that image-building is part of their mandate, there is still the question of securing interdepartmental co-operation and developing policy that will ensure mutual co-operation. As an example, cultural tourism only promotes, it does not invest in the development of heritage. It does not put anything back into the real basis for the image. In fact, only about 1 per cent of tourism revenues are reinvested in heritage (Dul 2007).

The linkages within economic development strategies are seldom appreciated by those involved in what should be a highly integrated process. Some of the barriers to development of effective strategy are organizational and institutional. For example, there is little point in devoting resources to image-building unless there are clearly defined objectives that are realistic. To launch a campaign to secure a major "hallmark" event to Winnipeg, for example, is pointless unless the city has the range of accommodations needed, the infrastructure to handle the event, and sufficient airline capacity to bring in the expected influx of visitors. In any image-building initiative, close cooperation between all relevant federal, provincial, and municipal governments, quasi-governmental agencies, and private corporations is absolutely vital. This is more easily said than done, not least because of the different objectives and mandates of public institutions and private corporations. Development of public policy that recognizes these dilemmas, and the creation of specialized advisory units at the federal level, could go some way toward addressing these difficulties.

Striking a balance between political continuity and political immobility is a crucial element in image-building and promotional efforts. Too frequent changes will disrupt implementation of policy, but when elected officials remain in office for decades, it is difficult to introduce fresh ideas or new policy (August 2007; Dul 2007; Stroski 2007).

Higher levels of government should play a role in assisting municipalities to develop policy, and to foster interdepartmental and intermunicipal collaboration. Image-building is the one policy field where clearly defined objectives are essential. Without a common objective, attempts to promote the image of a community will be confused, contradictory, and ineffectual.

There are some very real differences in approaches taken to image-building by the municipalities examined here. Whereas Swan River has exhibited an encouraging willingness to work with adjacent municipalities for the benefit of the region, Winkler has been reluctant to co-operate with its neighbouring community in any kind of promotional venture. Further, Stuartburn has pursued a "go it alone" policy. Insofar as effective marketing is concerned, intercommunity and intraregional co-operation is vital. Tourist promoters know well that very few destinations can be sold without the help of their neighbours; operators look for a bundle of attractions so competition is futile. Co-operation yields higher dividends (Gartrell 1988).

Provincial and federal governments could facilitate the image-building process in a number of ways. Municipal administrators and business owners commented that grant applications are often unnecessarily complex, and that the sheer volume of information descending upon smaller municipalities who operate with limited staff makes it very easy for opportunities to become lost in a welter of extraneous information (Mistlebacher 2007; Siemens 2007; Respondent D 2007). One municipal administrator said that federal opportunities were often "the government's best kept secret" (Respondent D 2007). Chuck Davidson (2006) of the Winnipeg Chamber of Commerce echoed this concern with keeping abreast of government programs and policies:

> Policy development is always very difficult in terms of ensuring you have all the information, have done all the research, and knowing what the starting point is and what all the different jurisdictions are doing – knowing what all the current laws and what the current restrictions are – and knowing all of this makes it tough. Sometimes [businesspeople and local officials] do not know who the right people to talk to are.

In almost every aspect of economic development, Winnipeg overshadows all other communities. Its image is crucial to the image of Manitoba as a whole. Unfortunately, it has no clearly defined policy for image-building, and its one organization, which would seem to be devoted to that task, Economic Development Winnipeg, simply disseminates information provided to it. Within the industry, it would be termed a destination marketing organization. It does not appear to take an active role in the image-building process.

Policy-makers must recognize that the nature of a community's image will differ, not only according to the social and geographic characteristics of the area being promoted, but that the image must also be tailored to suit the receiving market. Local attempts at image-building are really only for local consumption and have relevance only within Manitoba. Outside of the region, the people receiving image promotion are more concerned with a comprehensive regional image than any particular segment of it, and for people outside the country, even regional images are perceived to be only a component of the national image (Johnson 2007).

To develop an effective image, Winnipeg needs to focus its efforts on one particular civic attribute. To determine its priorities, perhaps it should look to its citizens rather than to outside marketing companies, as the province did for its much-derided 2005 "Spirited Energy" revamping of the provincial image (Gerbasi 2007; Smith 2007). Image-building policy should make provision for public consultation and more opportunities for private citizens to become involved in shaping policy. It should ensure that a city's cultural and human capital is used to its best advantage. Above all, the slogan that promotes the city must ring true with its citizens, advancing values and attributes that resonate with ordinary people, and promoting attitudes that they can embrace and with which they can identify. The city's past and present role as a reception area for immigrants, and the realities of social deprivation, poverty, and crime in the core area have to be acknowledged and addressed before a new image can be successfully marketed. Image-building policy cannot stand alone; to be effective it should be an integral part of a broad revitalization strategy that addresses deeper social and economic issues (Paddison 1993, 348). Extra-regional agencies and corporations that have little understanding of the way that Winnipeggers see their city cannot develop new city images that will be embraced by the population at large. Heritage Winnipeg, the Manitoba Historical Society, the Winnipeg Chamber of Commerce, and the Manitoba Eco-Network are examples of organizations with specific expertise that are currently being largely ignored in this policy area.

Image-building remains a neglected policy area in rural Manitoba, although there is clearly strong latent interest in developing the potential of Manitoba communities by creating a strong sense of place and advertising the communities beyond their immediate locality. Local efforts at image-building have been done in the absence of any formal policy and without any strong linkages to higher levels of government. Thus, efforts are sporadic, uncoordinated, and probably far less successful than they could be. For this situation to be addressed, higher levels of government must take the lead and encourage the development of effective image-building policy within and between Manitoba municipalities.

NOTE

1 The term "disorganized," when applied in this sense, simply refers to the transfer of the administrative responsibility from elected local control to that of higher authority. In this case the municipality came under provincial administration.

INTERVIEWS

Anonymous [Respondent A]. 2007. Interview by author, telephone. Winnipeg, MB. 26 October.

Anonymous [Respondent B]. 2007. Interview by author, in-person. Winnipeg, MB. 2 November.

Anonymous [Respondent C]. 2007. Interview by author, in-person. Winnipeg, MB. 8 August.

Anonymous [Respondent D]. 2007. Interview by author, in-person. Winkler, MB. 3 August.

Anonymous [Respondent E]. 2007. Interview by author, in-person. Stuartburn, MB. 3 July.

August, Jim. 2007. Interview by author, in-person. Winnipeg, MB. 8 November.

Baird, Frances. 2006. Interview by author, in-person. Swan River, MB. 8 August.

Bellefleur, Emili. 2007. Interview by author, telephone, St Andrews, MB. 29 October.

Collinge, Darlis. 2006. Interview by author, in-person. Swan River, MB. 9 August.

Davidson, Charles. 2006. Interview by Danielle Richot-Sopko, in-person. Winnipeg, MB. 10 June.

Dueck, Barbara. 2007. Interview by author, in-person. Winkler, MB. 3 July.

Dul, Donna. 2007. Interview by author, in-person. Winnipeg, MB. 7 November.

Dyck, Adelgunde. 2007. Interview by author, in-person. Winkler, MB. 3 July.

Einarson, Neil. 2007. Interview by author, in-person. Winnipeg, MB. 7 November.

Gerbasi, Jenny. 2007. Interview by author, in-person. Winnipeg, MB. 6 November.

Grey, Brian. 2005. Interview by author, in-person. Winnipeg, MB. 8 December.

Hiebert, Eddie. 2007. Interview by author, in-person. Vita, MB. 3 July.

Johnson, Max. 2007. Interview by author, in-person. Winnipeg, MB. 5 November.

Johnston, Dave. 2006. Interview by author, in-person. Swan River, MB. 10 August.

Kologie, Michael. 2006. Interview by Danielle Richot-Sopko, Winnipeg, MB. 30 May.

McCrae, Don. 2006. Interview by author, telephone. Cowan, MB. 15 August.

McKay, Darin. 2006. Interview by author, in-person. Swan River, MB. 10 August.

Mistlebacher, Shirley. 2007. Interview by author, in-person. Stuartburn, MB. 3 July.

Moore, Mike. 2007. Interview by author, telephone. Winnipeg, MB. 31 October.

Penner, Deb. 2008. Interview by author, in-person. Winkler, MB. 20 February.

Potten, Beverley. 2007. Interview by author, in-person. Swan River, MB. 11 August.

Redekop, Karl. 2007. Interview by author, in-person. Winkler, MB. 3 August.

Reeves, Laura. 2007. Interview by author, in-person. Stuartburn, MB. 15 August.

Reich, Rick. 2006. Interview by author, in-person. Swan River, MB. 11 August.

Richenhaller, Pat. 2007. Interview by author, in-person. Swan River, MB. 8 August.

Shewchuk, Linda. 2006. Interview by author, in-person. Stuartburn, MB. 14 August.

Siemens, Walter. 2007. Interview by author, in-person. Winkler, MB. 3 August.

Smith, Harvey. 2007. Interview by author, in-person. Winnipeg, MB. 6 November.

Stroski, Mark. 2007. Interview by author, in-person. Winnipeg, MB. 7 November.

Terlesky, Greg. 2006. Interview by author, telephone. Winnipeg, MB. 17 August.

Vaillancourt, Josée. 2007. Interview by author, telephone. Winnipeg, MB. 29 October.

REFERENCES

Artibise, Alan. 1970. "Advertising Winnipeg: The Campaign for Immigrants and Industry: 1874–1914." *Transactions of the Historical and Scientific Society of Manitoba*, Series III: no. 22: 75–106.

Blanchard, Jim. 2005. *Winnipeg 1912*. Winnipeg: University of Manitoba Press.

Brooke, Rupert. 1978. *Rupert Brooke in Canada*. Toronto: PMA Books.

Canadian Broadcasting Corporation. 1999. "'Best Ever' Pan Am Games end." CBCNews.ca. http://www.cbc.ca/news/canada/story/1999/08/09/panam990809.html.

Der Spiegel (Hamburg). 1982. "Weg von hier – um jeden Preis." *Der Spiegel* 42, 18 November: 8.

Destination Winnipeg. [Now Economic Development Winnipeg] 2008. http://www.destinationwinnipeg.ca.

Gartrell, Richard B. 1988. *Destination Marketing For Convention and Visitor Bureaus.* Dubuque, Iowa: Kendal Hunt Publishing Company.

Gould, Peter, and Rodney White. 1974. *Mental Maps.* Harmondsworth: Penguin Books.

Hall, Ian. 2007. "Prairie Main Street: Conservation is not the Answer." *Prairie Forum* 32, no. 2: 321–34.

Hart, E.J. 1983. *The Selling of Canada: the CPR and the Beginnings of Canadian Tourism.* Banff: Altitude Publishing.

Heald, Susan. 2005. "The New Economy? Continuity and Change in Gardenton, Manitoba." Report by the Manitoba Research Alliance on Community Economic Development in the New Economy.

Kaplan, Bess. 1975. *Corner Store.* Winnipeg: Queenston House.

Kaye, Vladimir J. 1964. *Early Ukrainian Settlements in Canada 1895–1900.* Toronto: University of Toronto Press.

Kotler, Philip, Donald Haider, and Irving Rein. 1993. *Marketing Places: Attracting Investment, Industry, and Tourism to Cities, States and Nations.* New York: The Free Press.

Kunstler, James Howard. 1993. *The Geography of Nowhere: The Rise and Decline of Americas Man-Made Landscape.* New York: Touchstone.

Lehr, John C. 1983. "Propaganda and Belief: Ukrainian Immigrant Views of the Canadian West." In *New Soil – Old Roots: the Ukrainian Immigrant Experience in Canada,* edited by. J. Rozumnnyj. Winnipeg: The Ukrainian Academy of Arts and Sciences in Canada.

Lehr, John C., and Julie Kentner-Hidalgo. 1998. "The Tourist Picture: Murals and Small Town Tourism Animate Boissevain Manitoba, in Western Canada." *Small Town* 28, no. 5: 12–21.

Lehr, John S. 2007. "Place Marketing in Manitoba: A Study of Three Communities." BA diss., University of Winnipeg.

Lowenthal, David. 1975. "Past Time, Present Place, Landscape and Memory." *Geographical Review* 65: 1–36.

Lewis, Sinclair. 1922. *Babitt.* New York: Harcourt, Brace and World.

MacLean, Alexis, and Richard Rounds. 1991. *An Analysis of the Population of Agro-Manitoba 1961–1986.* Brandon: Rural Development Institute.

Manitoba Government. 2007. RM of Stuartburn Community Profile. Manitoba Community Profiles. http://www.gov.mb.ca/asset_library/en/statistics/demographics/communities/stuartburn_rm.pdf.

Mitchell, Elizabeth B. 1981. *In Western Canada Before the War: Impressions of Early Twentieth Century Prairie Communities*. Saskatoon: Western Producer Prairie Books.

Niedomysl, Thomas. 2004. "Evaluating the Effects of Place-Marketing Campaigns on Inter-Regional Migration in Sweden." *Environment and Planning* 36: 1991–2009.

Paddison, Roman. 1993. "City Marketing, Image Reconstruction and Urban Regeneration." *Urban Studies* 30, no. 2: 339–50.

Peel, Bruce. 1966. "The Lure of the West." *Papers of the Bibliographical Society of Canada* no. 5: 19–29.

Peterson, Gary, and Thomas Saarinen. 1986. "Local Symbols and Sense of Place." *Journal of Geography* 85, no. 4: 164–8.

Philips, Rhonda. 2002. *Concept Marketing for Communities: Capitalizing on Underutilized Resources to Generate Growth and Development*. Westport, Connecticut: Praeger.

Rees, Ronald. 1988. *New and Naked Land*. Saskatoon: Western Producer Prairie Books.

Relph, Edward. 1976. *Place and Placelessness*. London: Pion.

Sanemose, Aksel. 2005. *Aksel Sandemose and Canada: A Scandinavian Writer's Perception of the Canadian Prairies in the 1920s*. Edited and translated by Christopher S. Hale. Regina: Canadian Plains Research Centre.

Silver, Jim. 1996. *Thin Ice: Money, Politics and the Demise of an NHL Franchise*. Winnipeg: Fernwood Publications.

Soprovich, Dan. 2006. "Overallocation of Forests to Louisiana-Pacific." *Eco Journal* 17, no. 1: 5–6.

Squire, Shelagh J. 1986. "Boosterist Landscapes and the Geography of Community Promotion: An Analysis of the Western Canadian Experience." BA diss., University of Winnipeg.

Statistics Canada. 2006. Swan River. 2006 Community Profiles. http://www12.statcan.ca/english/census06/data/profiles/community/Details/Page.cfm?Lang=E&Geo1=CSD&Code1=4620048&Geo2=PR&Code2=46&Data=Count&SearchText=wan%20river&SearchType=Begins&SearchPR=01&B1=All&Custom=.

Stich, Klaus Peter. 1976. "Canada's Century: The Rhetoric of Propaganda." *Prairie Forum* 1: 19–29.

Swan Valley Enterprise Centre Inc. 2006. *Investment Attraction Marketing Plan*.

Ward, Stephen V. 1998. *Selling Places: The Marketing and Promotion of Towns and Cities 1850–2000*. New York: Routledge.

Warren, George. 1927. *The Victoria Daily Colonist,* 5 October.

Werner, Hans P. 2006. *Living between Worlds: A History of Winkler.* Winkler, Manitoba: Winkler Heritage Society.

Winkler Flyers Junior Hockey Club. *History.* WinklerFlyers.com. http://www.winklerflyers.com/about.html.

Winnipeg Chamber of Commerce. 2004. "Is it time for Winnipeg's Extreme Makeover?" http://www.winnipeg-chamber.com/pdf/editorials/d.pdf.

Winnipeg Free Press. 2005. "Mayor defends city's marketing efforts." 20 April, D9.

– 2008. "Winnipeggers say they're Heart of the Continent," 6 September. B1.

Woodsworth, James S. 1972. *Strangers Within our Gates.* Toronto: University of Toronto Press.

Zukin, Sharon. 1991. *Landscapes of Power.* Berkley: University of California Press.

4

Intergovernmental Relations and Image-building Policy in PEI

JUDY LYNN RICHARDS, WITH
HEATHER GUSHUE AND DAVID BULGER

THE SIGNIFICANCE OF THE IMAGE-BUILDING FIELD IN THE PROVINCE

The principal focus of image-building in Prince Edward Island (PEI) is tourism. While in recent years the city of Charlottetown has made much of articles describing it as a good place for business (Bulger 2008), for the province as a whole – and for Charlottetown, itself – tourism is a major money-maker. The provincial Department of Tourism estimates that, in 2007, receipts from tourism amounted to $354.3 million, placing it well ahead of fisheries ($166.8 million), and not far behind agriculture ($364 million) (Government of PEI 2008). In numbers of visitors, this represents approximately 1.2 million tourists annually (Government of PEI 2001). Given the importance of tourism to the Island economy, it is not surprising that the image built must be "visitor friendly."

Tourism image-building may be said to be the process of creating and promoting a specific identity representative of a place in order to entice potential tourists to experience what is offered by the promoted identity, whether this image is an accurate reflection of the destination or not.

The image created is not infinitely elastic. It cannot extend beyond the bounds of physical and cultural reality. PEI, Canada's smallest province, is a low-lying island in the Gulf of St Lawrence. The original Mi'Kmaq name for it, *Epekwitk* ("cradled on the waves"), provides a hint of those boundaries. Mountain vistas, for example, will not be part of the image.

Further, PEI is essentially a rural place. Its largest municipality, Charlottetown, is a very small city (32,174 residents in 2006), and the rural population still outnumbers urban dwellers by sixteen thousand people (Government of PEI 2008). Consequently, the image of a leisurely summer day with the family, a visit with Anne of Green Gables, building sand castles on Cavendish Beach, and golfing on lavish green courses all conjure up images of a laid back life on PEI – the ultimate family vacation (Selby and Morgan 1996, 287).

For years, PEI has relied on a mix of organic and inorganic images to lure regional, national, and international tourists to the Island. "Organic images" are ordinarily beyond the control of those creating tourism policy, spread by word of mouth, usually by the media (radio and television shows, e.g., *Road to Avonlea*), and through the national and international press. In contrast, "inorganic images" are controlled, deliberate creations, produced and promoted by image-building policy-makers, and used in tourism media, such as posters (with a professionally produced photo of a family visiting "Green Gables"), commercials, pamphlets, and websites. Inorganic images create a "destination image," or "an attitudinal concept consisting of the sum of beliefs, ideas, and impressions that a tourist holds of a certain destination." While the organic images may be unfiltered (not produced purposefully with tourists in mind), the process of image-building allows for localities to attempt to increase the popularity of their region as a tourist destination by reinforcing organic and inorganic images (Leisen 2001).

Recent exit surveys reveal that "the most in-demand activities specific to Prince Edward Island" include "beaches and beach activities, Anne of Green Gables and the L.M. Montgomery homesteads ... a diverse history and culture, an abundance of seafood ... other popular activities included championship or world class golf, PEI's Acadian culture, community-based festivals, and special events" (Prince Edward Island Tourism Advisory Council 2005, 10).

The strength and widespread appeal of the province's images has been remarkable, especially considering that the Island's population was 138,161 in 2007 (Statistics Canada 2012). Rural communities with limited resources are unlikely to sustain a successful tourist campaign (Cai 2002). However, in spite of the years of success, the province and many of its municipalities have had to adjust to occasional downturns in the tourism industry (for example, a 3.2 per cent decrease in tourists in 2003 resulting in a loss of approximately $3 million).

In response to the downturn in 2003, the Department of Tourism established the Tourism Advisory Council (TAC), a ministerial committee set up to advise the Minister of Tourism on research, product development, and marketing. Two overarching policies were developed: "The first was a recognition that a renewed industry-government partnership needed to be created. The second was that the focus of this partnership needed to be expanded from a purely marketing focus to an integrated research-product-marketing platform" (Prince Edward Island Tourism Advisory Council 2005, 1). This produced a shift in images from the family-oriented Anne of Green Gables-type approach, to boomer-attractive "lifestyle-led" campaigns of calm, stress-free vacations away from obligations. Recent campaigns include promotions to entice tourists to "The Gentle Island," targeting tourists with an appetite for "cultural consumption" of historical and cultural sites, such as the Island's lighthouses (Tyler, Guerrier, and Robertson 1998).

These may, or may not, have the success of older "images." In 2006, the Canadian Broadcasting Corporation (CBC) reported that the decline had subsided, but it was short-lived (CBC News 2006). There were declines in Confederation Bridge and ferry traffic in 2006 (Ryder 2007), and 2007 and 2008 showed a decline in nights of stay (CBC News 2008).

Nevertheless, on an island that has a population more like a mid-sized Canadian municipality, the success of the Island's image-building policy agenda in the past, and the moderate success of the current program, are rather curious, for while PEI tourism rides the social and economic change brought by the downturn, the province remains a popular destination. As one of our key informants stated, the success of the image-building program in PEI is somewhat of an enigma, especially given that "the three levels of government do not always work together on image-building" (Interview 10). PEI's dominant characteristic in policy-making and government generally is its smallness. This facilitates intergovernmental relations. At times, municipalities have direct access to federal authorities. Overall, however, the provincial government dominates in the image-building field because it is so important for the whole provincial economy.

In addition, the governments – mostly municipal and provincial – must work alongside, and sometimes work around, the Island's social forces groups (e.g., business and social organizations) to develop successful image-building policies. Thus, our investigation includes an examination of how the Island's social forces may also have an impact. In general, individuals and groups representing non-business interests tend to be ignored when images are being constructed. However, business is not homogeneous in what images and strategies it seeks or supports. Moreover, the provincial policy is such that it favours certain geographic regions. In the geographic regions that are not favoured, business and other interests are relatively disadvantaged.

The investigation here provides for a particularly interesting case study regarding the process of image-building because it extends from images that promote sports, such as golf and cycling, through to highlighting distinct lifestyles, such as those exhibited by the Acadian culture. In our case, we focus on the structural impacts of government on tourism policies within four municipalities of PEI, together with an examination of provincial image-building.

MUNICIPALITIES IN PEI

Island municipalities were created according to the population base available to support infrastructure. In the case of most named places in PEI, the infrastructure was schools (Bulger and Sentance 2009). Historically, PEI was divided into townships of approximately twenty thousand acres each. These were awarded to creditors of the Crown by way of a lottery in 1767, hence the informal designation "lots." Originally unpopulated – at least by Europeans – villages began to appear throughout the Island in the later decades of the eighteenth century.

Today, the various Island communities cover some 72 per cent of its land area. Land use is governed by federal, provincial, and municipal governments, each of which has its own level of authority and recognizable abilities to govern tourism. As a result, incorporated municipalities have relative jurisdiction to build an image that is reflective of their own areas of the province. However, this must be seen against a very real background. First, most identifiable communities in PEI, whether incorporated or not, lack the population size to provide a tax base for independent image-building. (The effect of this on incorporated municipalities will be shown in our examination of two of the four selected communities.) Second, the provincial government in PEI is said to act much like a municipal government in other provinces. The smallness of the place means that the province has close connections with the local level, and also that it dominates in policies about images. This is reinforced by a final characteristic: many Island communities are not incorporated and, in these areas of the province, the responsibility for policy, including image-building, must fall to the province.

The Four Municipalities

The municipalities chosen to be case studies for this research are the Resort Municipality (also known as the Cavendish area) and St Peter's Bay, which are both on the north shore; Charlottetown, which is in central PEI on the south shore; and Wellington, which lies in the more central and western portion of the Island. The four were chosen because they are either representative of many of the other municipalities on the Island or they are unique. Two of the four, Charlottetown and the Resort Municipality, have well-established images, which are the strongest on the Island, whereas the other two jurisdictions have recent, less well-established, but substantial images to portray. They are typical of many of the Island's municipalities, struggling to create a branding image for themselves. Further, Wellington and St Peter's Bay lie outside the so-called "Golden Triangle," the heavily visited area defined by Charlottetown, the Resort Municipality, and the city of Summerside as its apexes. All four will be introduced in greater detail in the discussion of their image-building policies below.

Our approach in this chapter will be to examine first image-building policies, both provincially and at the municipal level. We will then discuss the implementation of these policies in light of the interaction of the three levels of government. Finally, we will look at the input and influence of social forces in both the creation and the implementation of tourism image-building.

IMAGE-BUILDING POLICIES

The Policy-making Context

To understand the context within which we study image-building policy, several important points are worth noting. First, as mentioned, PEI has two types of municipal jurisdictions: those that are and those that are not incorporated. In those areas that are not incorporated, the responsibility for policy of any type falls to the province, but, as will be observed in the cases of Wellington and St Peter's Bay, most incorporated municipalities have tiny populations, and an equally tiny tax base. Only nine out of forty-four incorporated municipalities exceeded one thousand persons, and only three of those nine approached or exceeded five thousand in population (Government of PEI 2008). Consequently, for most municipalities, any independent image-building lies beyond their financial means, and they must take advantage of the "coattails" of the province and other municipalities.

On a second, related point, while PEI's tourism policy-making lies principally with the province and some municipalities, it is also subjected to the influence of the federal government and of the Island's social forces, leaving policy-making affected by a complex mix of relations. The evidence reveals the significant effect of these intricate interactions on the policy development process and its outcomes across Cavendish, Charlottetown, St Peter's Bay, and Wellington.

Third, a common difficulty with studying policies is that some policies cannot be characterized as formal; instead, they are more akin to guidelines for programs. Thus, although guidelines tend to lead to some type of formal structure and programs to be followed, they are created through an informal process of verbal agreements among parties who are familiar with one another, producing understandings and practices that are considered by all of the players involved to be as *legitimate* as formalized policy. Still, policy-making in PEI also stems from a formalized process, for example, through a series of meetings among designated representatives and politicians. Thus, Islanders recognize the existence of both formal and informal policies concerning the image-building agenda. For this reason, we consider informal policies, which can be generated in a variety of possible locations and atmospheres (from golf courses to grocery stores to dining rooms), alongside the Island's more conventional, formal policies that may come to fruition in the Island's government boardrooms. These informal policies and understandings, and their diffusion, are facilitated by the close interconnectedness of Island society.

Fourth, any policy discussion about PEI, especially related to image-building, needs to acknowledge that the tourism industry must deal with seasonal differences in population, i.e., a larger summer and smaller winter population, which are reflected in two distinct tourism products and sales pitches. Many of the image-building policies, except for those supporting only mid-winter events (e.g., the Jack Frost Winter Festival), aim to meet the needs of both populations.

Fifth, there are many different types of image-building policies in the municipalities. Together, they can be likened to a "municipal chowder." Whereas a larger province would have several of its jurisdiction-specific images spread out across the province's various jurisdictions, capitalizing on each area's offerings, PEI has all of its images concentrated into a very small area, creating a microcosmic bouquet of images.

The Province

While it may be suggested that the province does not have an image-building policy, this is not entirely correct. On the contrary, it has a relatively simple policy goal: to continue to attract tourist dollars. Its implementation of that policy may produce differing "campaigns," but the policy objective remains constant. Thus, while at one time slogans emphasized agriculture ("Garden of the Gulf," "Million-Acre Farm"), more recent campaigns, like "Come Play on Our Island," have touted recreation and, in particular, the "sun and sand" of the large number of Island beaches.

As observed earlier, in spite of its years of successful images, the province and many of its municipalities have had to adjust to the recent downturns in the tourism industry. The increasing strength of the Canadian dollar, rising gas prices, the changing population structure (aging boomers seeking attractions for couples rather than family-oriented vacations), and the loss of "islandness" with construction of the fixed link – the Confederation Bridge – have all slowed tourism. As a result, PEI chose to change some of the images it wanted to portray and the tourists whom it wanted to target. Where previous campaigns targeted families, current ones target boomer couples, using "lifestyle-led" images of calm, stress-free vacations, away from family and work obligations (Walmsley 2003, 34, 61).

Current policies have created a campaign to entice tourists to fly to "The Gentle Island" via "flypei.calm" (The Sharp Group 2009). The campaigns portray images of balmy breezes and open, unpopulated sandy beaches, suggesting the possibility of rest and relaxation away from cell phones, email, and the "rat race." In addition, recent tourism policy seeks to promote the Island's historical and ecological sites, and its image as the "Green Province," through environmentally friendly programs of recycling and wind energy. Along well-laid-out coastal drives, tourists with an appetite for history and "cultural consumption" can learn about historical and cultural sites, such as the Island's lighthouses (Tyler, Guerrier, and Robertson 1998). Overall, the recent image changes remain in their infancy, with their full potential yet to be seen against the years of success of images like Anne of Green Gables.

There have been shifts in economic focus as well. Over the tenure of the Progressive Conservative government led by Pat Binns (1996–2007), there was policy to allocate a disproportionate amount of money to the building of golf courses, which many felt were not necessary. To convince the electorate that the $10 million spent to subsidize the new golf courses was beneficial for the Island, the Progressive Conservatives claimed that the golf courses would bring a higher economic stratum of tourist dollars and boost the economy. Government money was spent on building the new courses, which were additions to the several already existing. The Liberals, as the subsequent government, changed the focus back to families and boomers.

Even taking into consideration changes in provincial focus, with several levels of government having a part in image-building, policies that pertain to the municipalities are not necessarily formulated by the province with the municipalities in mind. Consequently, the intentions of the strategic policies to support tourism in various municipalities can easily be derailed by the tenuous relations between the province and those municipalities. The aim of one such provincial policy, for example, was to create a tourist map of the coastal drives and major distinguishable areas of PEI, so as to promote the whole Island, including its municipalities, by offering tourists a wider choice of attractions than Anne of Green Gables and Cavendish Beach. The policy was set in place to help distribute economic benefits across many of the Island's municipalities, including St Peter's Bay and Wellington. However, the municipalities were never consulted, never asked about what to promote in their own areas, or which of them required more attention to equalize the benefits of such a map. The unintended outcomes of the map were an imbalance in economic benefits across municipalities. The municipality of Cavendish, which houses Anne of Green Gables' home and other Anne-related businesses, continues to be the major benefactor of this strategic tool.

According to some respondents, another reason the map may have failed was because the strategic initiatives to provide tourism funding to the different municipalities were not enough. It seems there is little emphasis on the promotion of the municipalities apart from the creation of the map. Thus, when people come to the Island, they still tend to seek to explore the major attractions within the Golden Triangle. In essence, the uneven distribution of benefits suggests that the map policy, intended to promote all parts of the Island, was a workable solution for the province but not for the municipalities, which require more provincial support.

The province will act to protect the economy of the Island by introducing new images to entice a different group of tourists, if necessary. For example, the province acknowledged that the intended policy outcomes, such as high tourism rates associated with the summer-related "Come Play on Our Island" campaign, were not being met. Such policies and programs were replaced with the more recent "flypei.calm" and "The Gentle Island" advertisements on television and in the newspapers. The changes occurred for several reasons, including the recent shift in tourism demographics and the state of depressed tourism in Atlantic Canada, but they did not include provincial support to sustain attractions in various municipalities. If the province had better supported a diversity of municipalities, Wellington and St Peter's Bay included, in addition to those with major attractions, such as Cavendish and Charlottetown, the former may have attracted tourists seeking alternate vacations, such as a cultural experience in the Acadian region, or a quaint and peaceful stay in St Peter's Bay.

THE MUNICIPALITIES

Charlottetown

The city of Charlottetown was incorporated in 1995 after an amalgamation of surrounding communities. Strategically located on a large, natural harbour near the confluence of three rivers along the south shore of the Island, Charlottetown has served as PEI's capital since 1769. While the city is home to just under a quarter of the province's population, the "market" population (labour and commercial) of Charlottetown and its suburbs is closer to fifty thousand. Because the Fathers of Confederation first met to discuss the uniting of the British North American provinces in the provincial legislature building, Charlottetown is perhaps best known as the "Birthplace of Confederation."

The city is unique among the case studies because of its large size. Unlike some of the Island's smaller municipalities, the Charlottetown municipal government is composed of a paid city council and a permanent staff of bureaucrats. Charlottetown serves as the main hub of shopping for the Island, and it has the Island's largest hospital and its only university and college. The majority of the provincial and federal government offices are in Charlottetown, as are factories and industrial plants. Charlottetown is the major economic centre on the Island, and part of that economy is the $80 million in annual tourism revenue, derived from 450,000 tourists per year (Prince Edward Island Tourism 2003; Marketquest Research Group Inc. 2004).

As will be noted below, it is difficult to clearly distinguish jurisdictions in PEI. The degree of interaction is extremely high. Thus, in detailing policy, municipal images may be co-opted by the province or other municipalities. One informant stated that Charlottetown's policy to continue to "promote ... itself as the birthplace of Confederation, a history of early Canada, and the [modern day] Festival of the Arts" is significant. The city's commitment to this policy is evidenced by (1) its creation of Founder's Hall on the Charlottetown waterfront, which houses an elaborate electronic show to instruct tourists about Charlottetown as the birthplace of Confederation; and (2) its continued support of the Confederation Centre of the Arts. The decisions to continue to support both establishments have proved to be almost as fruitful as those which have kept Cavendish's images strong in the media. According to this informant, both the municipalities and the province still benefit from these, PEI's strongest images. But not all informants viewed this policy as beneficial.

One key official viewed the province's promotion of images of the birthplace of Confederation in this way: "The province [freely] uses the municipalities in their advertising, for example, Charlottetown's 150 years [celebration] and the birthplace of Confederation" (Interview 7). This informant went on to discuss how the images are used to help promote the province's – not Charlottetown's – historical significance in Canada's inception. Provincial license plates promote PEI, not Charlottetown, as the birthplace of Confederation, but the province did not consult the municipality to find out whether it could use the license plate images (two examples of images are the Confederation Bridge, as a gateway to PEI, and a map of PEI), and the success of this portable message off-Island is mainly significant for the province.

But, as the policies of each government affect the others, it is crucial that all levels of government recognize the responsibilities of every other level and the roles that each plays in image-building policy. Policies related to constructing and supporting the Confederation Centre of the Arts are an example of this process.

The Confederation Centre is Charlottetown's largest and most physically prominent image feature. It took seven years to build. Pre-dating the inauguration of the Canadian flag in 1965, the federal government funded the construction of the Confederation Centre, building on the idea of Charlottetown as the birthplace of Confederation. At the time, the province did not think the Centre would be profitable, nor did it foresee the Centre's value as an icon of Canadian history. The concerns revolved around how a person in Vancouver could relate to a centre on the other side of the country. So, the province did not decide to be its sole supporter. Instead, PEI intended to have the Centre funded by all of Canada's provinces. The argument was that it was built to commemorate Confederation, and PEI should not be solely responsible for its upkeep. Today, it remains an interesting example of interprovincial co-operation, with Ontario recently pledging approximately $200,000 per year.

In more recent decades, the province and the city of Charlottetown have realized how valuable the Centre is to both the municipality and the province. Now, the provincial policy guideline is to work together to sustain the Centre. This example illustrates a somewhat uneasy relationship between the municipal and provincial governments, and between the provincial and federal governments. But the province eventually looked past its initial dismissal of the Centre's potential and acknowledged the need to work co-operatively to support it. The province realized it was a classic case of common interest, with a need to work together for the greater good. This change in perspective was one of several the provincial government would realize was beneficial.

The Resort Municipality

The Resort Municipality, amalgamating Stanley Bridge, Hope River, Bayview, Cavendish, and North Rustico was officially incorporated in 1990. The economy is based mainly on tourism and the fishing industry. The municipality occupies a narrow strip of approximately thirty-eight square kilometers (about half of which is in the PEI National Park) along the scenic North Shore in the heart of the Anne's Land tourist region. As of the 2006 Census, there were only 272 permanent year-round residents (Government of PEI 2008). The municipality's population greatly increases during the summer months to an estimated ten thousand. Further, the area has been known to host 437,000 visitors in one year (Prince Edward Island Tourism 2003), and tourism expenditures in this region total about $100 million (e.g., $90 million in 2003 and $93.7 million in 2004) (Marketquest Research Group Inc 2004; Prince Edward Island Tourism 2003).

As a result, issues surrounding the substantial local tourist industry typically dominate municipal politics, and the municipal council is unique in being permitted to allocate some seats to non-resident property owners (Bulger and Sentance 2009). Further, there is a great deal of overlap between the interests of government and those of local business, as numerous municipal councillors are also tourist operators. The Resort Municipality provides a case study of a municipality where tourism and image-building are pre-eminent concerns. It is also interesting because the distinction between public and private forces in municipal governance is often blurred (Interview 1).

Wellington

The municipality of Wellington was incorporated in 1959 and is located in Eastern Prince County near the southern shore. As of the 2006 Census, it had a population of 401 (Government of PEI 2008). Originally known as Quagmire, the community had an early experience with image-building policy when locals renamed it after the hero of Waterloo. During the mid-to-late nineteenth century, substantial Acadian immigration to the region supplanted much of the British population. Today, the community is culturally located in the Evangeline region and is considered to be a centre of Acadian culture.

Image-building policy in Wellington has two main objectives. The first is to strengthen and develop the community's Acadian cultural identity; the second is to lure tourists away from the traditional Charlottetown/Cavendish/Summerside triangle. The region has enjoyed some success, with a recorded $1.5 million in tourism revenues, and with 83 per cent of the tourists classified as return visitors (Prince Edward Island Tourism 2003).

Cultural identity uniquely presents an opportunity for the municipality to produce images unavailable to the rest of the province. Unlike the major image-building programs that sustain Charlottetown and Cavendish, Wellington has adopted a policy to "boast [its] Acadian cultural product." One of the more recent image strategies of the Acadian community is to respond to the "cultural imperative"; that is, the desire of tourists to consume culture (Tyler, Guerrier, and Robertson 1998). The goal is to use the "cultural economy" to expand the output of, and to gain recognition for, the Acadian community on an Island that has long been associated with the brands of sandy beaches and Anne (Allen 2004, 39, 461; Finucan 2002).

The municipality of Wellington and others with a relatively high population of Acadians came together to lobby the provincial government to change the policy about how their Evangeline area was promoted, and how, in particular, it would be represented on the recently designed tourist map of the Island discussed earlier. The Acadian community wanted the Acadian flag added to the map. The provincial government, however, left the flag off the map, meaning that the Evangeline area, as such, was not represented.

A more basic issue about which Evangeline communities banded together was sustaining the Acadian language and culture, for example, by seeking to ensure the development of "pure," rather than immersion-based, French schools. According to Finucan (2002), security with tourist images does not necessarily exclude change if the new images are consistent with those already established. The portrayal of the Acadian culture and lifestyle through maps and language entrenchment fits with the images of tightly cohesive families and social networks, an integral part of the images of the rural way of life in PEI.

St Peter's Bay

The municipality of St Peter's Bay was incorporated in 1953. Located adjacent to the north shore where the St Peter's River meets the Bay, the municipality had a population of 248 as of the 2006 Census (Government of PEI 2008). The municipality is actually made up of several communities. In the past, fishing, particularly at Red Head and Naufrage, represented $7 million in annual revenue (Federation of PEI Municipalities – Human Resources Canada 1998), but declines in the fishing industry prompted a change of focus.

In more recent years, the community has embarked upon a strategy to capitalize upon the strength of the region's natural beauty to attract tourists who might otherwise not venture outside of the Golden Triangle. The council capitalized on a spillover from the Golden Triangle to adopt a policy to build its own image of a rural lifestyle. The municipality has quaint gift stores, restaurants (famous for Island fish and chips), St Peter's Landing (a strip mall of shops and boutiques), and the annual St Peter's Bay Blueberry Festival, which attracts international tourists. While much of its economy is drawn from these local small businesses, St Peter's Bay also boasts one of the few four-star inns on the Island, the Inn at St Peter's Bay, testimony to the municipality's expanding nature as a tourist destination in its own right.

Also, "St Peter's Bay claims Greenwich National Park and eco-tourism, also used in the image of PEI" (Interview 11), and created "the St Peter's Area Development Corporation to devise long-term economic plans in the hopes that the inclusion of Greenwich into the park area would result in economic spin-offs" (Federation of PEI Municipalities – Human Resources Development Canada 1998).

The municipality of St Peter's Bay attempted to gain funding from the province to support a cycling trail through the town of St Peter's Bay, situated within the municipality. According to a key informant, St Peter's Bay joined with Cycling PEI to expand its policy initiatives to include bicycle and hiking trails leading to the St Peter's Bay area. The policy initiative came about because those who wanted to promote cycling across PEI approached the municipality of St Peter's Bay to ask if it would participate in identifying cycling-friendly businesses and promoting cycling trails, such as in the park. The informant noted that there seemed to be a high level of municipal government-business co-operation on this project. But while the initiative involved a partnership involving the municipality, businesses, and Cycling PEI, and while it has been "verbally" supported by the Department of Tourism, it has been difficult to obtain funding from the province. In spite of the government's adoption of the overriding policy meant to promote and sustain "government-industry partnerships" (Prince Edward Island Tourism Advisory Council 2005, 1), of which this is a classic case, neither Cycling PEI, nor the businesses in the St Peter's Bay region have been able to have much influence on shaping cycling policy to allow provincial dollars to flow to promote cycling (Interview 33). What must be considered, however, is that cycling does not bring in as much tourist revenue as other activities, such as Anne-associated events or golf. On the list of things the province intended to promote, presented in TAC's 2005–10 strategy for tourism competitiveness, cycling and other outdoor activities were at the bottom (Prince Edward Island Tourism Advisory Council 2005, 10).

What is important to note here is that neither Wellington nor St Peter's Bay could survive solely on their own images. The benefits of the policy decisions made by the other two municipalities in the Golden Triangle spill over to these two smaller places. Of course, the provincial government's efforts to promote the Island's stronger images dominate and favour some regions, but benefits do flow to the peripheral places like Wellington and St Peter's Bay.

THE ROLE OF PEI'S INTERGOVERNMENTAL RELATIONS IN DETERMINING IMAGE-BUILDING POLICIES

The policy examples above show that it is the hierarchical divisions of power that typically determine who has jurisdiction over policy decisions (Thomas and Thomas 2005; Walmsley 2003). Image-building policy in PEI, as with all policy development, is affected by the Island's intergovernmental relations and social forces. Thus, a discussion of PEI's intergovernmental relations will help bring into sharper focus the political and social milieu within which policies are developed, and will provide insights about how policy development in this arena can be influenced.

According to Buker (2005, 111), PEI's political structure is greatly influenced by a diversity of socio-political pressures whose sources stem from the Island's small size (geographically and demographically), an emphasis on federal government funding, and a conservative political culture (Buker 2005, 111). Our own findings are relatively consistent with Buker's view of Island politics, revealing a complex set of intergovernmental relations and influences from social forces. This section will discuss intergovernmental relations in PEI. A discussion of the Island's social forces follows.

Overall, intergovernmental relations in PEI reflect both conventional political relations, where the government with the higher authority has the decision-making power, and a characteristically informal nature, related to the size of the Island. The findings about policy, and the data from key informants, reveal that one type of relationship is defined by dealings between the municipalities and the federal government, showing that the municipalities prefer to deal with it rather than the province; another is among the three levels of government, where the province is regulator; a third is between the municipalities and the province; and, finally, there are those relationships that solely involve the municipalities. The latter two types of relationship can be greatly influenced by the small size of the Island, including the creation of tension over jurisdictional issues, but also the need to work together as a matter of survival.

Conventional Intergovernmental Relations

One aspect of the interactions among the three levels of government in PEI is the existence of rather conventional, well-established, official relationships (Buker 2005). However, our examples of policy indicate that the relations among the three levels of government on the Island are not always harmonious. Walmsley (2003, 63) claims that tensions between different levels of government can have a negative effect on the "coherent development of policy in relation to tourism." One high-ranking informant shed light on the basis for these tensions. Although municipalities would like to project distinctive images and attract tourists, "the role of the municipalities in PEI for tourism is not that great" (Interview 7). Image-building policy is often set by the province, even though the province does not have a developed policy framework for the municipalities *per se*, and it leaves much of the image-building up to the individual municipalities. Another informant elaborated, noting that "in spite of the fact that the province tends to leave image-building to the municipalities, for all intents and purposes, it has the power to implement whichever policies it so chooses. In addition, the municipalities have to live with its decision" (Interview 13).

The province does not have to consult municipalities on any policy it wants to implement, and is under no obligation to reveal which policy it might presume to be a priority. Such relations breed an air of dependency and suspicion; in some cases, the municipalities have little choice but to abide by the province's agenda, without consultation.

The preference of the municipalities is to deal directly with the federal government, and to receive transfer payments designated for tourism policy. In some cases, the municipalities can apply directly to the Atlantic Canada Opportunities Agency (ACOA) for federal funds. Within the municipalities, the belief is that *if* the municipalities were to receive their monies for federally funded municipal programs from Ottawa, the municipalities could act in a more autonomous fashion from the province. Thus, although ACOA is typically viewed as an administrative body that can be a critical locus of intergovernmental relations, Islanders use their access to ACOA to circumvent the need to interact with the province. The belief is that, wherever possible, the less influence from the province, the better. The key informants echoed these views: "We operate at arm's length from the province and the federal government, and we do not know what they are up to" (Interview 15).

In other cases, where the province is designated to act as regulator, there can be little room for municipal autonomy. Typically, transfer payments from the federal government are allotted on the premise that the intended recipients deal with the province as regulator, so that provincial jurisdiction over the municipalities is respected (McMillan 2006, 59). Municipalities are, therefore, subject to the province's preferences and needs, which, again, can leave the province to determine what is best for its municipalities. In the case of PEI, the provincial government's ultimate authority and power to act to determine what it believes is best for tourism and image-building among its municipalities can be stifling for them.

Further, more than in any other province in Canada, all of the municipalities of PEI are located geographically close to the province's epicentre. It is characteristic on small islands to have extensive knowledge about others' activities, meaning that the independence of the municipalities to develop policies and programs can be compromised. With such a confined space within which the province and the municipalities must coexist, the province can very easily become aware of image-building projects that may be counter to the province's goals and objectives. The province can then easily influence municipal policies, a rather daunting situation. The Island's small size reduces both the potential for a policy vacuum and the room for independent manoeuvre. Buker

(2005, 113) claims that "an attendant thinness of insulating layers of organizational structure between the citizenry and their ministers allows the [government's] attention to be directed to a range of political concerns, from the petty to the important, from the small to the great," so the province is capable of finely directing transfers.

Given the downward flow of funding, and the ultimate provincial responsibility for tourism, the municipalities may have to make compromises to ensure fiscal sustainability. For example, the province passed policy requiring the municipalities to place tourist-related information about their areas on provincial signs in order to receive their allotment of federal funding. The municipalities complied. Had the municipalities been dealing directly with the federal government, they might rather have created their own ways to manage their promotion.

Intergovernmental Relations on a Small Island

Other findings about intergovernmental relations and their impact on PEI municipal policies are less typical of other jurisdictions because some processes involved in making policy are related to the small size of the Island (Buker, 2005). Positive relations on a small island are governed by social capital and social bonding within and across social groups, including the different levels of government (Baker 1992; Benedict 1967; Richards 1982). To paraphrase one official, "personal relations within social networks provide an additional layer of complexity that can influence policy-making on small islands" (Interview 31). Intra- and intergovernmental relations represent social capital because established contacts and familiarity among players allow them to act in concert with each other (Baldacchino 2005; Groome-Wynne 2007). Without this type of social capital, a reliance on certain levels of government for support and help in accomplishing objectives can be quite difficult. With respect to the relations between municipalities and the province, it is precisely when a municipality needs the province that a strong social network, with well-established familiar relations, is critical to successful policies and their outcomes. Thus, in spite of the desire for the municipalities to remain autonomous, one official stated, "we have a good relationship with our local MP ... our MLAS are good" (Interview 15). Another noted the necessity of maintaining good relationships on such a small island (Interview 16). In the case of municipalities in PEI, having well-established relationships among representatives of different levels of government can mean the difference between achieving or not achieving a municipality's goals, which conceivably is the Island's way to manage its lack of an official provincial policy on image-building.

Perhaps one of the most defining dimensions of complexity of intergovernmental relations in PEI is the idea that no matter which working relationships the levels of government may prefer, each is generally guided by the adage, "we are in this together." Recognizing this sentiment, a high-ranking official noted that "there is a high level of co-operation [in PEI]. It would improve the already strong image-building] industry to go one step further, to have a strong single spokesperson" or organization (Interview 16). Moreover, although it seems that the municipalities turn to the federal government mainly when they need resources, the province remains a critical and integral member of intergovernmental relations with the municipalities. Moreover, relations among individuals across these institutions are generally viewed as positive.

Those who represent the levels of government in PEI are very aware that they are all members of a "have not" province. However, they are also cognizant of the fact that, in spite of its size and limited resources, the province and all of the key Island contributors have built an image of PEI that entices people worldwide. The tourism industry is a successful one, in which all governments have a large stake – the province most of all.

What is interesting from the above patterns of relations is the following: in a place where networking is so important, it is rather curious that relations among all three levels of government are not that important for image-building *per se*. The exception can be the way in which the social forces groups (elaborated on below) interested in tourism may work in tandem with any and all three levels of government. However, as one informant noted, "the three levels of government seem to be more involved in the funding part than in the policy itself" (Interview 12), which, as noted, indicates a set of power relations based on who brings resources to the table. It also indicates the predominant role in municipal image-building played by social forces.

HORIZONTAL MUNICIPAL INFLUENCES

In PEI, municipal policies can have a significant impact on other municipalities that are geographically proximate. In PEI, proximity can be about an hour's drive, as in the case of the distance to Wellington from the Resort Municipality. In a much larger province, policies implemented in a northern municipality, for example, will not likely have much of an effect on policies in the southern part of the province. In PEI, however, policy outcomes manifest in the Resort Municipality can easily impact most parts of the Island. Whatever affects one area can easily spill across municipal boundaries. This is the case when the provincial government promotes images that are associated with particular regions or places; inevitably there are repercussions, often positive but sometimes negative, on other municipalities.

There is no doubt that the municipalities of St Peter's Bay and Wellington profit from spillovers brought to them by tourists drawn initially to visit Anne's Land and Cavendish's sandy beaches. But, in the view of these municipalities, further benefits could accrue from building up their distinctive attractions and images. When provincial support was not forthcoming, both Wellington and St Peter's Bay decided to capitalize on their own icons while continuing to attempt to partner with the province. The St Peter's Bay municipal council adopted the policy of building its own image of a rural lifestyle. In the case of Wellington, the council has adopted deliberate guidelines to bolster the flow of visitors who want to take part in the culturally unique Acadian Evangeline region. One informant stated that the profiles of St Peter's Bay and Wellington have benefited from this policy, which is important given that "the provincial Department of Tourism draws people to the province, and it is up to the other jurisdictions to use images, such as the 'Birthplace of Confederation'" to promote their own communities (Interview 24). One benefit of this type of "collaborative" approach is that images associated with "regional [in this case, provincial] tourism organizations can circumvent potential conflict for scarce resources" (March and Wilkinson 2009, 461). Thus, although these places are outside the Golden Triangle area, the focus of the municipal councils on policy that will allow them to capitalize on the attractiveness of the Resort Municipality and Charlottetown is optimal for all involved. According to Urban (2002, 19, 51), such municipalities have inserted themselves within an already successful marketing strategy, and gain a share of the prosperity of areas in close proximity.

THE ROLE OF SOCIAL FORCES IN DETERMINING POLICIES

Just as the patterns of intergovernmental relations can influence policy in PEI, so, too, can the Island's social forces, at least to some extent. The social forces interested in PEI's image-building policies constitute two distinct groups: those concerned with social issues and those interested in tourism. In both cases, the sense of familiarity among Islanders governs their impact on policy development in PEI.

Social forces address local public issues, and often form coalitions with local officials (Interview 31; Interview 32). In all four municipalities under study, politicians are deeply involved in local issues. In Charlottetown especially, a mutually beneficial relationship exists between local officials and those organizations that advocate for social issues. It is a widespread belief that the people who support these organizations also support those socially conscious politicians. In the same way that social networks among the levels of government are beneficial in policy development, so, too, are the networks among the social forces useful for influencing policy and moving issues forward. As one representative commented, "we pick up the phone to deal with issues because we know the people" (Interview 32).

One pertinent observation concerning social forces in PEI is that power relationships are not generally perceived as rigid and exclusive. Although "there may be no one group that is truly influential in image-building policy," the familiarity among people residing in these geographical areas breeds a sense that negotiation is possible (Interview 32). Politicians from small jurisdictions often convey the message that they are accessible and responsive, not just because they are one of the locals, but also because of the typically high ratio of politicians to constituents/voters (Interview 32). The idea of a close connection between the locals and their politicians leaves people with the perception, and perhaps the reality, that they have some influence on the political process and on policy development (Interview 31; Interview 32).

Still, one participant felt that a better public relations campaign concerning policy was needed. In a place where everyone seems to have easy access to politicians, there can be hard feelings when the policy is finally revealed and it is not exactly what was expected (Interview 32). In small towns, politicians walk a tightrope, attempting to abide by their government's agenda and also to please their constituents, who are their neighbours and members of social forces groups.

Finally, groups that focus solely on tourism "are important to image-building in PEI and work very closely with all three levels of government" (Interview 7; Interview 16). Two, in particular, are the Tourism Industry Association of PEI (TIAPEI), a provincial umbrella advocacy group that includes a number of smaller regional associations involved in tourism, and the Tourism Advisory Council (TAC), discussed earlier.

In some respects, TIAPEI and TAC have relationships with government that cut across those that normally exist among the levels of government. Of tremendous benefit is the freedom to work with any level of government, "to approach any level, such as ACOA, for funding," to support a policy or project they might consider beneficial (Interview 29). For example, one of the respondents felt that "the municipalities' assistance program developed by the tourism association" is key (Interview 12). For another, "TAC is an important advancement to municipal image-building," noting that "coordination, in the area of policy-making on image-building, should improve with TAC" (Interview 2). In the same way as the provincial groups have an important relationship with all levels of government, other groups, such as the Cavendish Tourism Association, can "play a huge role in marketing, and the Resort Municipality supports them" (Interview 6). Indeed, the provincial government engages TIAPEI, TAC, and other social groups to assist them in shaping and implementing policy. These powerful and highly interested organizations are not simple policy-*takers*, they are favoured interlocutors. As one respondent involved in tourism at the local level put it, "unless we direct or come up with local policy, we have little contact or say with the province, and may only hear about new policy from TIAPEI ... government will make decisions without notifying the local tourist industry" (Interview 32).

In Prince Edward Island, it seems that change happens only when it is beneficial to a substantial group, or when an individual wages a very public campaign. This is true whether the group is interested in tourism or social issues. "Groups, such as those that focus on attracting and catering to Island tourists, tend to have a strong voice on the Island and are considered to be a driving force for change" (Interview 13). One policy area where such a group had an impact concerned improvements to the port of Charlottetown to bring in cruise ships. The Charlottetown Capital Commission partnered with ACOA to improve the port by spearheading negotiations with the federal government to expand the cruise ship terminal. The resulting policy created expansion on the waterfront, including a Cruise Ship Welcome Centre to help attract passengers to the downtown's quaint shops, boutiques, and outdoor cafés.

Another policy where social forces were influential, and which provided a bridge for the three levels of government to work together, was "the policy to improve to North Cape Drive. Prompted by the local tourism associations, the provincial and federal governments decided to improve this area for tourists. ACOA and the province provided funding, and the local tourist associations directed the project" (Interview 30).

Some social forces are successful in their efforts to influence image-building policy, and to create the infrastructure that supports tourism. Others are not. For example, the St Thomas Aquinas Society, a francophone lobby group, tried unsuccessfully to influence the government to add more signage for tourists in the Evangeline area. The explanation was the lack of resources available to support such a move. Underlying this unsuccessful policy effort may have been negative relations between the Acadian community and the provincial government, but the simple reality may have been that the province was engaged in changing its province-wide signage policy.

Another area where the policy intentions of government and of social forces may not be compatible is the area of sports. In particular, there were proposals to expand facilities for harness racing, which involves gambling. This would be politically risky. As one informant put it delicately: "If the racing park wants to expand support for the sport of harness racing, the government may not view their involvement as politically expedient" (Interview 35). There was no consensus between the government and the racing park. For the most part, "the government tends to go with the safe decisions where business and government interests conflict" (Interview 35). For electoral reasons, governments can act against narrow business interests. On the other hand, the government did permit the simulcast of races outside of the province. This decision involves an expansion of racing, of sorts, but just not on the Island, where the government did not want to be seen as promoting gambling. In such cases, the policy efforts of social forces produce a compromise, with each side gaining some benefit.

THE COHERENCE OF IMAGE-BUILDING POLICY ON THE ISLAND AND IN THE MUNICIPALITIES

This study explores the theory that the structure of intergovernmental relations helps determine the quality of the policy; that is, policy outputs depend on the process through which they were created. The findings presented below will indicate clear support for this theoretical presumption.

Two problems that seem to arise when image-building policy is crafted in Prince Edward Island's complex, and often informal, environment is that there may be many stakeholders who are unhappy with the policy result, or there may be different images created that are competing. As noted, such problems are accentuated by the Island's small size: the resulting tourism images and their conflicts affect everyone, not just those living within the major tourist centres.

The problems that lead to potential conflict between the stakeholders in PEI are two-fold. First, all of the municipalities hope to gain increased tourism as a result of a strong marketing campaign, either directly by being included in the Island's marketing strategy (such as Cavendish's beaches), or indirectly by drawing tourists from the Golden Triangle into their less explored regions by using individualized municipal campaigns. While the smaller, less popular municipalities are forced to try to attract tourists on their own without significant support by the province, these same municipalities need to understand the limitations of image-building as a marketing tool. Although most communities would like to be part of the destination marketing package, not all cultures and communities can be represented; otherwise, the image designed to represent the whole Island could quickly become convoluted and ineffective. Like marketing for other popular products and brands, the messages flowing from the destination to the market's potential travellers must be simple, consistent, and recognizable. Those most represented by the Island's image will benefit, but so, too, will those that are not well-represented, because they have the opportunity to capitalize on the fact that tourists, and their money, are now within only a short drive from any point on the Island. Therefore, while there may be an imbalance with regards to the promotion and benefits of the tourism industry in PEI, it is one of relative gains, not absolutes. Even if not all of the municipalities are equally involved in the marketing strategy, any coherent and effective image that increases tourist numbers and expenditures for one municipality is a potential benefit for another. While the result of a simplified image may be that some municipalities feel like losers, the fact remains that the strong simplified messages, such as Anne of Green Gables and the beaches, are necessary for all to benefit from eventually. This is the message of the provincial government.

But non-central municipalities and others can continue their own attempts to attract visitors through image-building. This has produced the second problem: a complex mix of players forging tourism images – often using informal processes – has created programs whose resulting images of events and themes contradict PEI's long-standing policy promoting more traditional events and pristine images. The result is that tourists and locals attracted to one image may find that other events do not quite fit the image that they have come to experience.

There are a few recent examples of discordant images resulting in conflict and complaints from both those who have visited and those who reside in PEI. The first has to do with the image of PEI as the "green province." This is something that probably appeals to those from urban centres. However, it clashes with the reality of the many, many golf courses that have proliferated – often with provincial government support – on a small island. Further, where the government does have some ability to push the "green" image by working with social forces that are environmentally conscious, it has failed. Local organizations that promote cycling offer PEI the opportunity to use its traditional marketing image of outdoor family activities in a newer and eco-friendly way by promoting the Island, both as a family biking destination and as a professional destination for major biking events, such as the Tour de PEI. But the provincial government, the level of government with the funding and primary power to craft image, has yet to use cycling events as a way to promote tourism (Interview 33).

Nevertheless, the social forces representing the cycling community continue to work with municipal governments to improve biking conditions in PEI, and to emphasize biking as a green form of transport and leisure. They have also supported a private member's bill in the provincial legislature that sought to reduce taxes on the purchase of bikes. Further, other social forces, notably some in the business community, have recognized the potential importance of the sport of cycling for the tourism sector, and have begun working with organizations to create programs to promote it. The result has been an increase in the number of tourism-related businesses that are now considered "cyclist friendly." Given the intrinsic appeal to cyclists of the Island's flat and beautiful countryside, this image will spread, if only by word of mouth should the province not become formally involved.

The second conflict is the result of the increasing popularity of the Island's mega-event, The Festival of Lights. This is a series of rock concerts held in Charlottetown, and organized by Tourism Charlottetown as part of the Canada Day celebrations. Throughout the past few years, the festival has been gaining in popularity and attendance, and it now boasts some of the world's more recognizable rock acts. But, the acceptance of the festival is dependent to some extent on how it fits with the Island's image, and more specifically that of Charlottetown. While many summer tourists come for long walks down quaint streets, the tens of thousands of rock fans who descend upon Charlottetown for the concerts come for loud music, parties, and drinking. The two groups of tourists are forced to share one city at the same time, both expecting different things. In the end, some of the tourists leave less than pleased. One voiced his opinion in a letter to the city's mayor, stating that he "was quite dismayed by the crowd attracted to the Festival of Lights" (http://ward3brighton.ca). Most of that crowd, of course, has little interest in visiting the house of Anne of Green Gables, St Peter's Bay, or the Evangeline region.

Allowing for conflicts, there are instances of positive outcomes from the intersection of image-building policy, intergovernmental relations, and social forces. In 2003, the city of Charlottetown developed a policy to make the city a sports tourism destination. The city approached the province to sign on to this initiative, but the province declined. The city proceeded, however, inviting others – Downtown Charlottetown, Inc., TIAPEI, the Hotel Association, and local interested community groups – to join them. In addition, ACOA was approached for funding. It did help sponsor some successful events, though it did not extend continuous funding.

In 2006, realizing the economic spin-offs of such initiatives, the province finally signed on as a partner, albeit as somewhat of a mediator rather than a key player. Rather than working in tandem with community groups on the project, the province hired a consulting firm to assess the city's readiness. On the other hand, Charlottetown groups have been able to work closely with the Department of Community and Cultural Affairs and Tourism PEI to raise funds to host events. In the end, the policy and the co-operation of the players prompted the creation of a five-year plan to develop Charlottetown into a sports-friendly venue by developing relations with local sports organizers to take stock of what was available, and what needed to be further developed (for example, baseball fields). Thus, despite early tensions between the province and the municipality, the outcome of the whole process was very favorable – the groups were able to secure the 2009 Canada Games for the city – and, of course, for the province.

CONCLUSIONS

PEI is very well known as a tourist destination of natural beauty and cultural interest. On the mainland, one cannot speak of the Island without someone citing a story of a family vacation on PEI. Yet, while the images portrayed in marketing campaigns are often those of a quaint and simple province where visitors can have relaxing vacations, this chapter suggests that the process of image-building and image-building policy in Canada's smallest province is much more complex than one might expect, and also less formalized. There are a number of reasons for this high degree of complexity, most owing to the small size and small population of the province.

First, all the players involved in governance are relatively accessible. It is likely that residents of a particular community know their representatives at all three levels of government, and are not afraid to contact them should they need them. This closeness means that government officials, social forces, and citizens can take part in the policy process, or at least attempt to influence the creation of policy at any time, not just through formal participation mechanisms, such as town hall meetings and the ballot box. While this increased access is good for those who seek to influence policy, it also means that there are many more voices to be heard.

Second, this closeness between politicians (and governments) and those active in social forces means that much of the policy process may be initiated and furthered through informal means rather than traditional, formalized policy mechanisms. People will meet informally for coffee, while shopping for groceries, for a round of golf, or even for dinner. If someone is not personally acquainted with some decision-maker, they may know someone who is and can put them into contact without the formalities of making appointments.

Another source of complexity is the lack of coordination between the various levels of government. Formal intergovernmental mechanisms are absent from the image-building scene. The federal government most often provides funds for image promotion and tourism infrastructure through ACOA, but it does little hands-on work in formulating and implementing policy. The provincial government has the most financial resources and power with respect to image-building, but promotes what it regards as in the best interests of the province as a whole. Formal consultation with municipalities is intermittent at best. The municipalities have few funds for promoting their individual features, but they certainly do try to attract those drawn to the Island by the images promoted by others.

Further, all levels of government may take part in a particular policy, or some may opt to not take part in some initiative, but little of the work is done intergovernmentally. Rather, image-building is pushed by the social forces through their communication with the various governments, but not by politicians and officials in concert with their counterparts at different levels. In fact, social forces often play two important roles. First, they initiate and drive much image-building policy in PEI. Second, they act as a mediator, or a communication bridge, between levels of government that are often locked in conflict. Among these forces are those who lose in image-building because their orientation does not correspond with local and especially provincial priorities. There are also winners and losers on a geographic basis. Overall, at the provincial and municipal levels, business interests, and especially the tourism industry, dominates in policy-making.

The fact that the provincial government's ultimate responsibility is to maximize provincial benefits means that it will probably continue to promote images that are accessible to outside markets, that are popular with tourists, but that do not necessarily reflect the characteristics of all of the municipalities. This means that the Resort Municipality and Charlottetown will continue to be the main inspiration for image-building, while areas such as St Peter's Bay, will have to build an image on their own and market it towards those who have already arrived on the Island. The image promoted by the province cannot reflect the entire Island for the sake of image simplicity. That is not to say that smaller municipalities cannot make economic gains, but that those outside of traditional tourist areas cannot wait for a provincial strategy that will bring tourists to them. They need to do it themselves.

In a place as small in both size and population as PEI, outsiders may view its image-building policy process as confusing, incoherent, and ambiguous. There is often tension between governments and among social forces about the design of images, for much is at stake in the vital tourism industry. Still, the smallness, the closeness, and the informality of policy creation on what is now The Gentle Island has led to remarkable success in attracting tourists.

INTERVIEWS

Interview 1.   Provincial bureaucrat, Charlottetown. Summer 2005.

Interview 2.   Provincial bureaucrat, Charlottetown. Summer 2005.

Interview 3.   Social forces representative, Charlottetown. Summer 2005.

Interview 4.   Social forces representative, Charlottetown. Summer 2005.

Interview 5.   Municipal bureaucrat, Charlottetown. Summer 2005.

Interview 6.   Provincial bureaucrat, Charlottetown. Summer 2005.

Interview 7.   Provincial official, Charlottetown. Summer 2005.

Interview 8.   Provincial official, Charlottetown. Summer 2005.

Interview 9.   Municipal official, Charlottetown. Summer 2005.

Interview 10. Municipal official, Charlottetown. Summer 2005.

Interview 11. Provincial official, Charlottetown. Summer 2005.

Interview 12. Municipal official, Resort Municipality. Summer 2005.

Interview 13. Public official, Resort Municipality. Summer 2005.

Interview 14. Municipal bureaucrat, Charlottetown. Summer 2005.

Interview 15. Municipal official, Charlottetown. Summer 2005.

Interview 16. Federal official, Charlottetown. Summer 2005.

Interview 17. Provincial official, Charlottetown. Summer 2005.

Interview 18. Provincial official, Charlottetown. Summer 2005.

Interview 19. Federal official, Charlottetown. Summer 2005.

Interview 20. Provincial bureaucrat, Charlottetown. Summer 2005.

Interview 21. Provincial bureaucrat, Charlottetown. Summer 2005.

Interview 22. Municipal bureaucrat, Charlottetown. Summer 2005.

Interview 23. Provincial bureaucrat, Charlottetown. Summer 2005.

Interview 24. Social forces representative, Charlottetown. Summer 2005.

Interview 25. Municipal bureaucrat, Resort Municipality. Summer 2005.

Interview 26. Social forces representative, Wellington. Summer 2005.

Interview 27. Social forces representative, Summerside. Summer 2005.

Interview 28. Municipal official, Charlottetown. Summer 2005.

Interview 29. Provincial bureaucrat, Charlottetown. Summer 2005.

Interview 30. Social forces representative, Cap-Egmont, Evangeline
Region. Summer 2005.

Interview 31. Social forces representative, Summerside. Summer 2005.

Interview 32. Social forces representative, Summerside. Summer 2005.

Interview 33. Social forces representative, Charlottetown. Summer 2008.

Interview 34. Social forces representative, Charlottetown. Summer 2008.

Interview 35. Social forces representative, Charlottetown. Summer 2008.

Interview 36. Social forces representative, Summerside. Summer 2008.

REFERENCES

Allen, J. Scott. 2004. "Cultural-Products Industries and Urban Economic
Development Prospects for Growth and Market Contestation in Global
Context." *Urban Affairs Review* 39, no. 4: 461–90.

Atlantic Canada Opportunities Agency (ACOA). 2007a. "Government of
Canada and Partners Invest $1.83 Million to Develop Confederation
Birthplace Initiative." http://www.acoa-apeca.gc.ca/eng/Agency/
mediaroom/NewsReleases/Pages/2252.aspx.

Atlantic Canada Opportunities Agency (ACOA). 2007b. "Infrastructure
Funding Making a Difference in the City of Charlottetown." http://
www.acoa-apeca.gc.ca/eng/Agency/mediaroom/NewsReleases/Pages/
2174.aspx.

Baker, Randall A. 1992. "Scale and Administrative Performance: The
Governance of Small States and Microstates." In *Public Administra-
tion in Small and Island States*, edited by R. Baker. West Hertford CT:
Kumarian Press, 5–25.

Baldacchino, Godfrey. 2005. "The Contribution of Social Capital to Economic Growth: Lessons from Island Jurisdictions." *The Round Table:
Commonwealth Journal of International Affairs* 94, no. 378: 35–50.

Benedict, Burton. 1967. "Sociological Aspects of Smallness." In *Problems
of Smaller Territories*, edited by B. Benedict. London: Athlone Press for
the Institute of Commonwealth Studies, 45–55.

Buker, Peter E. 2005. "The Executive Administrative Style in Prince Edward Island: Managerial and Spoils Politics." In *Executive Styles in Canada: Cabinet Structures and Leadership Practices in Canadian Government*, edited by L. Bernier, K. Brownsley, and M. Howlett. Toronto: University of Toronto Press, 111–31.

Bulger, David. 2012. "Charlottetown: A Small, Quiet Seat of Government – No Boom, No Bust." In *Sites of Governance: Multilevel Governance and Policy Making in Canada's Big Cities*, edited by Martin Horak and Robert Young, 53–72. Montreal and Kingston: McGill-Queen's University Press.

Bulger, David, and James Sentance. 2009. "Prince Edward Island." In *Foundations of Governance. Municipal Government in Canada's Provinces*, edited by Andrew Sancton and Robert Young. Toronto: University of Toronto Press, 314–44.

Cai, L.A. 2002. "Cooperative branding for rural destinations." *Annals of Tourism Research*, 29(3), 720–42.

CBC News. 2006. "Tourism industry wants bigger marketing budget." http://www.cbc.ca/news/canada/prince-edward-island/story/2006/11/17/tourism-2006.html?ref=rss.

CBC News. 2008. "Weather, gas prices, blamed for decline in tourism." http://www.cbc.ca/news/canada/prince-edward-island/story/2008/09/04/tourism-docherty.html.

Federation of PEI Municipalities – Human Resources Canada. 1998. "Municipal Profile – Community of St. Peter's Bay." http://www.gov.pe.ca/profile/stpeters.pdf.

Finucan, Karen. 2002. "What Brand Are You?" *Planning* 68, no. 8: 10–11.

Government of PEI. 2008. *34th Annual Statistical Review*, Charlottetown: Department of the Provincial Treasury.

Groome-Wynne, Barbara. 2007. "Social Capital and Social Economy in Sub-National Island Jurisdictions." *Island Studies Journal* 2, no. 1: 115–32.

Leisen, Birgit. 2001. "Image Segmentation: The Case of a Tourism Destination." *The Journal of Services Marketing* 15, no. 1: 49–66.

March, Roger, and Ian Wilkinson. 2009. "Conceptual Tools for Evaluating Tourism Partnerships." *Tourism Management*, 30, 455–62.

Marketquest Research Group Inc. 2004. "Economic Impact: Tourism 2004. FINAL REPORT." Charlottetown: Marketquest Research Group Inc.

McMillan, Melville L. 2006. "Municipal Relations with the Federal and Provincial Governments: A Fiscal Perspective." In *Canada: The State of the Federation 2004. Municipal-Federal-Provincial Relations in Canada*, edited by Robert Young and Christian Leuprecht. Montreal and Kingston: McGill-Queen's University Press, 45–82.

Prince Edward Island Tourism. 2003. "Economic Impact Tourism 2003." Charlottetown: Prince Edward Island Department of Tourism, Policy, Planning, and Research.

Prince Edward Island Tourism Advisory Council. 2005. "The New Product Culture. The Prince Edward Island Strategy for Tourism Competitiveness. 2005–2010." Charlottetown: PEI Tourism Advisory Council.

Richards, John. 1982. "Politics in Small Independent Communities: Conflict or Consensus? *Journal of Commonwealth and Comparative Politics* 20, no. 2: 151–71.

Ryder, Ron. 2007. "Tourism industry optimistic amid early season traffic drop." *The Guardian*. 14 August. Charlottetown, PEI. http://www.theguardian.pe.ca/Living/Travel/2007-08-14/article-1291735/Tourism-industry-optimistic-amid-early-season-traffic-drop/1.

Selby, Martin, and Nigel J. Morgan. 1996. "Reconstructing Place Image: A Case Study of Its Role in Destination Market Research." *Tourism Management* 17, no. 4: 287–94.

Statistics Canada. 2012. "Table 051-0001 – Estimates of population, by age group and sex for July 1, Canada, provinces and territories, annual (persons)." http://www.statcan.gc.ca/tables-tableaux/sum-som/l01/cst01/demo31a-eng.htm.

The Sharp Group. 2009. "Our Work Portfolio – Projects. Marketing: Strategy, Execution, Evaluation. Charlottetown Airport Authority. Flypei.calm" http://www.sharpgrp.com/home.php?page=work.

Thomas, Rhodri, and Huw Thomas. 2005. "Understanding Tourism Policy-Making in Urban Areas, with Particular Reference to Small Firms." *Tourism Geographies* 7, no. 2: 121–37.

Tyler, Duncan, Yvonne Guerrier, and Martin Robertson (eds.). 1998. *Managing Tourism in Cities: Policy, Process, and Practice*. Chichester: John Wiley & Sons.

Urban, Florian. 2002. "Small Town, Big Website? Cities and Their Representation on the Internet." *Cities* 19, no. 1: 49–59.

Walmsley, D. J. 2003. "Rural Tourism: A Case of Lifestyle-led Opportunities." *Australian Geographer* 34, no. 1: 61–72.

5

Leadership and Image-building Policy in Four Saskatchewan Municipalities[1]

CRISTINE DE CLERCY AND PETER A. FERGUSON

It is impossible to understand Saskatchewan without understanding how the idea of Saskatchewan was created, shaped and sold.

Dale Eisler, *False Expectations: Politics and the Pursuit of the Saskatchewan Myth*, 2006, 1.

Two events – Confederation and the National Policy – fundamentally influenced the development of what became the province of Saskatchewan in 1905. Directly and indirectly, both helped to establish large-scale agricultural settlement as the area's premier economic and societal objective (Stabler and Olfert 2009). In order to populate the province quickly with immigrants from Europe and elsewhere, the federal and provincial governments, along with private entrepreneurs, land grant companies, the railways, religious groups, and ethnic networks worked to market the area's possibilities and resources while downplaying its deficiencies and limitations. These early efforts to attract people began a rich tradition of enthusiastic self-promotion that continues to mark this province's politics and policy.

Strikingly, image-building policy in Saskatchewan is focused overwhelmingly on retaining and attracting permanent residents, and this probably reflects the province's early history and population experience. Shortly after entering Confederation, the population increased precipitously before stabilizing in the range of 800,000 to 900,000 people for the next sixty years (Li 2009, 2). After early rapid growth, the pressures of economic stagnation and depression, crop failure, urbanization, and the decline of agriculture contributed to the "Saskatchewan Diaspora": the province began consistently to export people. This trend continued into the late twentieth and early twenty-first centuries. Between 1986 and 2001, for example, more than one hundred thousand residents left Saskatchewan (Abley 2009, 357).

Given this problem, preserving existing population levels clearly is a key objective in image-building policy, and, as we discuss below, communities devote much time and effort to promoting a positive image explicitly toward retaining their current residents. As well, projecting a positive municipal image to external populaces helps attract potential new residents, as well as tourists. Today's generation has been called the most travelled one in human history, and this fact carries large economic implications: tourism directly employs over twenty-one thousand people and contributes about $1.3 billion annually to the provincial economy (Government of Saskatchewan, news release 2002). The concern to preserve existing population levels is apparent in most formal efforts to promote Saskatchewan communities, and it was a constant factor in our study.

To help focus the analysis, we first approached image-building policy by considering it as the product of a deliberate choice by public authorities. This contrasts with another approach, which considers governmental action, or inaction, to constitute a public policy (Pal 1992, 2). Second, we defined image-building policy as a course of action chosen to foster a favourable perception or understanding of a community toward attracting or retaining human and capital resources. We employed this definition because it spans more classes of policies than those identified by similar but narrower definitions, such as "place-based marketing" or "branding policy"(see, for example, Thode and Masulka 1998; Abimola 2001).[2]

Third, within the broad scope of image-building activities we identified three specific subcategories: events policy, branding policy, and economic development policy. The events policy category encompasses policies supporting ongoing events, such as annual harvest or jazz festivals, as well as special spectacles, such as the Canada Winter Games. The branding policy category includes efforts to identify a place with a specific idea, image, theme, benefit, or resource. For example, in the late 1960s Saskatoon was known as "The POW City" to emphasize its resources; the acronym stands for potash, oil, and wheat. Finally, the economic development policy category includes a variety of initiatives designed specifically to enhance a locale's attractiveness to business. For example, the Vancouver Green Capital initiative was launched as "part of a strategic effort for the city to leverage the once-in-a-lifetime economic development potential of the 2010 [Olympic] Games" through promoting its location and resource conservation culture (City of Vancouver 2009).

Working within the parameters established by our definition of image-building policy and its three subcategories of policy activity, we explored image-building within four local governments: the Waskesiu community, and the cities of Humboldt, Swift Current, and Saskatoon. This study reports our findings, which are organized within three main parts. In part one, we briefly summarize Saskatchewan's physical setting, population dispersion, and main geographic subdivisions. Each of the four communities under study is introduced and described in terms of its history, demographics, and economic profile. As well, the recent image-building efforts of each community are reviewed.

The focus of part two is on who makes image-building policy in each of the four locales under study. In this section, we investigate which public and private actors do (or do not) contribute to making decisions in this policy area. We also consider whether two specific factors – intergovernmental relations and social forces – have a significant influence on image-building policy-making. Finally, based on the precedent material, an evaluation of each community's image-building policy is presented at the end of this section.

Part three summarizes our conclusions about the nature and quality of image-building policy in the communities under study. As discussed in more detail below, in Saskatchewan, successful image-building policy hinges heavily – perhaps too heavily – on the will of local leaders and their political networks.

PART ONE: PHYSICAL SETTING AND GEOGRAPHIC DIVISIONS

Saskatchewan covers 651,900 square kilometers and features a variety of climates and topographies. As Table 1 indicates, it may be roughly divided into five areas: the north, west-central, east-central, southwest, and southeast regions (Government of Saskatchewan, Tourism Saskatchewan 2005, 53). The northern region may be further subdivided into two parts: the far north and the near north. In the far north, which borders the Northwest Territories, there is relatively little settlement, few roads, and most areas are accessible mainly by airplane or wintertime skidoo travel. Beginning at the city

Table 1
Summary of the four communities under study

	Waskesiu	Humboldt	Swift Current	Saskatoon
Location	Near north	Central-east region	Southwest region	Central-west region
Population (2006 census data)	205 (winter) 2,500–8,000 summer)*	4,998	14,946	202,340
Community type	Small resort community	Small rural city	Medium rural city	Largest city in the province
Senior level of authority	Government of Canada	Government of Saskatchewan	Government of Saskatchewan	Government of Saskatchewan
Date of most recent branding exercise	2007	2009	2005	2001

*= estimated population

of Prince Albert and extending northward to the southern shores of Lake Athabasca, the near north is heavily forested, features extensive lake and river systems, and benefits from a well-dispersed system of roadways. Most of its populated areas are accessible by car.

The province's two central regions are marked by prairie topography in the west and a band of boreal forest in the eastern region. The most common image of Saskatchewan – flat wheat fields – reflects much of this area's physical character. Many First Nations reserves are located in these areas, and the town of Batoche is a centre of Métis culture. Several small communities, such as St Isodore de Bellevue, retain their identity developed when they were established as French settlements in the nineteenth century. As well, these regions are dotted with many small communities that arose from large-scale European immigration in the early twentieth century, particularly German and Mennonite areas to the west and Ukrainian settlements in the east region.

The southwest region is "cowboy country." The topography is very hilly and it encompasses the Great Sand Hills, which are giant, active sand dunes (Government of Saskatchewan, Tourism Saskatchewan 2005, 75). Near the town of Eastend, in badland areas, there are several active archeological sites yielding dinosaur skeletons and fossils. In Saskatchewan's southeast quadrant, the Qu'appelle Valley is a key geographic feature. Within it are several well-developed lakes, and the area has rich deposits of oil and coal.

There are fifteen cities in the province; their populations range from five thousand people (e.g. the city of Meadow Lake) to more than two hundred thousand citizens in the cases of Regina and Saskatoon (CBC News 2009). For most of its history, much of the province's political character has been shaped by its population level. As of 2008, it had approximately 996,000 residents, and the population level had not changed for more than twenty years, as out-migration has served to offset any increases owing to the birth rate and immigration (Li 2009, 6–8). As the province's agricultural basis has diminished over the last two decades, many small communities have faced sharp population reductions, or emptied completely (Garcea and Gilchrist 2007, 347). This trend is worrisome. The desire to maintain a provincial population of around one million people, and to retain younger and educated citizens within Saskatchewan's boundaries, have been key policy objectives widely shared by citizens and political leaders (see Li 2009; Eisler 2006; Waiser 2005). Community promotion efforts ought to be understood within the social context created by these two broad objectives.

To study how local governments make decisions about building their image, four communities were chosen as research sites. Ranked from least to most populous, we studied the Waskesiu community located in Prince Albert National Park (PANP), the city of Humboldt, the city of Swift Current, and the city of Saskatoon. Each case represents one region of the province, specifically the near north, east-central, west-central, and southwest regions. As well, these cases were chosen because they are different from each other in several areas, such as their physical location, population, developmental trajectory, economic profile, and the scale of their governments. While these communities are distinct from each other in important ways, they share many characteristics and, so, considered as a group, represent key facets of the province's political and economic profile.

Waskesiu

The first case lies within the boundaries of Prince Albert National Park (PANP), which is located in the near north and is the area's main tourism attraction. The park was created by order-in-council on 24 March 1927, and was opened officially on 10 August 1928 by Prime Minister William Lyon Mackenzie King. It spans nearly one million acres and is administered by the federal government through Parks Canada (Government of Canada, Parks Canada 2006b).

Waskesiu is a summer resort community located within PANP. For many years, the Waskesiu Chamber of Commerce acted as a town council of sorts, representing local interests to the park superintendant. In 1994, and partly owing to large cuts to its budget, Parks Canada initiated an operational review of communities located within the National Park system, including Waskesiu. Parks Canada appeared willing to devolve some of its management authority in return for increased financial participation by the community (Waskesiu Community Council 2009c; 2009a). In 1997, a Memorandum of Understanding described a new quasi-municipal governing body that aimed to devolve some governance responsibilities to the local level. The local council, however, would lack taxation and levying powers normally included within the scope of local government (Waskesiu Community Council 2009b). Shortly thereafter, the first elections to the new Waskesiu Community Council (WCC) were held.

However, the council's limited fiscal authority constrained its ability to address much needed infrastructural issues, and so mobilized interest in incorporating this community as a local government within the jurisdiction of the Saskatchewan government (Waskesiu Community Council 2007a). By changing jurisdictions and expanding its authority, the council would be empowered to levy taxes and aimed to use these to upgrade local services. As well, it was anticipated that changing jurisdictions would increase the town's capacity to promote itself to tourists through bypassing the extant constraints imposed by Parks Canada's policies.

The proposed change from federal to provincial control was controversial and for several years the council explored this option by consulting with residents, park officials, and elected provincial representatives. In 2006, an agreement-in-principle for self-governance was reached between the WCC and the PANP. Parks Canada supported this development and viewed it as an extension of similar self-governance agreements in place in the Banff and Jasper national parks (Government of Canada, Parks Canada 2006a). A local ratification vote on the self-governance proposal passed easily that July.

After extensive negotiations with federal and provincial officials, a bill establishing Waskesiu as a provincially administered municipality was presented to Cabinet.

However, progress on this issue was stalled in 2007, when the Cabinet chose not to present legislation to the legislature for consideration. This was viewed by the WCC as "a complete surprise" and a "major setback" (Waskesiu Community Council 2007a, 7). In 2009, the council withdrew its request for provincial incorporation because of a lack of clarity concerning the province's policy on levying education property taxes. At the time of writing the community remains in a difficult position: the WCC lacks the necessary authority to control key aspects of local administration owing to its location within a national park. Despite the park's clear interest in helping the community secure provincial status as a recognized local government, negotiations with the Government of Saskatchewan have not been fruitful (Waskesiu Community Council 2008; 2009b, 3; Kiunga 2007).

DEMOGRAPHIC AND ECONOMIC PROFILE

Along with the difficult jurisdictional situation described above, this community's governance is additionally challenged by its unusual population basis. Owing to its heavy dependence on tourism, the town's population varies considerably: in the winter, about 250 people live there, while the summer population swells to 2,500 residents or more.[3] In terms of future trends, Statistics Canada data suggest the number of year-round residents is steadily increasing as winter tourism activities expand and new retirement communities open (Government of Canada, Statistics Canada 2009c).

Tourism clearly is the main economic driver in the PANP region. An assortment of lodges, resorts, golf courses, campgrounds, and cottage associations provide a strong service base for tourism focused on the area's lakes and forests. The emphasis on lakes and forests, rather than the wheat fields of the central regions, are apparent in the northern area's imagery.

Within the park, statistics from 2000 to 2006 report the number of annual visitors regularly exceeds 215,000 people, while revenues from park fees normally generate about $2 million each year (Government of Canada, Parks Canada 2005; 2006c). Although located in the less populated northern region, Waskesiu's larger trading area supplies many visitors: within a hundred-kilometer radius of PANP, more than fifty thousand people reside within four cities and several smaller rural municipalities. As well, Saskatoon, Saskatchewan's most populous city, is approximately 320 kilometers away from the PANP.

RECENT IMAGE-BUILDING POLICY INITIATIVES
Concerning current image-building policies and new initiatives, as noted above, the WCC devoted much effort towards changing from a federal to a provincial jurisdiction, in part because its image-building goals have not always reflected Parks Canada's policies or mandate (Waskesiu Community Council, 2007b). Some community members have desired more effort from park officials concerning promoting the town and enhancing its services, goals which park officials historically have not considered the most pressing ones. In recent years, however, park administrators have become more concerned with promotional activities. For example, in 2007, PANP officials initiated a set of "big picture" community discussions aimed at collecting feedback on park stewardship and collaborative initiatives. A marketing report also was commissioned and released, and then a new logo was unveiled (Colour 2007). Such efforts have helped to moderate criticism that PANP administrators have been largely uninterested in helping to promote the community.

At the same time, there are other sources of tension concerning the community's image-building policy. For example, there is a clear and long-standing division between two groups of people about how to market the community. On the one hand are those residents and business people who perceive the community mainly as a lakefront extension of city life. This group tends to favour efforts to control local pests, such as the budworm, and to develop the community in terms of attracting new businesses, enhancing service provisions, and increasing the annual number of visitors. On the other hand, a significant number of people perceive Waskesiu as a unique ecology that merits preservation. Many of these people point to the presence of Grey Owl's cabin at Ajawan Lake as a symbol capturing Waskesiu's authentic image (Waiser 2005, 317). This group tends to oppose additional development and seeks to minimize human intervention in the park's landscape and ecology.

This division is reflected in the content of the community's central website (www.waskesiu.org). For example, in 2006, the WCC's main page displayed the motto, "Environmental stewardship for our community and our park." Alongside images of Grey Owl's cabin and local wildlife were pictures of local businesses that communicated urban luxuries: one picture's caption advised that "lunch or supper at the club is always just right"; another caption told viewers that "a favourite pastime is the great shopping found in Waskesiu." The two different approaches to marketing the community compete with one another and generate a moderate level of tension between their advocates.

Beyond Waskesiu's boundaries, several recent initiatives promise to enhance its efforts to build its image. For example, in 2007, the province of Saskatchewan announced an investment of $16.1 million into the Prince Albert area for transportation projects. This project has been advanced by the Transportation for Economic Advantage Strategy, which will invest $5 billion over ten years in the province. The Prince Albert region was chosen as an investment area specifically for the purpose of increasing tourism from beyond the province, as well as easing the commute for local residents travelling into the park region (Government of Saskatchewan, news release 2007). As well, Parks Canada announced in 2009 major improvements to visitor infrastructure: $14.2 million was allocated to upgrading a sewage lagoon and repairing degraded local roads (Missinipi Broadcasting Corporation 2009). These investments were welcomed by the community's residents as improvements to basic local services that were overdue, as well as necessary for increasing tourism activity.

Humboldt

In contrast to the case of Waskesiu, which is a resort community under federal jurisdiction, the municipality of Humboldt typifies the normal administrative arrangement where responsibility for the municipality lies within provincial jurisdiction. Located in east-central Saskatchewan, Humboldt is a rural agricultural community whose founding originated with the building of a nearby telegraph station in 1878. In the early 1900s, a marketing campaign by the German American Land Company attracted many German Catholics to the area, and in 1903, a group of Benedictine monks arrived from Minnesota and established St Peter's colony. A new Canadian Northern Railway line further helped to attract businesses and settlers, and on 7 April 1907, Humboldt was declared a town. As with many prairie settlements, the railways and agriculture were key sources of economic growth in its first century. On 7 November 2000, Humboldt became the thirteenth city in Saskatchewan (City of Humboldt 2009c).

DEMOGRAPHIC AND ECONOMIC PROFILE

As its ascension to city status suggests, Humboldt has experienced a modest but steady population increase. The 2006 Census reported there were 4,998 people residing in the community (Government of Canada, Statistics Canada 2009a). In 2008, health records were used to estimate that 5,765 people were residents, and this is an enviable increase given the ongoing problem of rural depopulation (City of Humboldt 2009a). The most common ethnic identities of its residents are Canadian, German, and Ukrainian. Also, a small Aboriginal population is present. Immigrants account for only a small portion of the population increase, as most residents – 86.4 per cent – were born within the province (City of Humboldt 2007b).

Agriculture, forestry, fishing, and hunting are the main economic activities, employing 22.5 per cent of the population, followed by retail, health care/social assistance, manufacturing, and construction (Government of Saskatchewan, Saskatchewan Bureau of Statistics 2006). While the local economy is largely based on mixed-farm agri-culture, there is a diverse manufacturing sector and a robust service sector. Potash mining also plays a fairly large role in the city's econ-omy. Humboldt also benefits from its wider trading area: 29,500 people live within an eighty-kilometer radius, and the province's lar-gest city – Saskatoon – lies approximately 110 kilometers to the west (City of Humboldt 2007f; Government of Canada, Statistics Canada 2009b). Owing in part to these neighbouring communities, tourism is a significant economic driver. In 2007, for example, it accounted for $13.8 million in local economic activity (City of Humboldt 2007e).

RECENT IMAGE-BUILDING POLICY INITIATIVES

Partly out of concern for increasing tourism activity, over the last sev-eral years the city has been reviewing its image-building policies and in 2008 it adopted a new community tourism plan. One key debate has centred on whether the city should retain its brand as "a little bit of Germany in the heart of prairies" (City of Humboldt 2008, 11). In the 1980s, the city chose to project its image as a quaint Ger-man settlement akin to a Bavarian town. To help communicate the image, the municipality offers businesses small grants in the range of

$10,000 to $15,000 if they adopt Bavarian-themed building facades. The image also is communicated by facilities, such as a donated building housing a "mini German museum," and events such as an annual polka festival (City of Humboldt 2008, 19; 2009b). At the same time, however, a number of competing brands and slogans exist; it has been advertised as "Canada's Mustard Capital," as well as the "Heart of the Sure Crop District," the "Iron Triangle," and the "Home of Action Humboldt" (City of Humboldt 2008, 11). For a city of merely five thousand people, quite a few images of Humboldt have been actively promoted.

The 2008 tourism plan noted this identity confusion, and generally aimed to rebrand the city through focusing on its natural and urban amenities. It seems clear, however, that the community has a long-standing investment in its German village image that many people are reluctant to abandon. As well, the issue of brand confusion is proving difficult to resolve. Long-standing images continue to be utilized despite a consensus that the community is to focus on using only updated images.[4]

Recently, the city developed a "relocation package," which has exemplified a successful economic development strategy where advertising competitive tax rates, affordable housing, and low utility rates have enticed people to relocate (City of Humboldt 2007c; 2007d). The council also allocated several thousand dollars in loans to attract new small businesses to the area (City of Humboldt 2007e). Growth and development are central tenets of Humboldt's three key pro-business organizations: Sagehill Development Corporation, the Chamber of Commerce, and Action Humboldt. Action Humboldt in particular has been very active in helping to formulate a new city image (City of Humboldt 2007a).

Swift Current

Approximately 280 kilometers southwest of Humboldt lies the city of Swift Current, a modern transportation hub servicing agriculture and the oil and natural gas industry. The area was originally called *Kisiskâciwan* by the Cree, and *Rivère au Courant* by fur traders to describe its major creek, which stretches across a hundred miles of windswept prairie before emptying into the South Saskatchewan River system. In 1882, a town site was reserved and a CP rail line followed. For many years the settlement was the freight terminus for western Canada. On 21 September 1903, Swift Current became a village, and eleven years later it was declared a city (Tourism Swift Current 2007).

DEMOGRAPHIC AND ECONOMIC PROFILE

Swift Current is Saskatchewan's sixth largest city; the 2006 Census reported there were 14,946 residents (Government of Canada, Statistics Canada 2009e). Over the past ten years, Swift Current has had a relatively stagnant population level, with a negligible population change from 1998 to 2008 (City of Swift Current 2009, 6). For several years, the proportion of senior citizens has been increasing while the proportion of children has been decreasing.[5] The largest segment of Swift Current's population is aged 40–54 years, and there is a "hollowing out" of the 20–39 age cohort, typical of most rural Saskatchewan communities (Government of Canada, Statistics Canada 2009e). Its people predominantly are Caucasian; specifically German, Canadian, British, and Ukrainian, and most were born within the province. There is also a small Aboriginal population (Government of Canada, Statistics Canada 2009e).

As with most prairie communities, the Great Depression of the 1930s devastated Swift Current's economy. Massive out-migration followed as many people abandoned the area seeking increased prosperity elsewhere. A boom period began in the 1950s when oil and gas reserves were discovered nearby (Tourism Swift Current 2007). Oil and gas remains a staple of Swift Current's economy, as companies continue to explore the area: well drilling records were set in 2003 and 2004 (Action Swift Current 2005, 5).[6]

Swift Current's role as a major transportation hub intensified in the 1960s with the expansion of the Trans-Canada Highway adjacent to the community. Along with manufacturing, the tourism and retail sectors benefit from the city's transportation linkages: visitors and travellers spent an estimated $23.9 million dollars in 2003 alone (Action Swift Current 2005). In the near future, planners have oriented the city's growth strategy toward expanding its reach into regional and international markets, in part to take advantage of its southerly location and proximity to Alberta's oil fields.[7]

The local economy also is fueled by a strong agricultural sector featuring both cereals and livestock farming. It is home to three inland grain terminals and the Semi-Arid Prairie Agricultural Research Centre. As well, with over one thousand licensed businesses, manufacturers, and professional offices, the city clearly values its diverse business sector as a key component of growth (City of Swift Current 2007b; 2009).

RECENT IMAGE-BUILDING POLICY INITIATIVES
In the last several years, the city's image-building policy has changed markedly. Swift Current's old brand depicted it as a "frontier city," but the attractiveness of this image was criticized after fifteen years without population growth raised local concerns. As a result, in 2002, Action Swift Current (ASC) was founded as a not-for-profit organization dedicated to encouraging the "business sector to become the catalyst for growth, and lead in economic development" (Action Swift Current 2009a).[8] Interestingly, preliminary studies reported Swift Current was perceived quite negatively by many people outside of its borders. Image consultants found it was widely viewed as a "red neck" city, marked by racial intolerance and hostility toward newcomers, and this report surprised the community (Smith 2003). So, the community faced two image-building challenges: updating its brand and countering a widely held negative image.

In response, in 2005 the ASC group developed a new brand and a new slogan – "Where Life Makes Sense" – to help focus the city's new image-building strategy on increasing tourism, business development, and population growth through advertising its quality of life (City of Swift Current 2007a; Action Swift Current 2007). The new branding strategy was funded heavily by Western Economic Development (the federal government's regional development agency), and the city also received significant funds for image-building activities from a few federal programs.[9] As well, community leaders actively sought to leverage their resources towards directly supporting local development. For example, the council implemented new business tax incentives, and moved to price industrial land for sale competitively. These initiatives and others helped increase construction activity significantly: an estimated $100 million was invested in local construction projects from 2005 to 2008 (Government of Saskatchewan, Enterprise Saskatchewan 2009).

Saskatoon

Whereas Swift Current represents a medium-sized rural city, the last case concerns the most populous city in the province. Located in the province's west-central region, and situated on the banks of the South Saskatchewan River, Saskatoon is a commercial and agricultural centre, and a gateway to the north. This city hosts the University of Saskatchewan and so benefits from a large number of related facilities, such as the Canadian Light Source and a major research park (Klein 2004). The area has been inhabited for about six thousand years by First Nations peoples; European settlers did not arrive until the 1880s. Saskatoon's name derives from the Cree word for a local berry, and its origins are found in two failed social experiments.

The first experiment began with the temperance movement. In 1881, the federal government of Sir John A. Macdonald allotted 313,000 acres to the Temperance Colony Society, and many Toronto Methodists moved west to found an alcohol-free community (City of Saskatoon 2007). The second experiment, initiated by two enterprising clergymen, aimed to establish Britannia, a territory filled with exclusively British settlers in northwest Canada. Known as the Barr colonists, in 1903 more than 2,700 British residents arrived in Saskatchewan and settled in what are now the cities of Saskatoon and Lloydminster (Government of Saskatchewan, Saskatchewan Archives Board 2005). Although each experiment failed to achieve its utopian goal, both groups helped to found and sustain the community of Saskatoon (O'Brien, Millar, and Delainey 2006, 1).

Despite the promotional activities of several large colonization companies, Saskatoon's early development was slow. Stagnant growth owed to the river's difficult navigation, and political conflicts, such as the North-West Rebellion of 1885, discouraged settlement. In 1890, railway companies bridged the river and this encouraged three new settlements on the west bank, which amalgamated to form the city of Saskatoon on 26 May 1906 (O'Brien, Millar, and Delainey 2006, 5–7). For many years the city's growth rate lagged that of similar communities, such as Regina and Moose Jaw. In the post-war era, however, population growth increased significantly and, in 1985, Saskatoon became the most populous city in the province (Coneghan 2005, 829).

DEMOGRAPHIC AND ECONOMIC PROFILE

The 2006 Census reported there were 202,340 residents; the city has experienced a steady annual population growth rate of about 2.8 per cent over the last five years (Saskatoon Regional Economic Development Association 2007).[10] Economic restructuring and declining agricultural income have produced a rural exodus to urban centres like Saskatoon, which is a leading destination for rural migrants and young people relocating from First Nations reserves (Stabler and Olfert 2009, 141). Close to 85 per cent of Saskatoon's population is Caucasian, and most of these residents identify their ancestry as German, English, Canadian, Scottish, Irish, or Ukrainian. A further 10 per cent of residents affiliate themselves with at least one Aboriginal identity group (Government of Canada, Statistics Canada 2009d). Beyond the city limits, Saskatoon also benefits from a populous trading area encompassing 550,000 people.

There are six dominant industrial sectors within the local economy: mining and energy, manufacturing, transportation, life sciences, construction, and agriculture (Saskatoon Regional Development Authority 2009a). Of the 139,700 people employed in all industries in 2008, about thirty thousand were in goods-producing industries, while 109,400 worked in service fields (Saskatoon Regional Development Authority 2009b, 5). Saskatoon accounts for about one-third of the total provincial manufacturing value, and tourism is a significant revenue source.

In regard to its image-building efforts, the city has a long history of promoting itself to different clienteles. As mentioned above, the early temperance and Barr colony leaders advertised the settlement's image as that of a "good society," unspoiled by alcohol consumption or non-British residents. Saskatoon's next image reflected the sudden deluge of immigrants from 1908 to 1913, whose startling numbers helped to promote it as the "Fastest Growing City in the British Empire" for a few years (O'Brien, Millar, and Delainey 2006, 20). In the post-war era, the city advertised its central location and transportation linkages with the slogan, "The Hub City," and its resources via the "POW City" moniker.

RECENT IMAGE-BUILDING POLICY INITIATIVES

The most recent major change in Saskatoon's image-building policy occurred in 2001 when a municipal agency, Tourism Saskatoon, adopted a new slogan and a strategic plan. The "Saskatoon Shines" slogan refers not only to the generic bright and glowing connotation of the term, but also to the Canadian Light Source facility at the University of Saskatchewan, and goals of establishing Saskatoon as a "science city" (The Marketing Den/Fast Consulting 2001, 2–7). As well, the city recently developed a marketing strategy to target local, regional, and interprovincial tourism markets (Tourism Saskatoon 2007).

Although it is relatively small when compared to other regional centres, such as Calgary and Winnipeg, Saskatoon has an impressive record of hosting what are, by Canadian standards, mega-events, such as the Jeux du Canada Games, the Vanier Cup, the Juno Awards, the Special Olympic Games, and international amateur games for soccer, rugby, hockey, and figure skating. Within the last five years, Saskatoon Sports Tourism, a non-profit organization promoting local tourism, was launched along with a new website (Saskatoon Sport Tourism 2009). Municipal leaders also have undertaken several large-scale infrastructural development projects focused on increasing the city's capacity and attractiveness for hosting mega-events and large conferences, such as adding fifty-two thousand square feet to the main convention centre (City of Saskatoon 2005).

Without a doubt, the main focus of municipal attention recently has been on resolving a thirty-year-old riverbank development conundrum. Since the 1970s, community leaders had struggled to establish and then pursue a plan to revitalize a large area of the south downtown core. Owing to its excellent riverbank location, this area offered many possibilities for business, cultural, and tourism investments. However, three problems perennially challenged progress on this issue. First, there were large costs involved in preparing the site for development. Some citizens wanted old buildings removed, while others wanted them refurbished. As several decrepit industrial buildings required demolition and the removal of hazardous materials, local politicians balked at the large costs required to clean up brown field areas and remodel existing buildings.

Second, some key lots were held by private interests and it took time for the city to acquire these properties (City of Saskatoon, River Landing Project 2009a). Third, there was little agreement on who should develop the parcels of land in question. Should it be a purely public investment, a purely private one, or a mixture of public and private participation?

In 2000, community leaders began to agitate for resolution to this long-standing issue, and that December a call for expressions of interest was issued for the redevelopment of a key building. This signaled the beginning of rapid progress toward resolving the development conundrum. In 2004, city council adopted the South Downtown Concept Plan, which was a cornerstone for the River

Landing Project (CBC News 2007; City of Saskatoon, River Landing Project 2004). The River Landing Project is divided into two
parts: phase 1 concerns developing eastern land parcels, and phase 2
concerns western parcels (City of Saskatoon, River Landing project
2007).[11] By adopting a mix of private and public sector investments,
along with a thorough marketing strategy, careful land use planning, and a consistent concern to ensure the development's physical
attractiveness, River Landing is well positioned to promote the city's
image as a modern community with superior lifestyle amenities.

A combination of public and private investment has helped to
realize the development plan's goals. By 2004, funding for phase
2 totalled over $29.3 million as a result of a joint investment from
the federal, provincial, and local levels of government (Government
of Saskatchewan, news release 2004). Then-Finance Minister Ralph
Goodale commented the project represented the federal government's
commitment to the New Deal for Cities policy, which had been a key
element within Liberal Prime Minister Paul Martin's 2005 federal
budget (Government of Canada, Department of Finance 2005). On
3 April 2009, the Art Gallery of Saskatchewan publicly announced
its intent to construct a new art gallery at the River Landing Destination Centre, and that September, the governments of Canada and
Saskatchewan each contributed $13.02 million towards the new
plans. At the time of writing, the area's development continues with
the support of four key public bodies: the city of Saskatoon, the
Meewasin Valley Authority, the government of Saskatchewan, and
the federal government (City of Saskatoon 2009b). In total, public
investment in both phases of the project currently stands at $112
million (Schultz 2009).

Similar to the River Landing Project, there are several other initiatives related to image-building policy that involve the city of Saskatoon with one or more senior governments. For example, a new
urban development agreement was announced in Saskatoon in May
2005. The federal, provincial, and municipal governments agreed to
partner and invest $10 million to revitalize Saskatoon's older neigh-
bourhoods; encourage artistic, recreational, and cultural activities;
and promote its positive business climate (Government of Canada,
Western Economic Diversification 2004). As well, in March 2006,
the Capital City Legacy Projects were announced, where four local
facilities received funding of $10.5 million in total from Western
Economic Diversification to increase local tourism (Government

of Canada, Western Economic Diversification 2006b). These funds flowed from the federal government's $24 million "Canada Cele- brates Saskatchewan" centennial initiative (Government of Canada, Western Economic Diversification 2006a).

In summary, these four communities represent important aspects of municipal government in Saskatchewan. The differences between them lends us the opportunity to search for characteristics of image- building policy that are common in all these communities, and so perhaps typical of this policy field generally within the province. Having introduced each of our four cases as above, in the next sec- tion we move on to explore how policy is formulated and influenced within each community.

PART TWO: WHO MAKES POLICY?

To investigate how local governments undertake image-building policy and who is empowered to make decisions, we consulted pub- lished documents, such as annual city reports, organization charts, and marketing studies in order to understand the formal roles and responsibilities of public and private actors. To help us understand the informal pressures and the realpolitik of decision-making in this area, we interviewed several people in each community, and identi- fied potential interviewees through a variety of methods.

Mayors, council members, administrative personnel, and journal- ists were located through searching organizational information pro- vided on municipal websites and telephone directories. We located representatives of various community groups and social forces by several means. We asked politicians and administrators about which main organizations they interact with in the area of image-building policy, and located some representatives through media accounts of particular events and controversies. Also, we relied on our own accumulated knowledge of local politics in Saskatoon, Waskesiu, and Humboldt to locate people who were active, or who ought to have particular interests, in image-building initiatives.

We completed interviews with twenty-eight people located in the four communities under study. Most of these were conducted in per- son, with five completed via telephone. On average, we spent ninety minutes speaking with the respondents.[12] The interview group repre- sents a wide variety of perspectives, experiences, and organizations. One unexpected but helpful characteristic of the interview group was role multiplicity, where respondents had experience participating in image-building policy-making in more than one capacity. As a hypothetical example, a respondent may have served as a past council member and so participated as governmental representative, and now currently contributes to policy-making through leading the local chamber of commerce in advocating for a new local branding policy.

About 75 per cent of our interview pool held such multiple roles, while the remaining 25 per cent can be assigned to a single role, such as "politician," "social force representative," or "public administrator." Owing to the variety of roles played by those in our respondent group, the information we collected is particularly rich, insightful, and helpful in understanding the context and process of image-building policy.

Before discussing specifically how intergovernmental relations and social forces affect policy-making, it is worth communicating a few general observations about who makes policy in the communities under study. First, policy-making in Saskatoon fundamentally is different than in the three smaller communities under examination. Owing to its size and resources, the city of Saskatoon delegates much control over tourism development and promotion to tourism businesses, and allocates economic development policy to economic development organizations and business improvement districts. Only events policy remains within the city's direct control. In the other three communities, the local government retains control of all three subcategories of policy activity: events, branding, and economic development policy.

A second point is that in all four locales under study, a surprisingly small number of people contribute to making image-building policy. This is true even in the most populous case: despite Saskatoon's size, policy is controlled normally by a very small group. For all the cases, we note that the key players are leaders from government, the business sector, or the community. As discussed in more detail below, local elites exercise much power and command an impressive array of resources in this policy field.

Intergovernmental Relations

To study how image-building policy is created, in our interviews we investigated the effects of intergovernmental relations within each of the four locales under study. We studied what sorts of resources

were available within each local government and at the provincial
and federal levels, probed the nature of local-provincial-federal relationships, and also examined the presence or absence of horizontal collaboration among local governments. We considered whether
(and if so, how) partisan and ideological differences among governments facilitate or retard intergovernmental relations, and whether
the change from Liberal majority to Conservative minority governments has affected this policy area. If politicians are important in
this policy field, then a change of government could have repercussions; moreover, the Conservatives were committed to intervene less
in areas of provincial jurisdiction, such as municipalities.

WASKESIU

In comparison to many other Saskatchewan resort communities,
Waskesiu is distinct because of the numerous business, government, and academic leaders who summer there. For well over sixty
years it has been a favorite playground for Saskatchewan's elite; a
long-standing nickname, "Whisky Slough," refers to the lively social
climate. Intergovernmental relations have to be understood in reference to the summer community's wealthy and socially privileged
composition. For example, Don Ravis, a former Progressive Conservative Member of Parliament, has served also as chairman of the
WCC (Waskesiu Community Council 2009a). Two former provincial finance ministers, Janice MacKinnon and Eric Cline, own cab-
ins and are regular summer residents. Janice MacKinnon recently
was elected as a WCC councillor, and she is married to the president
of the University of Saskatchewan, Peter MacKinnon. Many of the
province's wealthiest families maintain cottages here, as do many
former mayors, city council members, and public administrators. As
a result of this elite concentration, intergovernmental relationships,
particularly among politicians and officials active at the municipal
and provincial levels, frequently are facilitated through informal
personal contact at barbeques, parties, and summer leisure activities.

In terms of formal intergovernmental relations, the main exchange
occurs between the WCC and Parks Canada representatives. Alan
Fehr, currently the Field Unit Superintendent, Northern Prairies,
and a handful of staff officials administer the park and coordinate and consult with the WCC. Relations between these two bodies
have changed substantially over the last fifteen years, generally for
the better.

There are four main factors that have worked to change the structure of relations between Parks Canada staff and the WCC: (1) the expanding size of the community's off-season population; (2) deteriorating infrastructure along with demands for new and upgraded infrastructure; (3) Parks Canada's recent effort to increase international tourism; and (4) the entry of new businesses to Waskesiu and the PANP area. One respondent who has been in business in the area since 2003 summarized the change in intergovernmental relations in this way: "Parks Canada's attitude used to be that 'we deal with squirrels and deer but as far as people, we don't want them [here].' That attitude has really changed now" (Interview 4). One Parks official commented that the administration's attitude for many years was "we know best" rather than "we consult" the community (Interview 10).

A cabin owner who has been active on the WCC stated that Parks Canada's decision to hire a communications officer made a huge difference. The new officer then hired a marketing professional on a three-year contract to help advertise the park and its amenities, issue regular media advisories, and engage in public consultations. These efforts have increased the park's visibility, smoothed relations with community members, and also generated some partnerships between the park and WCC to set up new attractions.

We encountered much evidence that Parks officials have become more responsive to local concerns. For example, one respondent told us that three years ago the chief executive officer of Parks Canada, Alan Latourelle, visited Waskesiu. Local residents complained about the many infrastructure issues to him, and he was visibly embarrassed by the poor condition of the roads, beaches, and water treatment facility. Shortly thereafter the park superintendent indicated he was willing to discuss some infrastructural upgrades with WCC, and the park did shoulder some infrastructural and maintenance costs.[13]

The park administration clearly has been quite supportive of the WCC's efforts to alter the form of local government in place. One WCC member told us Parks Canada has worked closely with the WCC to specify how resources and personnel would be transferred to the new municipality and which governmental organization would bear responsibility for particular costs and duties. This person commented that park officials recognized they could not satisfactorily administer the Waskesiu community and its needs, in part because the administration's organizational structure is not designed to serve as a local government.

A park official told us that in the past couple of years there has been more effort devoted to consulting the WCC, as well as the adjacent rural municipalities of Lakeland and Christopher Lake. The stakeholders have responded with different levels of enthusiasm. Some have welcomed closer collaboration. Others have not, such as the local council of Christopher Lake. We were told by one local businessperson that the Christopher Lake council was taken over in a recent election by cottage owners opposed to additional tourism, and so this body has not been receptive to new partnership proposals.

The role of the provincial tourism office, Tourism Saskatchewan, generally was described in negative terms by most of our interview subjects. One experienced resort owner observed that Tourism Saskatchewan was solely concerned with promoting a single Saskatchewan image – that of flat wheat fields – and largely ignored the different image of the near north. She said: "Eighty-five per cent of Saskatchewan's imagery is prairie fields ... but 60 per cent of our territory is woods and water. Europeans love woods and water, but Saskatchewan's image is not being sold as it ought to be. Saskatchewan is not just farming, not just agriculture" (Interview 11). In contrast, beyond Parks Canada, the most important federal partner for the WCC and the larger PANP area is Western Economic Diversification (WED). Many people told us WED was responsive to their needs, and, in some cases, actively sought out specific businesses to help them apply for particular federal programs. In general, federal government has a large role, while the provincial government seems to play a small role in PANP image-building policy.

HUMBOLDT

Concerning Humboldt, respondents indicated that they have little contact with elected federal or provincial politicians representing the area. The Humboldt council does have some interaction with provincial agencies and departments, mainly Tourism Saskatchewan and the Department of Agriculture and Food. However, the province tends to deal with Humboldt's Regional Economic Development Agency (REDA) rather than the council because the REDA "can move things ahead a lot faster" (Interview 21). Ms Kerri Martin, Humboldt's director of tourism and economic development, spends most of her time working with community members and groups, such as the German Heritage Society and the Junior Chamber, rather than liaising with other governments. Several respondents commented that there were few formal linkages between Humboldt and other councils (except for weak linkages through the Saskatchewan Urban Municipalities Association [SUMA]). The few linkages that do exist are personal ones between Humboldt politicians or administrators, and their counterparts in other areas. These linkages are held to be valuable and critical to success: one person summarized it as "leadership at the top is the key to success" (Interview 19). At the same time, the perception that Humboldt is in active competition with some other nearby local governments, particularly Saskatoon, for tourism spending and manufacturing businesses clearly diminishes the will to secure bilateral co-operation.

When asked which governments supplied resources to Humboldt for image-building purposes, the federal government was mentioned frequently, and two agencies – the Rural Secretariat and WED – are key actors and funding sources. A representative from Action Humboldt told us his organization has revitalized interest in, and capacity to undertake, economic development in Humboldt with the help of federal programs and funding (Interview 20).

SWIFT CURRENT

In comparison with the Waskesiu community and Humboldt, for Swift Current we found more contact generally with other levels of government and other local governments. At the political level, then-Mayor Sandy Larson was very active within some larger umbrella groups, such as SUMA and the Federation of Canadian Municipalities (FCM). Interestingly, a large portion of her interactions with the Saskatchewan government depended heavily on personal relationships she built with provincial politicians. For example, she relied heavily on MLA Clay Serby for help with many projects and initiatives. She "would go to him for informal coordination on image-building policy, especially concerning economic development" (Interview 18). At the federal level, during Paul Martin's Liberal government, she met often with federal politicians, particularly concerning the 2005 New Deal for Cities. She commented, however, that generally "the feds are very aloof" and there is no real mechanism in place for receiving input from municipal politicians concerning image-building policy. With the arrival of the Harper government into office, she told us her interactions with federal politicians are less frequent.

At the administrative level, Swift Current representatives have some contact with their provincial and federal counterparts, but these tend generally to be limited and to focus on specific projects, such as annual festivals. An exception is Matt Noble, the chief administrative officer, who is in fairly regular contact with provincial officials representing rural development and aboriginal affairs, and also with WED officials (Interview 23). His interactions with the province over the new Cities Act have been frustrating. He suggests the new act gave cities more authority and responsibility, but not more fiscal capacity. So, in many areas, cities lack the fiscal capacity to undertake key projects and administer areas for which they are responsible (Interview 22).

So far as Swift Current's politicians and administrators are concerned, the most significant, accessible, and reliable governmental partner in image-building policy is WED. The mayor told us she rarely interacts with federal or provincial administrators, with the exception of WED, because she says politicians tend to interact with politicians, while administrators tend to interact with administrators. Here she heavily values – and relies on – personal relationships with key WED administrators, particularly with regard to navigating the grant submission process. The linkages with this federal agency clearly have been beneficial, as several people noted the city has been exceptionally successful at securing WED project funding.

SASKATOON

In the case of Saskatoon, we found the same sort of relationship "layering" evident in Swift Current: politicians tend to interact with politicians and administrators tend to interact with administrators. Saskatoon's mayor, Don Atchison, told us he has much contact with federal politicians, and, moreover, "we go to great lengths to ensure [visiting] federal ministers have a very positive experience [when they're in Saskatoon]" (Interview 1). He said also he ensures federal politicians are given a lot of credit for their involvement in programs. He notes, "Saskatoon is the only city in Canada that has a GST project – phase 2 of River Landing," and affirms working as a team with his federal political counterparts is important (Interview 1). He does not interact with WED; this occurs at the administrative level.

As mayor, he has worked closely with Liberal Minister Ralph Goodale and Conservative MP Carol Skelton, both of whom acted as the provincial "go to" person for their parties. When asked about proximity to politicians, he argued local politicians in Regina were better at accessing the Liberal government when the Liberals were in government, but is pleased that several Saskatoon-area MPS are influential in Stephen Harper's Conservative government. Beyond the mayor, other council members do interact with federal politicians, but often these relationships are personal, and cultivated over a significant period of time. Interestingly, as in the case of Waskesiu, many of the relationships originate though informal contact at events, such as facility launches or community awards dinners. Members of Saskatoon's council regularly interact with the surrounding rural municipalities, particularly Corman Park.

At the administrative level, senior administrators have contact with their federal counterparts mainly on a project basis. There are no mechanisms regularly linking federal and municipal administrators. However, one senior administrator told us his department (communications) has quite a lot of interaction with WED, and this is his impression concerning other city departments as well. He added that under the new Urban Development Agreement, and in view of the new provincial Cities Act, currently there is much interaction between city administrators and those at the other levels as details are finalized and "tinkering" occurs (Interview 7).

In summary, we discern a few commonalities across these four cases concerning intergovernmental relations. First, there is less interaction between the local and provincial levels than we expected, especially in the smaller communities. While the absence of the provincial government in the PANP region's image-building policy-making may be explained by the fact of federal jurisdiction, this does not account for the smaller communities of Humboldt and Swift Current.

Second, we were surprised by the scope of Western Economic Diversification's presence and activity within this policy field. In all four communities, respondents reported that WED was a valuable partner. This agency consistently is the main representative of, and connection to, the federal government for local governments. This connection may be more valued since the federal Liberals were replaced with the Conservatives in 2006, because generally, respondents perceived federal-municipal relations in this policy area had weakened in the early years of the Harper government.

Another commonality we noted is that, with the exception of linkages created through umbrella organizations such as SUMA, or those established briefly to address a specific project, intergovernmental linking mechanisms in this policy field largely are absent. We found little evidence of positive and consistent interactions between local governments or between the province and municipalities. Intergovernmental relationships are not regular or institutionalized. It seems clear that when relationships are created, they depend heavily on political or administrative leaders, and so any change in the leadership threatens to terminate such connections. Similarly, and perhaps because of the lack of intergovernmental linking mechanisms, in all the cases there was a consistent emphasis on the important role played by personal relationships between political and bureaucratic actors to secure image-building objectives.

Social Forces

In this section we move from examining how governmental relationships affect image-building policy to analyzing which social forces influence policy-making. The term "social forces" is meant to indicate the broad array of organized, non-governmental interests, and here we subdivide this category into two parts. The first group encompasses business and business-related groups. The second grouping contains all other non-business groups, such as trade unions, conservation societies, amateur sports clubs, and anti-poverty groups. The social force category was divided in this way to allow us to examine a maxim common within the local government literature: business groups are dominant within local politics and therefore have much policy influence (see, for example, Fainstain and Fainstain 1986; Peterson 1981). So, we are interested particularly in comparing the influence of business and non-business groups, which below we refer to as "business" and "community" groups.

WASKESIU
In the case of Waskesiu, there are several long-standing community groups with interests in image-building policy, such as the Waskesiu Foundation, as well as groups with a broader mandate that includes the PANP area, such as the Saskatchewan Environmental Society. Clearly, most businesses in this resort community depend heavily on tourism. In answering our queries about group activity

and influence, one respondent suggested that while the local chamber of commerce enjoyed much access to key decision-makers, other groups had just as much access, and so business and community interests were evenly balanced.

Our findings, however, suggest business interests clearly dominate Waskesiu's image-building policy agenda. Several people commented that community groups are unimportant in making key decisions. As well, it is widely perceived that there is a policy bias favouring business, especially larger businesses. As an example of this bias, several respondents pointed out that a large lodge received lucrative tax concessions that were unavailable to smaller businesses. The influence of business upon government is perceived to extend beyond the local council and include Parks Canada. Relations between park administrators and the business community have become more cordial in the last few years, and the park has received much credit for being aware of local business concerns and responding to specific infrastructural needs and marketing opportunities.

HUMBOLDT

In regard to the relative policy influence of business and community groups in Humboldt, this case is similar to Waskesiu's situation. Business interests seem dominant. Humboldt faces the same economic challenges confronting many other small rural communities, and so residents perceive their community to be in a serious "race to attract business" (Interview 28). Several respondents suggested the main purpose of image-building policy was to help existing businesses and attract new ones. There was a clear consensus that the current city government was making policy explicitly to spur economic development, and this was a positive change. Five years earlier, elected officials were unconcerned with economic development, the chamber of commerce was "dead," and the regional economic development association (REDA) was heavily in debt (Interview 20). So, the council's new, pro-business orientation was necessary, legitimate, and highly desired.

Within this context, our research found community groups play a small role in image-building policy. This is not to say they are excluded from the process, as community groups are considered to possess appropriate policy influence if they choose to exercise it. In the words of one respondent, such groups can become involved in decision-making "if they pick up the phone" (Interview 13). At the same time, we did not find much emphasis on the virtues of under-taking formal or informal consultations beyond the business community. One view we encountered holds that because many local business people also are members of community groups, there is little necessity to consult community groups formally owing to these overlapping memberships. Because local business leaders are linked to community groups, they are aware of the community's needs and concerns.

SWIFT CURRENT

In the third case as well, it seems clear that business interests dominate image-building policy in Swift Current. In part because citizens view themselves as being in a situation where the city must "grow or die," there appeared to be a consensus supporting the local business sector and its policy dominance (Interview 18). In the words of one respondent, "Swift Current is not apologetic about having a strong business approach," and several respondents underscored the city is very responsive to business (Interview 25). The city aims deliberately to create policy that businesses will find helpful and enticing. In the words of one senior administrator, the city deliberately "sells a responsive government" to help attract new businesses (Interview 23).

At the same time, there was recognition that community groups have an important role to play, and several people told us that local policy-making about image-building is very open and inclusive. The mayor assured us that "input is sought from all groups," and that the process does "not exclude any sectors of the community" (Interview 18). This city's unusually strong commitment to using planning tools to guide the search for growth may contribute to efforts to formally consult community groups. Yet there are real limits on community group power. We were told that in the event of conflict between business group and community group goals, business goals clearly would prevail.

Some respondents pointed out that community groups are included in the policy process mainly through interlocking elites. There is "not a community board that does not have a council member on it. These memberships serve as a conduit for social forces to influence governmental policy" (Interview 22). As well, government leaders rely on the local media to communicate policy issues and debates to social forces as a means to include them in the process.

One respondent told us more effort was necessary to include marginalized groups in key image-building decisions, particularly concerning events policy. However, past efforts to consult some community groups were met with apathy, and this experience probably had diminished the leadership's enthusiasm for community consultation exercises.

SASKATOON

As discussed above in the introduction to part two of this study, Saskatoon differs from the other cases owing to its size, and this was apparent in examining who participates in image-building policy-making. Saskatoon has several established formal consultation mechanisms, which draw social forces into image-building policy to a greater extent than in the smaller communities we studied. For example, a city administrator reported that "at the administrative level, there is a double or quadruple level of contact. It used to be that elected politicians and [administrative] departments would each seek out public input. Now there is a new set of guidelines on seeking public input, [there is] a constant interconnection" (Interview 5).

It appears that such consultation takes place very late in the process. A prominent member of the local media told us that generally "people are afraid to debate ideas until they are featured in the newspaper. Some [of the explanation] is street-level – politicians don't want to distract the process [so] they won't take the [consultation] initiative until it is presented publicly" (Interview 4). Other respondents suggested much more effort could be devoted to including community groups in decision-making. As one former city councillor observed "there is not nearly the kind of consultation there should be. Lots of decisions are made in camera" (Interview 3). Several people held up the "Saskatoon Shines" image policy as an example of how public consultations actually occur: key decisions were made early on by political leaders and the marketing firm; there was little debate about the goals of the new policy, and in the end the community was asked mainly to decide which was the best among marginally different logos.

As in the other three cases, the business community in Saskatoon was perceived to exercise real influence on image-building policy. Several past councillors told us business lobbying clearly influences local policy, and this was echoed by community group representatives who commented that business groups were the most influential ones. In part, this was because "personal relationships with politicians really count" if one hopes to influence policy (Interview 6). As well, we were told business exercised much influence specifically because city politicians and administrators trusted a group of prominent citizens who actively sought out mega-event opportunities for Saskatoon. When one of these promoters presented an events policy proposal, it was then routinely referred to administration for further consideration. However, if a group of people who are not known to council were to propose an event, then "council is very wary" (Interview 3).

While business groups tend to communicate with city government at the "executive to executive level," there was relatively little contact between senior administrators and community group representatives. From the perspective of the city, one difficulty with the inclusion of non-business social forces is that they "have less knowledge of the workings of municipal government than business groups" (Interview 5). In the past, the city tried to remedy this problem. For example, on one occasion, administrators tried to organize and coordinate the city's various social groups and then meet with them informally in council chambers to receive their views, but this initiative failed. Officials believed many community group representatives objected to a "top down," bureaucratic effort to organize them (Interview 6).

As with the other communities we studied, we encountered the argument that the presence of interlocking elites helped ensure community groups' interests were communicated to political elites. This is established partly through formal means. A city administrator explained that "the council's committees, along with fifty community associations, are the eyes and ears of council. City administrative staff [are members of] these associations, so in this way, there can be constant contact" with community groups (Interview 5). As well, the interlocking leadership groups are a product of a relatively compact city with a small, stable elite. It is common that a single person may be at the top of several distinct groups. For example, she may be a well-known business person, an elected ward councilor, and also serve as a director on a local repertory theatre's board.

In summary, across the cities examined, the needs of business appeared to dominate image-building policy, while community groups generally possess little influence. In large part, this was not problematic for local leaders because of the presence of interlocking elites. As key local government and business people who make policy decisions also belong to community groups, the elites are aware of the interests of the broader community. Given this pervasive level of trust we encountered in this system's capacity to accommodate the polity's needs, it is unsurprising that formal public consultation exercises were generally considered unnecessary. It seems that actual consultation that could influence policy at various points in the policy process was undertaken rarely and reluctantly.

It is also clear that resources matter. Business groups used their resources to gain access to the policy process. Other groups, however, were left out. For example, Aboriginal groups and groups representing poor people generally appeared to be left out of the decision-making process across all the cases we studied. It may be logical to expect that in such circumstances, community groups will band together when seeking to influence public policy. However, we found little evidence of such coalition formation, with the notable exception of an example in Saskatoon. A coalition of community groups was opposed to the South Downtown development plan, and engaged in a fairly well-organized, well-publicized battle with the pro-development side. In the end, however, they lost the riverbank development debate and their representative on city council lost her seat to a pro-business candidate.

Clearly, local business interests exercise much influence in image-building policy. This is not because business groups successfully competed for influence with active community groups on a level playing field, as pluralists might argue. Rather, it was because business groups largely have the field to themselves. Their interests were given priority by politicians, administrators, and citizens while community groups largely remained content to depend on interlocking elites to represent them. In view of the province's difficult economic condition for the last fifty years or so, there was a consensus that image-building policy should serve the needs of business.

The widespread concern about Saskatchewan's long-term growth coalesces around the issue of young people who leave in search of better economic opportunity. As discussed earlier in this chapter, the desire to maintain a robust population level is deeply rooted in the province's culture. This helps to explain, in terms of image-building policy, why the interests of business are dominant, and why this dominance is considered legitimate. Business growth is viewed as the main driver of community growth and well-being, and so what serves business also serves the community.

PART THREE: CONCLUSIONS[14]

In view of the detailed discussion of each community's particular characteristics and recent approach to image-building policy as located above in parts one and two, the task of this last section of the analysis is to summarize our main findings and recommendations for each community, as well as across the cases. So, below we briefly evaluate each community's image-building policy, and then move on to summarize some general patterns and issues common to all the cases.

In the case of Waskesiu, image-building policy is constrained by the incongruence between the needs and objectives of the WCC, and its means and authority to secure these ends. Clearly the community council should move, and should be allowed to move, towards becoming a regular municipality with normal powers over taxation, expenditure, and land planning. While park administrators and WED have aided local efforts to establish and pursue some key policy objectives, these actions are episodic initiatives that do not address the core problem. As a result, the policy output is small in scale, serves a small part of the community, and may be offset or undercut by other policies enacted by other governments.

Given that image-building policy in Humboldt was, to quote one respondent, "dead" only a few years ago, the community has made good progress in revitalizing this policy area and devoting resources to it. It remains to be seen whether the new tourism and economic development plans are effective in guiding action and allocating resources to priority areas. Because this community has a long history of image-building initiatives, and because it has sought to learn from the experiences of some similar communities with relatively successful image-building policies, there is much potential for success. We believe policy outcomes here may well be improved with more intergovernmental collaboration and co-operation, particularly with nearby Saskatoon.

Image-building policy in Swift Current is successful in several respects. There are sustainable and well-researched plans in place that have addressed some key image problems and limitations with resolve and focus. The speed of policy-making in recent years has been quite impressive, and the scale of many of the policies is large enough to secure positive results. As in other cases, we believe Swift Current would benefit from more intergovernmental collaboration, especially through an established, institutionalized mechanism. The mayor recognized the limitation of her personal approach when she commented it was very difficult when the partisan complexion of senior governments changed because many of her contacts no longer were useful.

Image-building policy in Saskatoon seems successful, and many respondents spoke with pride about Saskatoon's positive image and ability to "fight above its weight" when hosting mega-events. We think there are some problems, however, in the contracting out of tourism-related initiatives to private business. Politicians and administrators affirmed this has been common practice for many years, and that the other aspects of image-building policy (business communication and communications with citizens) are done "in house" because of their clear importance. We believe this practice somewhat hinders the potential for positive collaboration with other municipalities. It also undercuts policy equity and stakeholder involvement, and has some potential to weaken the coherence of policies taken *in toto*.

Across the cases, we located many examples of good public policy in the area of image-building. This is to say we encountered several examples of coherent, well-designed, well-resourced initiatives supported by intergovernmental co-operation. In general, these examples tend to be found in the larger cities. We found little evidence of long-term feedback or formal evaluation mechanisms, even for some of the largest, most expensive initiatives, such as Saskatoon's River Landing Project. We were struck by the high degree of fragmentation, by which we mean the common pattern of small-scale, short-term policies undertaken without intergovernmental collaboration or consultation. Along with this pattern we note that this policy area, at least in Saskatchewan, relies heavily on the actions of "policy entrepreneurs." There is little long-term planning by groups of politicians, citizens, or administrators. So, we believe policy-making tends to be episodic and heavily reliant on personalities rather than processes.

In summary, we note the following patterns in regard to image-building policy in the four cases under study. First, image-building policies are heavily dependent on policy entrepreneurs. This may benefit policy-making in terms of enhancing its speed and responsiveness, but there are large costs if entrepreneurs fail to take action when opportunity presents itself. Second, the policy environment is highly fragmentéd. There is relatively little long-term planning. Many policies are formed in isolation, without collaboration among governments. There is a paucity of formal intergovernmental linking mechanisms. Change in the partisan complexion of government, whether at the federal or provincial level, exacerbates this problem as new governments bring in new programs, while old ones may be left to wither despite their clear utility. Third, we note political and business elites dominate the policy-making process. There are few means for citizen interests to be represented in the process of decision-making, and, if such opportunities appear, normally the agenda already has been established.

A fourth conclusion is that senior levels of government are unusually distant from municipal image-building policy. Unlike some other public policy areas, such as education, health care, or immigration where municipalities often complain senior governments are far too involved in local concerns, in the case of image-building, local governments enjoy unusual freedom to pursue their goals. In the communities we studied, the provincial government normally was regarded at best as a neutral influence, neither helping nor hindering local initiatives. In the case of Waskesiu, however, the province's tourism policy was considered to be unhelpful to the community's image-building efforts because it did not emphasize the lakes and hills of the Prince Albert National Park region.

The main method of federal intervention in local image-building policy is via WED, and this agency's personnel and programs generally were widely respected and appreciated. Beyond this agency, the federal government generally is perceived to become involved only on a project-specific basis, and only when it suits federal interests. There is some evidence that federal-municipal relations are somewhat more distant and less coordinated since the Conservative party took power in 2006.

A fifth finding is that there are few opponents to activity in this policy area. Image-building policy serves two audiences: citizens already resident in the community and those whom the community seeks to attract. In all the cases, politicians and city administrators listed many benefits of such policies – generating votes for incumbent leaders, affirming a positive community self-image, and increasing tourism revenues – but few detriments. In view of the many benefits image-building initiatives can supply for a community and its leadership, and the absence of constraints presented by senior government activity in this area, it seems to us there is much future potential for local governments to be far more active and innovative in making policy in this field.

NOTES

1 We greatly appreciate the help and co-operation provided by many politicians, public administrators, community activists, media representatives, and officials at the local, provincial, and federal levels. Of course, these people bear no responsibility for our findings and conclusions.
2 As well, the "image-building" rubric includes room for examining a relatively new dynamic of interurban reputational competition that seems to have arisen in response to technological change and globalization (Whitson 2004).
3 This population figure does not include campers. The Park population can reach eight thousand during summer months.
4 For example, the city of Humboldt's 2009 Community Profile document bears a standardized image as recommended by the Community Tourism Plan, but also bears this slogan on its cover: "Heart of the Sure Crop District" (City of Humboldt 2009a). This is a long-standing, but perhaps outdated, image reference.
5 In 1981, the senior population comprised 14.9 per cent of the total, while children represented 22.0 per cent; in 2006, seniors reached 21.1 per cent and children were 16.7 per cent of the total population.
6 It is estimated 85 per cent of the Swift Current area's oil reservoirs have not yet been tapped.
7 The immediate market area serves approximately fifty-five thousand people, but an eight hundred-kilometre radius contains approximately 6 million people (Action Swift Current 2005, 4).
8 It is useful to note ASC undertook its activities within the parameters of a formal business retention and expansion program. According to ASC, "business retention and expansion (BR&E) is an economic development philosophy and process that focuses on the support and enhancement of existing business opportunities and infrastructure (as opposed to a development model that seeks to attract new business to the jurisdiction

in question). The initial goal of a BR&E initiative is to identify and address the community's needs, concerns, and business opportunities. It is an effective means of gathering business input for the purposes of creating and implementing a strategic community economic development plan" (Action Swift Current 2009b).

9 The city received $99,000 for its branding strategy from WED. The ASC organization also benefited from a $600,000 government of Canada initiative in May 2004, delivered by WED to develop plans for core industry sectors in co-operation with neighbouring communities and businesses (Government of Canada, Western Economic Diversification 2004). Swift Current also received federal funding from the "Canada Celebrates Saskatchewan" initiative: it received $296,420, while its surrounding rural area received $34,120 (Government of Canada, Western Economic Diversification 2006a).

10 Note population figures recorded for Saskatoon vary depending upon the classification of the Saskatoon as a Census metropolitan area or a city. These figures represent the city population for the CMA population statistics.

11 In more detail, "River Landing is divided into two phases. In River Landing phase 1, the city will be developing the former Gathercole site, and area east of the Senator Sid Buckwold Bridge and south of 19th Street. The parcels of land that include the riverbank bounded by the Senator Sid Buckwold Bridge to the east, Victoria Park to the west, the former A. L. Cole Power site, and a number of old city electrical buildings and adjacent properties form River Landing phase 2. Overlooking the river in Saskatoon's vibrant downtown, these parcels represent the most significant undeveloped real estate opportunities in the province." From the River Landing Project website at http://www.riverlanding.ca/project_update/index.html .

12 In a handful of cases we contacted people who then declined to be interviewed. These people represented social force groups and declined to be interviewed on grounds that their group did not have a role in image-building policy and/or were not supposed to engage in political activities, such as lobbying government or advocating for specific policies.

13 The Parks Canada Agency was established in December 1998 as a "departmental corporation" under Schedule II of the *Financial Administration Act*. This means Parks Canada is a separate legal entity, dedicated to delivering the programs set out within the agency's legislation and policy authorities. The minister of Canadian heritage is responsible for the

overall direction of the agency and accountable to Parliament for all Parks Canada activities (Government of Canada, Parks Canada 2003).

14 We note our study took place in a period of extended but unusual (by Saskatchewan standards) economic expansion. So, we caution that some of the "success" we report in image-building policy may owe to general economic health, as opposed to effective policy decision-making. This may be particularly true for the economic development policy, as it probably is the sub-category of image-building policy that is most sensitive to the health of the economy.

INTERVIEWS

Interview 1.   Saskatoon. 7 August 2007.

Interview 2.   Swift Current. 17 December 2007.

Interview 3.   Saskatoon. 2 February 2008.

Interview 4.   Prince Albert National Park. 6 July 2006.

Interview 5.   Humboldt. 2 August 2007

Interview 6.   Humboldt. 2 August 2007.

Interview 7.   Saskatoon. 7 August 2006.

Interview 8.   Prince Albert National Park. 1 July 2006

Interview 9.   Prince Albert National Park. 10 March 2008.

Interview 10. Prince Albert National Park. 6 July 2006.

Interview 11. Prince Albert National Park. 1 July 2006.

Interview 12. Regina. 27 February 2008.

Interview 13. Humboldt. 2 August 2007.

Interview 14. Saskatoon. 4 June 2007.

Interview 15. Saskatoon. 13 March 2008.

Interview 16. Saskatoon. 3 June 2007.

Interview 17. Prince Albert National Park. 1 July 2006.

Interview 18. Swift Current. 8 August 2007.

Interview 19. Humboldt. 2 August 2007.

Interview 20. Humboldt. 2 August 2007.

Interview 21. Humboldt. 2 August 2007.

Interview 22. Saskatoon. 6 December 2007.

Interview 23. Swift Current. 8 August 2007.

Interview 24. Saskatoon. 4 June 2007.

Interview 25. Swift Current. 8 August 2007.

Interview 26. Saskatoon. 4 June 2007.

Interview 27. Prince Albert National Park. 4 July 2006.

Interview 28. Swift Current. 14 December 2007.

REFERENCES

Abley, Mark. 2009. "Saskatchewan's Diaspora." In *Perspectives of Sas-katchewan*, edited by Jene Porter, 351–68. Winnipeg: University of Manitoba Press.

Abimola, Temi. 2001. "Branding as a Competitive Strategy for Demand Management in SMEs." *Journal of Research in Marketing and Entrepreneurship* 3, no. 2: 97–106.

Action Swift Current. 2005. *Profile 2005*. http://www.actionswiftcurrent. com/documents/swiftcurrentprofile2005.pdf

– 2007. *Community Brand*. http://www.actionswiftcurrent.com/ community_brand.html.

– 2009a. "About Action Swift Current." http://www.actionswiftcurrent. com/about.html.

– 2009b. "Business Retention and Expansion." http://www. actionswiftcurrent.com/business_retention_expansion.html.

Canadian Broadcasting Corporation. CBC News. 2007. *Saskatoon Council Approves New River Landing Proposal*. 17 September. http://www.cbc. ca/canada/saskatchewan/story/2007/09/18/river-landing.html.

– 2009. *Martensville, Sask. gets city designation*. 4 September. http:// www.cbc.ca/canada/saskatchewan/story/2009/09/04/martensville-city. html?ref=rss.

City of Humboldt. 2007a. *Action Humboldt*. http://www.cityofhumboldt. ca/default.aspx?page=23.

– 2007b. *Community Profile*. March. http://www.cityofhumboldt.ca/ images/Articles/2423_City%20of%20Humboldt%202007%20 Community%20Profile.pdf.

– 2007c. *Humboldt Today: Thinking of Relocating?* http://www.cityof humboldt.ca/default.aspx?page=76.

– 2007d. *Relocation Package*. June. http://www.cityofhumboldt.ca/ images/Articles/2427_2007_Relocation_Package.pdf.

– 2007e. *Tourism and Economic Development News*. Fall. http://www. humboldttourism.com/files/Fall%202007%20Newsletter.pdf.

– 2007f. *Trading Area*. http://www.cityofhumboldt.ca/default.aspx?page= 27.

– 2008. *Community Tourism Plan*. December. http://www. cityofhumboldt.ca/images/Articles/2413_Community_Tourism_Plan_ December_2008.pdf.

– 2009a. *City of Humboldt Community Profile*. June. http://www.cityof humboldt.ca/files/Community_%20Profile_%202009(1).pdf.

- 2009b. *City of Humboldt 2009 Visitor Guide*. http://www. cityofhumboldt.ca/files/2009_Visitor_Guide_1.pdf.
- 2009c. "Humboldt History." http://www.cityofhumboldt.ca/default. aspx?page=31.

City of Saskatoon. 2005. *Annual City Manager's Report to Citizens*. http://www.saskatoon.ca/dpt/city_manager/pdfs/report_citizens_2005. pdf.
- 2007a. *City History*. http://www.city.saskatoon.sk.ca/org/city_history/ index.asp.
- River Landing Project. 2004. *South Downtown Concept Plan*. http:// www.riverlanding.ca/reports_public_input/reports/south_downtown_ concept_plan/concept_plan.pdf.
- 2007. *River Landing Marketing Strategy*. http://www.riverlanding.ca/ reports_public_input/reports/marketing_strategy/marketing_strategy. pdf.
- 2009a. *South Downtown History*. http://www.riverlanding.ca/south_ downtown_history/index.html.
- 2009b. *Partners*. http://www.riverlanding.ca/about/partners/index.html.

City of Swift Current. 2007a. *2007 Official City Guide*. Swift Current: Tourism Swift Current.
- 2007b. *Development Plan*. http://www.city.swift-current.sk.ca/pdfs/ cityhall/eng/distdevplan.pdf.
- 2009. *Economic Profile*. http://www.city.swift-current.sk.ca/pdfs/ cityhall/busdev/profile.pdf.

City of Vancouver. 2009. "Vancouver Green Capital – The Brand," http:// vancouver.ca/greencapital/.

Colour (Marketing). 2007. *Waskesiu Lake Brand Strategy, September 14, 2007*. Halifax: Colour/CCL Group.

Coneghan, Daria. 2005. "Saskatoon." In *The Encyclopedia of Saskatch- ewan*, 828–30. Regina: University of Regina, Canadian Plains Research Centre.

Eisler, Dale. 2006. *False Expectations: Politics and the Pursuit of the Saskatchewan Myth*. Regina: University of Regina, Canadian Plains Research Centre.

Fainstain, Norman I., and Susan S. Fainstain. 1986. "Regime Strategies, Communal Resistance, and Economic Forces." In *Restructuring the City: The Political Economy of Urban Redevelopment*, edited by Susan S. Fainstain et al. New York and London: Longman.

Garcea, Joseph, and Donald Gilchrist. 2009. "Saskatchewan." In *Founda- tions of Governance: Municipal Government in Canada's Provinces*,

edited by Robert Young and Andrew Sancton, 345–83. Toronto: Institute
of Public Administration of Canada and University of Toronto Press.

Government of Canada. Parks Canada. 2003. *Parks Canada Corporate
Plan, 2003–2004.* http://www.pc.gc.ca/docs/pc/rpts/ann-rpt/sec2/
profil1_e.asp.

– Department of Finance. 2005. *Budget 2005: A New Deal for Canada's
Communities.* http://www.fin.gc.ca/budget05/pdf/pacome.pdf

– Parks Canada. 2005. Prince Albert National Park, *Year End Report
Card, 2005.* http://www.waskesiu.org/parks/documents/2006/Park%
202005%20Report%20Card%20Final.pdf.

– Parks Canada. 2006a. *Information Bulletin: Agreement in Principle for
Self-Governance in Waskesiu Reached.* June 12. Prince Albert: Prince
Albert National Park of Canada.

– 2006b. *Prince Albert National Park of Canada Official Visitor Guide
2006.*

– Parks Canada. 2006c. Prince Albert National Park, *Year End Report
Card, 2006.* http://www.waskesiu.org/parks/documents/2007/2006%
20Park%20Report%20Card%20English.pdf.

– 2009a. *Humboldt, Saskatchewan* (table). *2006 Community Profiles.*
2006 Census. Statistics Canada Catalogue no. 92-591-XWE. Ottawa.
http://www12.statcan.ca/Census-recensement/2006/dp-pd/prof/92-591/
details/Page.cfm?Lang=E&Geo1=CSD&Code1=4715008&Geo2=PR
&Code2=47&Data=Count&SearchText=humboldt&SearchType=
Begins&SearchPR=47&B1=All&Custom=.

– 2009b. *Labour Force Characteristics, Manitoba, Saskatchewan.* http://
www40.statcan.ca/l01/cst01/lfsso5e.htm?sdi=swift%20current.

– 2009c. *Prince Albert National Park, Saskatchewan* (table). *2006 Community Profiles.* 2006 Census. Statistics Canada Catalogue no. 92-591-
XWE. Ottawa. http://www12.statcan.ca/Census-recensement/2006/
dp-pd/prof/92-591/details/Page.cfm?Lang=E&Geo1=CSD&Code1=
4716053&Geo2=PR&Code2=47&Data=Count&SearchText=
waskesiu&SearchType=Begins&SearchPR=47&B1=All&Custom=.

– 2009d. *Saskatoon Saskatchewan* (table). *2006 Community Profiles.*
2006 Census. Statistics Canada Catalogue no. 92-591-XWE. Ottawa.
(http://www12.statcan.ca/Census-recensement/2006/dp-pd/prof/92-591/
details/page.cfm?Lang=E&Geo1=CMA&Code1=725__&Geo2=PR&
Code2=47&Data=Count&SearchText=Saskatoon&SearchType=Begins
&SearchPR=01&B1=All&GeoLevel=&GeoCode=725.

– 2009e. *Swift Current, Saskatchewan* (table). *2006 Community Profiles.*
2006 Census. Statistics Canada Catalogue no. 92-591-XWE. Ottawa.

Released 13 March 2007. http://www12.statcan.ca/english/Census06/data/profiles/community/Index.cfm?Lang=E

– Western Economic Diversification. 2004. *Government of Canada Commits $99,000 to Action Swift Current Branding Strategy.* May. http://www.wd.gc.ca/mediacentre/2004/may07-01a_e.asp.

– 2005a. *Government of Canada Invests Over $216,000 in Three Saskatchewan Economic Development Initiatives.* June. http://www.wd.gc.ca/mediacentre/2005/june03-01a_e.asp.

– 2005b. *Saskatoon Urban Development Agreement.* 13 May. http://www.wd.gc.ca/eng/77_3005.asp.

– 2006a. *Canada Celebrates Saskatchewan-Funding Allocation by Community,* May. http://www.wd.gc.ca/centennials/ccs_grantamounts4_e.asp.

– 2006b. *Canada Celebrates Saskatchewan Invests in Four Capital City Legacy Projects.* March. http://www.wd.gc.ca/eng/82_4266.asp.

Government of Saskatchewan. News release. 2002. "Tourism Web Sites Receive Funding." 13 May. http://www.gov.sk.ca/news?newsId=43f00f06-a583-4d40-b95a-6e8412ce416d.

– 2004. "Saskatoon's River Landing Project to Receive $29.3 Million." December. http://www.gov.sk.ca/news?newsId=0816b873-f4e0-4dca-9b7a-0483c63a0f0c\.

– 2007. "Province Investing $16.1 Million in Prince Albert Transportation Projects." August. http://www.gov.sk.ca/news?newsId=061402a3-55f8-4252-9a4c-fd2edf940d0b.

– Enterprise Saskatchewan. 2009. *Community Profiles: Swift Current.* http://www.saskbiz.ca/communityprofiles/CommunityProfile.Asp?CommunityID=11.

– Saskatchewan Archives Board. 2005. "Saskatchewan Settlement Experience: The Barr Colonists." http://www.sasksettlement.com/display.php?cat=Settlement%20Patterns&subcat=Barr%20Colonists.

– Saskatchewan Bureau of Statistics. 2006. *Humboldt.* http://www.stats.gov.sk.ca/ped/humboldt.pdf.

– Tourism Saskatchewan. 2005. *Saskatchewan 2005 Vacation Guide.* Regina: Tourism Saskatchewan.

Klein, Gerry. 2004. "Synchrotron: Canadian Light Source 70 years in the making." *The StarPhoenix* (Saskatoon), 20 October. http://www.cns-snc.ca/history/Canadian_Light_Source.html.

Kiunga, Jessica. 2007. "Waskesiu folds on Municipality Plans" in *The Prince Albert Daily Herald,* 8 October. http://www.paherald.sk.ca/index.cfm?sid=52771&sc=4.

Li, Peter. 2009. "People of the land: population changes in Saskatchewan." In *Perspectives of Saskatchewan*, edited by Jene Porter, 1–12. Winnipeg: University of Manitoba Press.

Missinipi Broadcasting Corporation. 2009. "Millions Committed for Work at Batoche, Waskesiu." 17 April. http://www.mbcradio.com/index. php/news-archives/83–2009/7015-millions-committed-for-work-at-batoche-waskesiu-.

O'Brien, Jeff, Ruth Millar, and William P. Delainey. 2006. *Saskatoon: A History in Photographs*. Regina: Coteau Books.

Pal, Leslie A. 1992. *Public Policy Analysis: An Introduction*. Scarborough: Nelson Canada.

Peterson, P. E. 1981. *City Limits*. Chicago: University of Chicago Press.

Saskatoon Regional Economic Development Authority. 2007. *Saskatoon Demographics*. January. http://www.sreda.com/resources/pdfs/SREDA_Saskatoon_Demographics_Jan-07.pdf.

– 2009. *City of Saskatoon*. http://www.sreda.com/en/pages/238/city_of_saskatoon.html.

– Saskatoon Sports Tourism. 2009. *About Saskatoon Sports Tourism*. http://www.saskatoonsportstourism.ca/about_us.php.

Schulz, Sandi. 2009. Personal correspondence with author. 8 December.

Smith, Graeme. 2003. "Glance in mirror shocks Prairie city." *The Globe and Mail*, 12 December, A8.

Stabler, Jack, and Rose Olfert. 2009. "One Hundred Years of Evolution in the Rural Economy." In *Perspectives of Saskatchewan*, edited by Jene Porter, 126–47. Winnipeg: University of Manitoba Press.

The Marketing Den/Fast Consulting. 2001. *Marketing Saskatoon: Strategic Plan, Final Report*. December. http://www.saskatoonshines.ca/downloads/strategic_plan.pdf.

Thode, Stephen F., and James M. Masulka. 1998. "Place-Based Marketing Strategies, Brand Equity and Vineyard Valuation." *Journal of Product and Brand Management* 7, no. 5: 379–99.

Tourism Saskatoon. 2007. *Cultural, Tourism and Marketing Strategy*. March. http://www.tourismsaskatoon.com/files/106.pdf.

Tourism Swift Current. 2007. *Swift Current History*. http://www.tourismswiftcurrent.ca/history/index.php.

Waiser, Bill. 2005. *Saskatchewan: A New History*. Calgary: Fifth House Ltd.

Waskesiu Community Council. 2007a. "Minutes, Waskesiu Community Council Annual General Meeting, 5 August 2007, PANP." Waskesiu: Waskesiu Community Council, http://www.waskesiu.org/wcc.shtml.

– 2007b. Main page. http://www.waskesiu.org/.
– 2008. "Minutes, Waskesiu Community Council Public Meeting, 9 January 2008." Waskesiu: Waskesiu Community Council. http://www.waskesiu.org/wcc.shtml.
– 2009a. "Minutes, Waskesiu Community Council Annual General Meeting, 2 August 2009, PANP." Waskesiu: Waskesiu Community Council. http://www.waskesiu.org/wcc.shtml.
– 2009b. *The Waskesiu Community Memorandum of Understanding: Statement of Guiding Principles, May 17th, 2009 Update.* http://www.waskesiu.org/wcc.shtml.
– 2009c. *Waskesiu Community Council Background.* http://www.waskesiu.org/wcc_background.shtml.
Whitson, David. 2004. "Bringing the World to Canada: 'The Periphery of the Centre.'" *Third World Quarterly* 25, no. 7: 1215–32.

6

Conclusion

ROBERT YOUNG

Municipal leaders in Canada are increasingly conscious of the images that people hold of their cities, towns, and villages. They are concerned about how their place is perceived by both outsiders and citizens. Why is this so? Well, social scientists often invest globalization with a causal force far more sweeping than is reasonable, but in this case it seems appropriate. New trade arrangements have caused economic restructuring in municipalities: their economic nature has changed and the economy now presents new threats and opportunities. Information technology and the prevalence of the Internet have made it possible for municipalities, even relatively small ones, to project themselves on a grand scale. Personal mobility and inexpensive travel have increased the importance of the tourism industry, and municipalities want to profit from their attractions. There is also competition for immigrants, especially skilled ones, and most municipal governments in Canada have become aware of the benefits that new inhabitants can bring. Finally, there is a keen desire to attract capital investment in a world where firms in many industries have become more mobile than they were.

These are the deep forces influencing governmental policy at all levels and in all fields. In this book, we are concerned with the more proximate factors that explain how the images of municipalities are constructed. We consider the image as a public policy. We focus on who creates it, and we seek to explain its substance and deployment. In doing this, we stress two particular factors, though many other factors such as resources, personalities, and historical trajectories are also important. The first factor is intergovernmental relations. How do provincial governments and the federal government interact with municipal authorities to help construct and propagate the images that municipalities create? The second factor consists of the social forces involved in image-building. What organized interests or social milieux influence the content and projection of municipal images?

As was mentioned in the preface, the research presented here is part of a larger project, which has investigated multilevel governance and public policy in Canadian municipalities. The project is concerned with six policy fields, of which image-building is one. Each field has been studied in three or four provinces, with researchers examining four municipalities in each province. As well, in Canada's major cities, four of the six fields were also studied, with image-building being explored in Calgary, Halifax, Montreal, Saint John, St John's, Toronto, and Vancouver.[1] In this concluding chapter, I will draw on some of the material from the work on major cities in the other provinces, especially when dealing with questions about municipal size and the coherence of images.

The research reported in this book is extremely thorough. The studies use government and other documents, newspaper coverage, advertisements, and websites. Most of all, we rely on interviews. In all, 114 interviews were conducted with politicians, officials, and members of organizations with an interest in the image of their municipality. The authors present comprehensive views of image-building and provide many intriguing results. It should be noted, though, that we cannot claim the results are representative of all Canadian municipalities. The authors work in depth, but the book covers only twelve municipalities. As well, PEI is a most unusual province, as Richards, Gushue, and Bulger make clear; in many ways the provincial government is like a small metropolitan authority, policy-making is very personal, and tourism is disproportionately significant in the provincial economy (which is one reason this policy field was chosen for it). On the other hand, it seems likely that many of the patterns found in our studies are also present in similar places in British Columbia, Ontario, and other provinces.

Now we need to make some sense of our findings. So here I will provide brief summaries of the chapters, followed by an assessment of some of the patterns made evident through comparative analysis. The next section proceeds to more general considerations about intergovernmental relations and social forces in municipal image-building. Finally, I will evaluate the policies and assess avenues for improving the process of image-building in Canadian municipalities.

Jean Harvey provided a very useful introduction, including the definition of image-building that guided these studies. He situated the book as a new contribution that concentrates on smaller municipalities, and this is worth re-stating:

It is important to point out that smaller cities and towns, as well as rural municipalities, are also involved in a variety of place promotion strategies, branding their attributes not only to the regional, national, or global levels, but also to their own citizens or prospective new citizens.

Harvey depicts the current context as one marked by economic transformation, scarce municipal resources, and globalization, features that compel action and that offer opportunities as well as daunting challenges. One problem for many small places in Canada is demographic decline, which certainly is a preoccupation in Manitoba and Saskatchewan. Harvey argues that image-building is vitally important because it bears on many municipal objectives and affects many other policy fields in which municipalities are active. He also asserts that image-building is a particularly complex field. Not only does it involve many departments and agencies, but it also entails intergovernmental relations (where municipalities tend to be at a disadvantage because their resources are so scarce).

Adding to the complexities are social forces. Business in particular has an interest in the policy because of its stakes in tourism and economic growth. Also potentially interested are a host of community organizations representing people engaged in heritage, sports, the environment, culture, and so on. Harvey also lays out our questions concerning how intergovernmental relations and social forces affect image-building policy. These guided the research in the chapters exploring municipal image-building.

Caroline Andrew's discussion of federal policies about image-building deals first with the images propagated by the central government. For the most part, these still feature rural and remote images – Canada's wilderness rather than the lively fabric of its urban areas. With the partial exception of multiculturalism, even images of Canada's cities tend to adopt a "green" slant. Turning to other policies, Andrew shows that Ottawa does pay attention to municipalities, and especially to smaller communities. For instance, funding for sports events is spread very widely, and the federal government's substantial support for culture shows some bias toward small and medium-sized municipalities. Andrew shows how the federal government facilitates image-building (and the realization of images) by funding infrastructure and providing cultural grants. But it does not affect the content of municipal images except indirectly, by projecting an image, largely of the Canadian wilderness, which provincial and municipal efforts may have to complement or overcome.

Image-building in Manitoba, as described by John Lehr and Karla Zubrycki, builds on a long history of boosterism. They note that a "place identity" must be distinctive to attract attention while being carefully targeted at a specific audience or market. Yet they isolate an important feature common to municipal image-building, whatever the precise content of the images: all markets "are generally responsive to an overarching sense of vitality and a 'can-do' attitude." This chapter focuses on efforts to boost tourism, economic development, and immigration, and the researchers study four municipalities ranging from tiny, rural Stuartburn to Winnipeg, the metropolis of the province (and at one time of the entire prairies). The diversity is fascinating. In Stuartburn there are very scant resources and little agreement on how to brand the municipality. In the case of Swan River, the regional municipalities co-operate by off-loading the function to a quasi-autonomous development agency. In Winkler, strong German and Mennonite traditions underlie an image that has successfully attracted immigrants. Finally, in Winnipeg, image-building is essentially marginal, except for those officials and social forces active in the tourism sector. The Winnipeg case also leads to reflections about how much exposure and prominence is gained through sporting events, and especially through professional sport.

Prince Edward Island is an unusual setting. It is very small in size, and most parts of the province are easily accessible. The population is small and stable, and much information is widely shared. The provincial government is very dominant, and tourism is one of the most important sectors in the Island economy. The chapter on PEI covers Charlottetown, the Resort Municipality (formerly dominated by and still associated with the town of Cavendish), Wellington, and St Peter's Bay in descending order by population. These municipalities are active in promoting their attractions, but the dominant image is the provincial one, which tends to favour certain municipalities – Charlottetown and those areas around the beaches of the Resort Municipality that contain the legacy of Anne of Green Gables. Other municipalities aim to attract tourists who have come for these dominant features. Wellington (ironically Acadian, and an early re-brander from its original name, Quagmire) has to fit its Acadian character into the tropes of tradition and ruralism, for example. Richards, Gushue, and Bulger also emphasize the problem of conflicting images, such as the clash between promoting golf, which is fertilizer and water intensive, and propagating the image of a green, ecologically sound destination.

Saskatchewan, as described by de Clercy and Ferguson, has a "rich tradition of enthusiastic self-promotion." Governments and citizens possess a historic and very strong preoccupation with retaining residents and maintaining the place as a going concern. The authors examine branding, events planning, and economic development in the very different municipalities of Waskesiu, Humboldt, Swift Current, and Saskatoon. They find few formal mechanisms of intergovernmental co-operation in the image-building field, and maintain that personal relationships are important for coordinated activities. As well, many initiatives are undertaken by policy entrepreneurs, so policy is intermittent and not systematically planned. Generally, image-building is under the control of a small group, and these individuals often have multiple roles – for example, as a councillor and a leader of the chamber of commerce. Finally, local business interests generally predominate in municipal image-building, a conclusion that applies beyond the borders of the province of Saskatchewan.

COMPARATIVE CONSIDERATIONS

The chapters collected here report unusually thorough research on a comparatively large number of cases. What general patterns emerge from these studies? What conclusions can be reached about policy-making in the field of municipal image-building? We begin with some observations about provincial and municipal activism, and then consider the effect of municipal size, the political dynamics involving leadership and opposition, and the links between municipal images and both economic development and community solidarity.

The involvement of provincial governments in image-building depends on how much it can contribute to realizing core provincial goals. In PEI, tourism is so important that the provincial government is highly active and advertises heavily. It is also systematic and strategic, assessing the changing nature of its target audiences and adjusting the image appropriately, as in the shift from family beach experiences to "The Gentle Island," with leisurely ruralism and relaxing pursuits like golf. In other provinces, tourism may be significant but different considerations predominate. The governments of Manitoba and Saskatchewan are preoccupied with demographics; each aims to attract immigrants and to retain citizens. The same motives are reflected in the campaigns of Winkler to recruit new inhabitants, and of Saskatoon and Winnipeg to build citizens' civic enjoyment through festivals, big events, and installations like the Forks. But the provincial governments do not involve themselves in any formal way in the image-building efforts of municipalities. They neither assist them nor constrain them. By the same token, there is little consultation with the municipalities about provincial campaigns, even in PEI. So municipalities have a great deal of autonomy in image-building, even though they must sometimes frame their own efforts within the dominant provincial and Canadian images.

The activism of municipalities varies similarly with the importance accorded to luring tourists, enticing investment, and attracting and retaining people. This is very strong in smaller, peripheral places facing economic and population decline, but activism also varies with the resources available. The rural municipality of Stuartburn strained to install uniform signage in the villages. Places like Swan River and Winkler are not so constrained, and cities like Saskatoon and Winnipeg are capable of much, much more.

Yet the will to engage in image-building is remarkably strong. As is discussed below, there is very little opposition to municipal action in this field. The great majority of municipalities examined here are either active in image-building or feel the need to be so, and this is true even of the smallest. Indeed, Lehr and Zubrycki suggest that "ironically, the effort put into it, and certainly their perception of the need for the formulation of an effective image-building policy, seemed to be inversely proportional to the municipality's size." It is tempting to end the matter with such a concise proposition, but the effects of size are more complex than this and deserve some extended exploration.

It is sometimes held that smaller municipalities are more homogeneous than larger ones, but this is not necessarily the case. Moncton, for example, is a relatively small city, but it has a clear ethnic divide between Acadians and anglophones, one that has been sharp and difficult to manage in the past. Little Stuartburn is divided between those wanting intensive hog production and those who want to emphasize the natural prairie. In Waskesiu there is a division between the ecologically minded and those in the business of tourism. So, small municipalities are not necessarily very homogenous. On the other hand, larger municipalities are inevitably heterogeneous. This can make it difficult to create a stable image, or to avoid conflicting images, or, in the extreme, to generate any image at all. There are examples of this in the research reported here, as well as the research on the big Canadian cities.

Winnipeg has a most unfavourable image. It is cold, prone to floods, and the municipality sprays chemicals against mosquitoes for a good portion of the snowless months. But building and projecting a more favourable image is not a priority, at least under recent administrations. Those concerned with emphasizing the city's great architectural heritage make little headway, while the chamber of commerce cannot manage to push manufacturing and research and development to prominence. There is no consensus on an image, and no clear image is strongly and consistently projected.

Calgary is a city that has been marked by tremendous growth. Over the 1986–2006 period, the population increased by 55 per cent and the city has become a very wealthy place. Historically, the city's image was tied to the western frontier, epitomized in the Calgary Stampede. Some local forces have aimed to supersede this by portraying the place as a world-class city and branding it as "Renaissance Calgary." This is resisted by others, and a major recent initiative is the Stampede Park Western Legacy Project, to which the provincial and federal governments have each committed at least $15 million, and which clearly builds on the past. Still, the tension with the alternative is evident as the project is also billed in part as "A Gathering Place for Calgary and the World." Coherence and clarity are lacking.

St John's is a rather similar case. A quasi-autonomous organization called Destination St John's does tourism promotion, while the Economic Development Division of the municipality markets the city insofar as business and technology are concerned. So on the one hand, the city is promoted as a Cultural Capital (and it was designated as such in 2006 by the federal government, resulting in substantial cultural subsidies) where festivals and the arts are celebrated and publicized. On the other hand, St John's is also the "City of Ocean Excellence," focusing notably on offshore energy and technology, and biological technology based on the oil industry and the fisheries. In this case the tourism and business markets are probably segmented enough that the bifurcation is not dysfunctional, but there is no single image for the city.

Toronto's image is weak, in part because interests are divided, but mainly because of administrative incoherence and political inattention. Toronto receives on the order of 20 million tourists a year, and promoting this industry was traditionally done by Tourism Toronto, a public-private partnership dominated by hotel and convention interests. The city bureaucracy also had a special events unit. In 2003, consultants recommended that a representative tourism advisory committee draw up a comprehensive tourism action plan, and that the city collect a destination marketing fee (a tax on hotel rooms) of 3 per cent. After the SARS crisis devastated tourism, the fee was implemented and it went to Tourism Toronto. In 2005, this agency introduced the "Toronto Unlimited" brand, which failed. The city sought to access the destination marketing fee, and relations with Tourism Toronto worsened. Another review was done in 2008, and again there was a recommendation to establish a trans-sectoral advisory committee (which had never been done). There has been substantial in-fighting at City Hall within the Economic Development, Culture, and Tourism Department between the tourism division and the special events unit. While there have been some successes in this field, there is still no co-coordinated, long-term policy, and co-operation with the provincial and federal governments has been difficult to attain.

Montreal is another case of a large city that has not managed to brand itself successfully. Its size and structure prevent the emergence of a coherent image-building strategy. Government structures in the city and the metropolitan region are exceedingly complex. Boroughs in the city divide Montreal internally, while the city government must work within the Montreal Metropolitan Community, which includes many municipalities, notably the big suburbs of Laval and Longueuil. In 2006, there was a consensus that branding was essential. But was the image to be that of a technological centre, a cultural metropolis, a site of creativity and festivals, a new media hub, or something else? Consensus has not been reached. As Bherer and Hamel put it in their study, "no single actor is currently strong enough to convince the others to adhere to a particular vision. The result is, if not a perpetual state of confrontation, at least a series of parallel endeavours with no sign of convergence in the medium term."

So image-building is difficult to accomplish in larger cities. There, images are likely to conflict, and it may be much easier for smaller places to reach understandings about their essential character. Administrative incoherence and political stasis are more likely to occur in larger centres, and when other municipalities are involved, as in a metropolitan area, no actor may be capable of forging a consensus. Smaller municipalities may experience some of these problems, but the odds of success are higher.

The studies collected here also show that successful image-building often depends on leadership. This can be political, supplied by mayors and councillors, as was true in Stuartburn, St Peter's Bay, and Swift Current. More generally, the drive is supplied through quasi-autonomous agencies, even in smaller places. In the Swan River Valley, the Swan Valley Enterprise Centre (SVEC) takes on the image-building function, along with general economic development activity. The Development Corporation in Winkler helps project the town's brand, along with the council and the chamber of commerce. St Peter's Bay established a Development Corporation to make plans in relation to the new national park. Action Swift Current hired image consultants, while Action Humboldt leads in that municipality. Tourism Saskatoon produced the "Saskatoon Shines" slogan. Where such institutions are established, the image-building function has an enduring champion. This is important because image-building is a diffuse activity that would involve many normal departments of a municipal government. The function can become marginalized when a relatively small unit is lodged in bureaucracies that are preoccupied with delivering goods and services within the municipality.

The use of such agencies highlights the strong link that is perceived in municipalities between image-building and economic development. Economic development organizations often take on the function, and sometimes it is done by units that are lodged in the economic development branches of municipal bureaucracies. Current image-building activity continues a long tradition of boosterism in municipal government in Canada. Attracting tourists, investment, and immigrants are all seen as creating growth and jobs and wealth. Hence, audiences are carefully targeted. Winkler aims for German speakers. In the Swan River Valley, SVEC generates an image of an environmentally wholesome and socially welcoming place –

"A Community of Communities." SVEC targets ecologically minded European immigrants and has even participated in an immigration trade fair in the United Kingdom.

Another case where image and growth are thought to be closely linked is Saint John, New Brunswick. This is a city that has been in a long economic decline. It is widely regarded, with some justification, as a firmly blue-collar smokestack city marked by heavy pollution and considerable poverty. The image is very negative. Saint John is largely controlled by a business-dominated growth coalition centred in the Board of Trade, which is determined to reverse economic decline. The city's 2005 growth strategy also aimed to refurbish its image. The old "Loyalist Man" figure, who had long represented the city and its colonial founding, was jettisoned and replaced with a rather generic explorer figure, who was accompanied by the slogan, "Explore Our Past, Discover Your Future." There was some emphasis on tourism as an economic engine, and there were attractive improvements made to the waterfront (as long as refurbishment did not interfere with the serious business of the port), but the main thrust was to turn around perceptions of the city and to propagate that "sense of vitality and a 'can do' attitude."

A final case of pure marketing (with the expectation that growth in the form of tourists, capital, and immigrants inevitably will follow) is presented by Vancouver. This city's image is shifting from the metropole of a staples-producing economy to a "transnational metropolis" that is also an "Asia-Pacific City." Vancouver has used mega-events to project its character and beauty onto the world stage. The first was the 1986 International Exposition, which produced a great deal of international exposure (helped by $100 million in marketing), and which powered the development of a convention centre, downtown hotels, and the North False Creek area. The 2010 Winter Olympics was even bigger, with the core theme of "sustainable development," one befitting a metropolis nestled in a sort of ecotopia. There were many long-term tangible benefits, including the Canada Line link to the airport, and the development of South East False Creek for the Olympic Village. Olympics are high-risk events, but the success at Vancouver and Whistler might produce long-term economic growth, even though the track record of mega-events doing so is mixed.

Our chapters show how image-building is done in order to attract things – tourists, capital, and immigrants – to the municipality from the external environment. But image-building also has internal effects. It has "domestic" purposes. Images, events like festivals and celebrations, and facilities can promote a sense of community, solidarity, inclusion, and pride among the current citizenry. They represent citizens to themselves (Nelles 1999). This is particularly stressed in the treatment of Saskatoon by de Clercy and Ferguson, but leaders of the other municipalities studied here are clearly aware of how image-building activities can be functional for their communities, and for themselves. Writing recently about big cities, Eleonora Pasotti (2010) explored how successful branding campaigns can reinforce collectivism and a sense of common citizenship. This can generate support for innovative policies and a greater supply of public goods; at the same time, it can increase the political capital of leaders. The internal benefits that image-building can entail for the leadership of municipalities is one reason why de Clercy and Ferguson conclude that there is much potential for municipal governments to become even more active in this field.

This brings us to the final interesting characteristic of policymaking in this field that comparative analysis reveals. Simply enough, there is little opposition to municipal governments and other actors engaging in image-building. There may be opposition to the construction and projection of particular images, as in Stuartburn when farmers fearing land-use restrictions were resistant to celebrating the Western Prairie Fringed Orchid, and when those in Waskesiu aiming to promote summer recreational activities were opposed by ecologists invoking the mantle of Grey Owl. Such conflicts may lead to deadlock in the short term, and little activity. As well, there is often disappointment when the themes favoured by groups and individuals lose out to others, failing to be reflected in the chosen image, as was seen when images of the retirement mecca, built heritage, and Acadian culture were not seized upon by Swan River, Winnipeg, and PEI respectively. There can be fierce opposition to particular brands and slogans, and outright failure. This was not observed in the cases analyzed here, but "Technically Beautiful" flopped in Ottawa, "Toronto Unlimited" was swiftly dropped in 2005, and the city of London's "All Mixed Up" lasted a very short time indeed.

Despite such conflicts, disappointments, and failures, though, there still seems to be little opposition to municipal spending on the function of image-building. Most citizens and organized groups agree that image-building is worthwhile. This was noted by de Clercy and

Ferguson, and, to use Lehr and Zubrycki's terms, this activity is seen as "non-ideological." In other words, projecting an image is very widely supported. This is a feature of this policy field that is most unusual. Normally, there is some opposition to initiatives – a green bin program, road widening, more soccer fields – but this does not seem to be the case with image-building efforts. This is remarkable because resources at the municipal level are very scarce; yet image-building, ostensibly always in pursuit of growth, is seen as a good investment. It is also remarkable because, as we shall see shortly, it is very difficult to evaluate the effectiveness of image-building efforts.

GENERAL CONSIDERATIONS

Comparative research can reveal generalizations, such as those discussed just above. This tells us a lot about the policy field and how image-building works in Canadian municipalities. But this research can also illuminate larger questions that are of interest to people who are concerned with policy-making in general. Our research was designed to address matters of broad concern to scholars, policy-makers, and citizens. These questions were laid out in Jean Harvey's introduction. They have also been discussed in other works in the larger project (Young and Leuprecht 2006; Lazar and Leuprecht 2007; Sancton and Young 2009; Tolley and Young 2011; Peters 2011).

The first questions concern intergovernmental relations (IGR), and how these contribute to policy formation. To start with, there is the issue of municipal-federal relations. Until recently, this was a neglected aspect of IGR, but it has come to receive much more attention. In part, this is because municipalities in most provinces have been delegated an expanded range of powers (Garcea and LeSage 2005). Rather than having their activities restricted by provincial legislation to a set of enumerated areas, often narrowly defined, many provinces have conferred broader power in more general functional areas. So municipalities can be more active, and this is more likely to bring them into contact with the federal government. In most provinces, municipal interaction with the federal government is not closely supervised. Even in Quebec, widely regarded as an outlier, there is substantial contact. Quebec law decrees that all contracts signed between municipal corporations and the federal government must be approved by the provincial authorities, but this does not prohibit contact and consultation. In most provinces, supervision by provincial governments of municipal dealings with the federal government is quite weak. At first blush, the chapters collected here show little contact between municipalities and the federal government, but this is not the case. There are many forms of influence and co-operation. Most obviously, the government of Canada has extensive advertising campaigns. Municipal governments must be conscious of the overall image constructed of the country, which, as Caroline Andrew notes, is primarily about the outdoors and the environment rather than urban life. However, the federal campaigns are rather vague and widely focused, so it is not too difficult for most communities, especially smaller ones, to build images congruent with that of "Canada." Most provincial campaigns pose greater problems for municipalities.

Second, there are many federal programs that municipalities can access for image-building purposes. Canadian Heritage supports museums, heritage initiatives, and many cultural programs. For example, there is the Cultural Capitals program, under which funding is allocated for municipalities so designated. One place per year is chosen in each of three population categories: less than 50,000, 50,000–125,000, and over 125,000, with funding covering up to 75 per cent of the costs of projects to maxima of $500,000, $750,000, and $2 million. In 2006, for example, St John's was designated as a Cultural Capital, and $500,000 flowed in, largely to support festivals and cultural events. Another example is a program that supports innovation in sustainable communities: in Swan River, this helped fund SVEC's activities.

There is also funding of various kinds for sport, which is extremely important for image-building. Professional sport is most effective, probably, because television coverage provides continuous exposure in the other cities in the league. It also builds much loyalty and civic pride, as is shown when teams win championships, and also by the deep regret felt when franchises are lost (as in the case of NHL teams in Winnipeg and Quebec City). But other sports events also highlight municipalities. The Canada Summer and Winter Games traditionally are awarded to small and medium-sized cities, with substantial federal funding. International events receive heavier support. There are also international single-sport events. Saskatoon has hosted these in soccer, rugby, hockey, and figure skating, all providing wide exposure for the city and all receiving federal government support. Canadian cities have also hosted the ultimate mega-event, the Olympics, in 1988 and 2010. These operations require very intense intergovernmental co-operation. This is absolutely essential in mounting a successful bid, and planning and implementation require all governments and other stakeholders, such as Aboriginal communities, to collaborate intensely. In the Vancouver case, intergovernmental coordination was cemented in VANOC, the Olympic organizing committee, which also included stakeholders. The very large federal government commitment to the games helped produce enormous worldwide exposure, as well as enduring legacy developments for the city and its partner municipalities.

The federal government also helps municipal image-building through some special programs. In Winnipeg and Saskatoon, tripartite Urban Development Agreements have been signed. These have supported the Forks development in Winnipeg, along with some downtown revitalization; in Saskatoon, there was substantial assistance for the River Landing Project. The federal government is also in the business of celebration. The Confederation Centre of the Arts is central, literally and figuratively, to Charlottetown. There was federal funding for this as a 1967 Centennial project. Similarly, Swift Current received federal monies from the "Canada Celebrates Saskatchewan" initiative that marked the province's one hundredth anniversary.

Other federal agencies are involved in municipal image-building efforts. The Atlantic Canada Opportunities Agency (ACOA) has provided considerable support for tourism planning throughout the region, and it has helped build infrastructure, like the cruise ship facilities in Charlottetown. It has also extended financial support for tourism businesses. The comparable agency in the west, Western Economic Diversification Canada (WED), was found by de Clercy and Ferguson to be a "valuable partner" in all four communities they studied. In Swift Current, WED provided $99,000 for the city's branding strategy and another $600,000 for sectoral planning for its core industries. Parks Canada is another agency that has been present in municipal image-building policy, because national parks are tourist magnets. This was true in Waskesiu, the Resort Municipality, St Peter's Bay, and even Stuartburn, where Parks Canada contemplated an initiative to create a historic site marking Ukrainian settlement.

One other set of federal programs deserves mention. Since 1993, the federal government has operated a wide array of infrastructure programs, administered by Infrastructure Canada. These have included the Infrastructure Canada Program, the Public Transit Fund, the Municipal Rural Infrastructure Fund, the Canada Strategic Infrastructure Fund, the Border Infrastructure Fund, the Building Canada Fund, the Public-Private Partnership Fund, the Gateways and Border Crossing Fund, and the First Nations Infrastructure Fund, not to mention the very large Economic Action Plan (EAP) introduced in 2009 by Stephen Harper's Conservative government to deliver stimulus spending in the face of the 2008–09 recession. The EAP provided funding for infrastructure, and also for industries and communities, including money for tourism, small business, and culture. It is impossible to quantify the sums involved in all of these programs, because of double-reporting and the way that money was rolled from expiring programs into new ones, but Ottawa has provided billions of dollars in such expenditures since 1993. Generally, the programs involve equal cost-sharing between the federal, provincial, and municipal governments. Municipalities propose projects and the "senior" governments make the real decisions. Many transfers are for streets, bridges, and public transit, but other expenditures are for recreation facilities, waterfront improvement, sewage treatment plants, and other infrastructure. All of this not only improves municipal infrastructure but can also brighten municipal images.

Such spending raises an important point: the connection between image and reality. To be effective in the long run externally, and more immediately with the local population, municipalities must actually deliver on their image. They need to produce the "brand reality." As Hankinson (2009, 108) puts it, "delivering brand reality was identified with the quality of the destination's buildings, infrastructure, and support services, as well as the collection of retail, leisure, and special interest services it offered. Delivering this went beyond the creation and communication of place images." In the Canadian context, there is a clear intergovernmental division of labour. The municipalities create their images, while the federal (and provincial) government helps to provide the reality, through funding for infrastructure, sports and recreation facilities, and cultural events. There is a loose coupling between the municipal and federal governments. Ottawa does not interfere in the images themselves, but it does help produce the reality – the features and facilities and events expected by those who consume the municipal images.

Another IGR issue is how the provinces mediate the municipal-federal relationship. And what role do provincial governments themselves play in municipal image-building? The answer to both questions is much the same: provincial governments are remarkably non-interventionist in this field. First, provincial governments interfere very little in municipal-federal relations. They are involved co-operatively in the Urban Development Agreements and the infrastructure programs, and they certainly have more influence in choosing projects than do the municipalities. But there are no programs about municipal images themselves, no supervision, and no coordination. There is no interference: municipalities can define and project themselves as they will (though they are dependent on their own limited resources). The only real effect of provincial policies occurs when provincial governments build images that are not compatible with the desired image of a municipality. Waskesiu, for example, wants to advertise with depictions of the hills and lakes of near-northern Saskatchewan, but the provincial images project flat wheat fields. PEI's main campaigns do not square well with the distinctive Acadian culture that municipalities like Wellington want to advertise. But apart from non-congruence in the images projected, there is remarkably little provincial impact on municipal image-building in Canada. It is hard to think of another policy field where the hand of the province rests so lightly on its municipal "creatures."

Given the many relationships in the IGR context, it is noteworthy that there are few, if any, formal federal-municipal or provincial-municipal mechanisms or institutions in the image-building field. A small number of federal programs are accessed intermittently, but most interaction involves special initiatives. As de Clercy and Ferguson note, institutionalization is weak, and there is instead a reliance on particular municipal leaders and on informal, personal connections to develop co-operation and new initiatives. In this context, politicians play an important role. In other policy fields, much policy development rests with permanent officials, but in image-building there is little room for bureaucratic initiatives. Instead, some politicians come to realize how vital images are to the municipality's economic development, and they champion the effort, seeking support from other levels of government where possible. The reeve of the rural municipality of Swan River provides one example, and others are scattered throughout the studies reported in this volume. The political impetus depends to some degree on the general orientation of elected representatives toward the role of local governments. When they favour a "minimalist" approach that emphasizes municipalities as service providers, then activism is less. Where they have a "comprehensive" orientation and regard municipal governments as responsible for defining the collective goals of the citizenry and proceeding to achieve them, political activism is greater, and so are intergovernmental efforts.

A final issue about intergovernmental relations concerns horizontal co-operation. In this field, is there collaboration between municipalities? Do vertical relations induce horizontal co-operation, as suggested by Agranoff and McGuire (2003)? The short answer is no. Municipal image-building does not lend itself to horizontal collaboration. The only instance in our studies was the Swan River Valley where there was coordination of branding through the Swan Valley Enterprise Centre. In this case, most municipalities were not heavily involved, at least at the political level, as a lot of autonomy had been delegated to svec. In other cases, image-building is generally seen as a competitive policy area. Municipalities are competing for tourists, investment, and people, and though there could be some gains from regional co-operation, this does not appear to be forthcoming. There is even, at times, a conflictual attitude, such as exists between Winkler and Morden. Where there is coordination, as in pei, it is because the provincial government's overall policy involves demarcating tourist regions and applying a strong brand to them, so the various municipalities are tossed into the same boat. Still, it should be noted that in pei, the Acadian communities united to pressure the province to promote "Evangeline country," largely because as an ethnic community they had come together to fight other battles for the preservation of their culture. In normal circumstances, though, image-building is seen as a policy field in which gains for some municipalities represent losses for others.

Our second major set of general questions concerns the role of social forces in creating image-building policy. By "social forces" we mean local organizations and associations of all kinds and the interests that they represent. So, what groups are involved in this field? When groups are interested, at what stage of the policy-making process are they involved? How much influence do they have in municipal image-building?

The perennial question in the study of social forces and municipal government is about the role of business. Do business interests dominate in policy formation? The answer is often mixed, or complex – but not in this policy field. Our studies show that local business interests control the generation and projection of municipal images. This is true in every municipality studied. There are only a couple of minor exceptions: in Winkler, there is some effective resistance among the Mennonite community to aspects of industrial development, and in Winnipeg even the chamber of commerce is among the groups that are "being largely ignored" through the city's lack of activity in image-building. Apart from this, business representatives are thoroughly in control of the field. Moreover, business dominates from the beginning. Its representatives typically are the ones who perceive problems and opportunities with existing images, define alternatives, make choices about the municipal image, and even implement the policy. When other interests are involved, it is much later in the process and for consultation only, as happened in Saskatoon and Swan River. This does not mean that other social forces are completely neglected. They can be taken into account through other channels. As was described in the Saskatchewan chapter in particular, there is often overlapping membership: business people are also members of other organized interests like churches, recreation groups, environmental groups, and charitable associations of various kinds. This is a common characteristic of leadership in smaller communities, and it was noted in the Resort Municipality in PEI. So business people reflect in part their other associational involvements. But business interests are at the fore. And, as our researchers point out, decisions about image-building are generally taken by a relatively small group.

Another noteworthy feature of decision-making about municipal images is that the function is often entrusted to a quasi-autonomous agency: SVEC in the Swan River Valley, Action Swift Current, the Capital Commission of PEI, the St Peter's Area Development Corporation, Destination Winnipeg, and so on.[2] These organizations have boards that are composed of representatives of local business, often including a couple of public sector officials or politicians (sometimes sitting *ex officio*). Funding typically comes in part from the private sector and partly from the municipality (with, occasionally, some provincial funding as well). In larger communities there is sometimes a division of labour. Tourism might be done within the municipal bureaucracy or hived off to a separate organization. Events management might be divided from activities meant to promote the municipality's economic development, including image-building. This specialization may reflect differences in the interests of segments of local business. For instance, as mentioned earlier, St John's is marketed as a centre of ocean excellence by the Economic Development Division, while Destination St John's handles tourism and emphasizes culture. But a major finding here is that the key image-building function is very often isolated from the political process and the direct purview of elected politicians, housed in organizations and agencies that are controlled by local business interests.

In contrast to the privileged position of business are other social forces – environmental groups, historical associations, cultural organizations, heritage preservation societies, sports organizations, First Nations, and others. Our research shows that many such organizations are interested in image-building and try to advance images. These images would reinforce those characteristics of the place which they value and wish to preserve and strengthen. These organizations also argue that the image and character they favour would attract tourists and bring other benefits. However, these social forces are subordinated to business; in most cases they lose out in the politics of image-building.

Why does business dominate in something so important as the very identity of the collectivity? There seem to be several reasons. The first is the link between a municipality's image and economic development. This is not a necessary connection, but it has been forged over a long period of time and now generally permeates the thinking of political leaders and most of the public. Second is the simple view that business has most at stake in the community's economic prosperity and so should have a preponderant role in ensuring that development continues. A corollary is that growth is beneficial to all, as tourist dollars, incoming investment, and the activities of immigrants trickle down in the form of jobs in the community. There is also an argument to be made for expertise: entrepreneurs are more knowledgeable about the factors that are likely to attract and to best accommodate incoming firms. As well, business has more resources and is willing to spend on the image-building function because it perceives it as important. Moreover, municipal images can sometimes be segmented to appeal to diverse audiences and to accommodate different segments of business, but images are not amenable to compromise, and conflicting images are confusing

and dysfunctional. So image-building often is a zero-sum game at
the municipal level, and it constitutes a policy field that business
exerts itself to dominate. Finally, there is very little coherent opposition to business leadership. As de Clercy and Ferguson summed up
their findings about Saskatchewan:

> Clearly, local business interests exercised much influence in
> image-building policy. This is not because business groups suc-
> cessfully competed for influence with active community groups
> on a level playing field, as pluralists might argue. Rather, it was
> because business groups largely have the field to themselves.
> Their interests were given priority by politicians, administrators,
> and citizens, while community groups largely remained content
> to depend on interlocking elites to represent them. In view of the
> province's difficult economic condition for the last fifty years or
> so, there was a consensus that image-building policy should serve
> the needs of business.

In larger municipalities this consensus might be less than complete,
but there is no doubt that business has the lead in the field of municipal image-building everywhere in Canada.

ASSESSING THE POLICIES

The last area of analysis concerns the quality of image-building policies. How good are they? How might policy be improved? Could
changes in the structure of intergovernmental relations or in the participation of social forces improve the policies? For the most part,
the authors of the chapters collected here have not approached these
issues directly. But some such evaluation is necessary. First, though,
we must clarify the criteria that define what good public policy is.

It is sometimes believed that multilevel governance tends to produce public policy that is superior to that emanating from a single
tier of government. This is because more information is available
from the different administrations and because co-operation can
overcome jurisdictional obstacles to properly coordinating and integrating policies. But on the strictly intergovernmental side, there is
no compelling reason to conclude that complex IGR mechanisms
produce superior policy. Most of the information needed for municipal image-building is either obvious (what senior governments are

doing, for instance), or held at the local level. Image-building is far less directly interconnected with other fields where provincial and federal governments are active than is the case with fields like immigrant settlement or urban Aboriginal policy. Further, when policy is produced and implemented through complex multilevel government structures, it is hard to hold governments accountable for what they have done. Finally, the negotiating processes can be cumbersome and time-consuming; that is, the transaction costs mount rapidly as more actors become involved.

On the governance side, the debate is richer and more nuanced. Some would argue that policy tends to be superior if it is implemented in partnership with representative social forces, or, more strongly, if it is formulated through their participation in policy-making; at the extreme, direct participation is a matter of dignity and equity (Albo 1993). It is hard to counter the argument about rights to participation, except to note that the essence of the Canadian system, like other large-scale polities, is representative democracy rather than direct democracy. On the matter of making policy better, the argument for participation rests on the notion that citizens and groups can bring information and expertise to the process that would otherwise be lacking. This seems to be indisputable, but it does not imply that these contributions should be determining: valuable input is not the same as decision-making itself, which may be subject to other considerations, taking other information into account. A final argument here is that direct democratic participation helps develop better citizens, ones who learn tolerance, compromise, and the other democratic arts (Pateman 1970). This could be particularly useful for participants with little experience of democratic systems. On the other hand, while participation can have developmental consequences for citizens, this takes time, and meanwhile they participate instrumentally, to achieve certain objectives, so the negative consequences can be twofold. Decision-makers, on the one hand, can be overwhelmed by conflicting and perhaps quite unrealistic views about what images are desirable, while on the other hand participants can become frustrated and alienated when their views are not realized. So what other criteria can we use to evaluate policy, and how does municipal image-building policy stack up against them?

One criterion often employed is speed, or timeliness. But this is not really appropriate in the case of image-building, for policy here is not a response to a crisis or the sudden emergence of a problem. Moreover, images need to be carefully developed and deployed consistently over a lengthy period of time to be effective: they should not change rapidly. Another criterion is whether the scale of the policy is adequate to address the problem. By this measure, most of our municipalities seem to perform adequately, with the exception of Winnipeg, where little is done apart from standard destination marketing. Most municipalities aim for a provincial and regional audience, which is appropriate, and some go far beyond this. Another measure of quality is coherence. This does appear to be a problem in some cases where images proliferate, as in Humboldt, and where they conflict, as in Charlottetown. More generally, as noted in the Saskatchewan chapter, there often is considerable fragmentation among relatively small-scale initiatives and a reliance on the leadership of particular individuals. Image-building at the municipal level, especially in smaller communities, tends not to be done through systematic analysis and long-term planning, so coherence can be a real problem.

A standard criterion of the quality of policy is whether it is effective. Did it achieve its objectives? This, unfortunately, we cannot assess. As de Clercy and Ferguson note, evaluations of image-building policy are simply not conducted. Policy change, even in large cities, tends to be based on vague feelings that existing images are inadequate. In any case, the effectiveness of images is terribly difficult to assess. Evaluating advertising in the private sector is difficult enough, even though hard figures about sales are available to correlate with campaign efforts. When municipal images have several purposes – investment, immigrants, tourism, civic pride – effectiveness is much harder to gauge, especially in smaller municipalities. Incoming investment and new development tend to be "lumpy," and linking them to campaigns that have existed for some time is not possible. As well, many factors are at play in such developments, including the general state of the economy, sectoral market conditions, the labour force, tax rates, and so on. To isolate the independent effect of a municipal image cannot be done, except anecdotally. Even in tourism, where indicators like flows of people and hotel bookings can be measured reliably, there are many confounding factors such as gas prices, unemployment rates, travel and passport regulations, and changing demographics, all of which make it unfeasible to evaluate the impact of branding policy. This means, notably, that it is also impossible to assess the efficiency of municipal image-building efforts. This standard criterion is about whether the results obtained were achieved at a reasonable cost. While the cost of image-building can be measured, if there is no effectiveness measure then there is no good information about what results were obtained, and hence it is impossible to judge whether the cost was justified. Effectiveness and efficiency, common criteria of policy's adequacy, have little traction in this field.

Another very common criterion for judging the quality of policy is equity. Does the policy treat people fairly? This does not figure highly in municipal image-building. One consideration in this field is equity on the input side of the policy; that is, in developing the policy. Many groups and interests are marginalized in the process of image-building. Indeed, most are in this position, except for business communities. Yet for most citizens this is not highly salient. On the output side, it is clear that public expenditures often benefit the local tourism industry, though the claim can be made, depending on the economic structure of the community, that there are widespread benefits from this in the form of employment and secondary spending. Some public initiatives that qualify as image-building involve special events and festivals. These can leave out citizens who are not able to attend or take part in them. Basically, most public galas build solidarity with the city among the middle classes, and are often unfairly exclusive of poorer citizens.

Generally, the standard criteria by which we judge the quality of public policy are either inapplicable to the image-building field or they provide little purchase upon common practice in this policy area. But a final criterion of good public policy is optimality. Is the policy the best that can be achieved? We must judge this according to what is possible, and essentially this means evaluating policies in comparison to the best practices found on a comparative basis, and in the light of promising, innovating approaches. Along these lines, we can also consider the suggestions for improvement made by the authors of our chapters.

Municipal image-building in Canada is a rather closed process involving a small group, or even a single determined champion. Some suggest that there should be more consultation in the process. For Winnipeg, where Lehr and Zubrycki find a very weak performance in constructing a positive image, broad consultation is highly desirable:

Image-building policy should make provision for public consultation and more opportunities for private citizens to become
involved in shaping policy. It should ensure that a city's cultural
and human capital is used to its best advantage. Above all, the
slogan that promotes the city must ring true with its citizens,
advancing values and attributes that resonate with ordinary
people and promoting attitudes that they can embrace and with
which they can identify.

In contrast to this inclusive vision, de Clercy and Ferguson find that
"actual consultation that could influence policy at various points in
the policy process was undertaken rarely and reluctantly."

But can consultation work in an area as amorphous as image-
building? Can a broad array of social forces be involved in decision-
making or even in proposing alternatives? It seems unlikely. To
begin with, there are several well-understood problems with public
consultation. Such processes are not very efficient. They take up a
lot of time and resources, and there are high transaction costs in
finding a collective solution. Public consultation is not very effective
at making linkages between the images considered and other policy
areas: this can be better done by insiders. Finally, consultation provides no guarantee that conflict will be resolved; in particular, the
sort of side-payments and log-rolling that facilitate negotiated solu-
tions are not available when consultations focus on a single policy
area (Huxham 2000). These general problems are exacerbated by
the nature of the municipal image-building field. First, policy formation is intermittent. Images are created and are maintained for
some years, ideally, before reform is undertaken. Second, building
an image often does not represent a marginal change to an existing
policy. In principle, the slate is wiped clean when new images are
to be designed, so the debate can be quite unbounded. Further, few
citizens are very familiar with the content of the field, and few other
than business have a lot at stake: these conditions are very different than those obtaining in many other policy fields, such as transportation for example. Finally, image-building is highly connected
with other policy areas, including infrastructure, economic development, planning, tourism, and immigration. Images cannot be built
in isolation.

For all of these reasons, image-building policy probably should continue to be made by a relatively small group who are knowledgeable

and comprehend the implications of images for related areas of municipal activity. However, more can be done to ensure that the image(s) resonate with the local citizenry. Large numbers of groups and individual members of the public should be canvassed for their reaction to proposals about images. Only this can avoid the kinds of fiascos that have sometimes occurred, and ensure that the image "rings true" with ordinary people. It is essential for the image to win the adherence of broad swathes of the population if it is to fulfill its internal function of reinforcing civic pride and generating social solidarity.

From the studies collected here, it is obvious that regional co-operation in image-building is quite rare. Only in the Swan River Valley, with its distinctive and isolated geography, and in the Acadian towns of PEI, with their common culture, were exceptions found. In most instances, the fruits of image-building are seen as the payoffs in a zero-sum game, available either to one municipality or another but not both. Yet in this field, co-operation can involve the "bundling" of different municipalities' characteristics in such a way that a broader appeal is achieved. Or, it can simply reinforce the shared characteristics of a group of places, as in the Swan River Valley. In either case, through co-operation more resources could be allocated to the effort and efficiencies could be achieved, while potentially increasing the impact. Narrow self-interest seems to prevent this. This provides an argument, therefore, for incentives to be offered by other levels of government to promote co-operation. From the studies collected here, the federal government is best positioned to provide a stimulus for municipal co-operation. It is distant enough to be somewhat insulated from charges of favouritism and interference, yet it has very flexible mechanisms that are capable of offering grants and that have the local knowledge to evaluate proposals. These are the federal development agencies that now blanket the country – ACOA, the Economic Development Agency of Canada for the Regions of Quebec, FedDev (the Federal Economic Development Agency for Southern Ontario), FedNor, and WED. Already these agencies are present in the image-building field, and they could do more to promote regional co-operation.

So does this mean that there should be a more formal, institutionalized relationship between municipal, provincial, and federal government actors? As noted by all of the authors, this is now lacking: relationships are intermittent, ad hoc, and often dependent on personal initiatives and connections that are transient. Certain advantages of more institutionalization are obvious: in all likelihood, there would be more provincial assistance. There could also be more congruence between municipal images and provincial and national ones. Better coordination of municipal images would be possible on a regional and provincial basis. Clear, structured relationships could stimulate more municipal activity in the field, as Lehr and Zubrycki suggest.

But this possibility deserves more scrutiny. Greater intergovernmental coordination would mainly involve municipalities and provincial governments, because the federal government is well positioned to manage funding programs to which municipalities make applications, but not to deal with municipalities on a sustained basis. Continuous interaction is the mode of relationship with which provincial administrations have experience. Currently, there is a remarkable lack of intervention by provincial governments in municipal image-building activities. There are not even signs of much interest in what municipalities do in this field. This is an area of unparalleled municipal autonomy. Compared to any other field of municipal activity – from land-use planning to solid waste disposal to policing – municipal image-building allows local governments to freely design and implement policy. Municipalities can define and project their own essence, or at least what they perceive to be their core characteristics and distinctive attributes.

What would intergovernmental coordination entail? First, there would be increasing provincial control over municipal images. There would be greater harmonization with the provincial brand. There would be coordination, and possibly harmonization of images across the province, through common website design and external messaging. In all likelihood, the level of conflict about municipal images would increase. Not only would municipal authorities chafe at provincial interference, but the level of intracommunity discord would also rise as image-building became more open to local debate. There would also be political costs for provincial governments because choices would have to be made between the proposals of various municipal authorities, and between local factions. Given all of this, it is probably best to abjure greater and more institutionalized intergovernmental coordination. More coordination would least affect those municipalities where the main orientation is simply to provide local goods and services, because there would be some cost savings.

But it would hamstring those municipalities with a more comprehensive vision of their role, one that involves defining and achieving collective objectives. An intrinsic part of such a vision is the definition, elaboration, and projection of a collective identity. Where the belief is strong that this should be a function of the municipality, then any provincial government interference is to be resisted.

Instead of influencing directly the nature of municipalities' images, other levels of government should continue to help provide the facilities that the images are built upon; that is, infrastructural, cultural, recreational, and heritage resources. There is some opportunity here for the provincial and federal governments to adopt a regional perspective and to prevent duplication and destructive competition. Most important, however, are their contributions to helping realize the image. Brands, of course, are built on the real character of the municipality, depicted in ideal form by the image. But the character must be reinforced. Writing about communications strategies, Kavaratzis (2004, 69) observes that "the content of this communication is the most significant factor, stressing the self-evident, but often forgotten, fact that there simply needs to be something to communicate about; to put it simply, promotion comes only after one has something to promote." Senior governments can certainly assist municipal (and regional) efforts in this regard. To be successful, given the vagaries of tri-level funding negotiations, municipal representatives will need solidly justified and strongly articulated proposals supported by a local consensus.

CONCLUSION

Municipal image-building is a very interesting field of policy and of study. Consciousness of it has grown rapidly as global forces have created corrosive change while providing new opportunities for places to project themselves on broader scales, which they have certainly done. The studies gathered here, mostly of smaller municipalities, show determined efforts to promote places in order to attract tourists, investment, and immigrants. At the same time – and this is well understood by practitioners as well as analysts – image-building efforts can help create a sense of community, generate civic pride, and decrease social exclusion.

Image-building is a noteworthy policy field for several reasons, which deserve a brief summary. Even the smallest municipalities are active in image-building, or would like to become more active, because they realize its importance. Larger municipalities, in contrast to the record in almost every area of policy, are less likely to be effective in image-building. They are bureaucratically complex and contain many different and contesting interests, and so finding a clear and simple brand that defines the essence of the place is very difficult. In all municipalities, those engaged in image-building have an unusual degree of autonomy: there is little opposition to spending money on place promotion. Along with this latitude, image-builders are able to concentrate power. Typically, policies are made by a very small number of actors. The process is dominated by local business interests. This is true of many other policy fields, but the acquiescence of other interests to business shaping municipal images is remarkable, and is even more so when an important function that affects the entire community is delegated to specialized agencies dominated by business, which is often the case. Finally, there is very little interference in image-building by other levels of government. Unlike most other fields of local government activity, provincial governments are not involved in control and coordination. In light of all this, as de Clercy and Ferguson conclude, "there is much future potential for local governments to be far more active and innovative in making policy in this field." And so, inevitably, there is also much potential for further research in this fascinating area of policy-making.

NOTES

1 These studies are found in *Sites of Governance: Multilevel Governance and Policy Making in Canada's Big Cities,* edited by Martin Horak and Robert Young. Montreal and Kingston: McGill-Queen's University Press, 2012. The authors of the studies in which image-building was analyzed are Byron Miller and Alan Smart (Calgary); Robert Finbow (Halifax); Laurence Bherer and Pierre Hamel (Montreal); Greg Marquis (Saint John); Christopher Dunn and Cecily Pantin (St John's); Martin Horak (Toronto); and Thomas Hutton (Vancouver).
2 Destination Winnipeg is now Tourism Winnipeg, a subsidiary of Economic Development Winnipeg, which has a private-sector board. See http://www.economicdevelopmentwinnipeg.com.

REFERENCES

Agranoff, Robert, and Michael McGuire. 2003. *Collaborative Public Management: New Strategies for Local Governments*. Washington: Georgetown University Press.

Albo, Gregory. 1993. "Democratic Citizenship and the Future of Public Management." In *A Different Kind of State? Popular Power and Democratic Administration*, edited by G. Albo, D. Langille, and L. Panitch, 17–33. Toronto: Oxford University Press.

Carroll, Barbara Wake, and Katherine A.H. Graham, eds. 2009. "Special Issue on Federalism, Public Policy and Municipalities." *Canadian Public Administration* 52, no. 3.

Garcea, Joseph, and Edd LeSage Jr., eds. 2005. *Municipal Reform in Canada: Reconfiguration, Re-Empowerment, and Rebalancing*. Toronto: Oxford University Press.

Hankinson, Graham. 2009. "Managing Destination Brands: Establishing a Theoretical Foundation." *Journal of Marketing Management* 25, no. 1–2: 97–115.

Huxham, Chris. 2000. "The Challenge of Collaborative Governance." *Public Management* 2, no. 3: 337–57.

Kavaratzis, Michalis. 2004. "From City Marketing to City Branding: Towards a Theoretical Framework for Developing City Brands." *Place Branding* 1, no. 1: 58–73.

Lazar, Harvey, and Christian Leuprecht, eds. 2007. *Spheres of Governance: Comparative Studies of Cities in Multilevel Governance Systems*. Montreal and Kingston: McGill-Queen's University Press for the Institute of Intergovernmental Relations, Queen's University.

Nelles, H.V. 1999. *The Art of Nation-Building: Pageantry and Spectacle at Quebec's Tercentenary*. Toronto: University of Toronto Press.

Pasotti, Eleonora. 2010. *Political Branding in Cities: The Decline of Machine Politics in Bogotá, Naples and Chicago*. New York: Cambridge University Press.

Pateman, Carole. 1970. *Participation and Democratic Theory*. London: Cambridge University Press.

Peters, Evelyn J. 2011. *Urban Aboriginal Policy Making in Canadian Municipalities*. Montreal and Kingston: McGill-Queen's University Press.

Sancton, Andrew, and Robert Young, eds. 2009. *Foundations of Governance: Municipal Government in Canada's Provinces*. Toronto:

University of Toronto Press and the Institute of Public Administration of Canada.

Tolley, Erin, and Robert Young, eds. 2011. *Immigrant Settlement Policy in Canadian Municipalities*. Montreal and Kingston: McGill-Queen's University Press.

Young, Robert, and Christian Leuprecht, eds. 2006. *Canada: The State of the Federation 2004: Municipal-Federal-Provincial Relations in Canada*. Montreal and Kingston: McGill-Queen's University Press for the Institute of Intergovernmental Relations, Queen's University.

Contributors

CAROLINE ANDREW is the director of the Centre on Governance at the University of Ottawa. Her areas of research include municipal government, urban politics, and particularly the relationship of community-based equity seeking groups and municipal policy decisions.

DAVID BULGER taught political science and law at the University of Prince Edward Island for many years. He is a keen observer of politics on and off the Island, and an aficionado of PEI history.

CRISTINE DE CLERCY is an associate professor in the Department of Political Science at the University of Western Ontario. She studies Canadian politics and public policy.

PETER A. FERGUSON is an assistant professor in the Department of Political Science at Western University. He studies comparative politics and tourism/image-building politics.

HEATHER GUSHUE now lives in St John's, NL, where she is enrolled in the interdisciplinary PhD program at Memorial University. In her spare time, she volunteers with the Arthritis Society and spends time with her family.

JEAN HARVEY is a professor of sociology of sport at the University of Ottawa and is the founding director of the Research Centre for Sport in Canadian Society at the same university. His research interests include sport policy, as well as sport in the context of globalization.

JOHN C. LEHR is a professor in the Geography Department at the University of Winnipeg. He is a historical geographer with research interests in the ethnic settlements and cultural landscapes of the prairie west.

JUDY LYNN RICHARDS is chair of the Sociology Department at the University of Prince Edward Island. A gerontologist and social demographer, her main research areas are social policy, population aging, and the wellness of community-dwelling seniors.

ROBERT YOUNG is director of the Major Collaborative Research Initiative on Multilevel Governance and Public Policy in Canadian Municipalities. He holds the Canada Research Chair in Multilevel Governance at the University of Western Ontario.

KARLA ZUBRYCKI graduated from the University of Winnipeg in 2006 with a degree in Communications, and from the University of Waterloo in 2010 with a Master of Environmental Studies. She is currently working at the International Institute for Sustainable Development in Winnipeg.

Index